youth moves

Critical Youth Studies
Series Editor: Greg Dimitriadis

Beyond Resistance! Youth Activism and Community Change:
New Democratic Possibilities for Practice and Policy for
America's Youth
Edited by Shawn Ginwright, Pedro Noguera, and
Julio Cammarota

Youth Learning On Their Own Terms: Creative Practices and
Classroom Teaching
Leif Gustavson

Youth Moves: Identities and Education in Global Perspective
Edited by Nadine Dolby and Fazal Rizvi

youth moves

identities and education in global perspective

edited by
nadine dolby and fazal rizvi

Routledge
Taylor & Francis Group
New York   London

Routledge
Taylor & Francis Group
270 Madison Avenue
New York, NY 10016

Routledge
Taylor & Francis Group
2 Park Square
Milton Park, Abingdon
Oxon OX14 4RN

© 2008 by Taylor & Francis Group, LLC
Routledge is an imprint of Taylor & Francis Group, an Informa business

Printed in the United States of America on acid-free paper
10 9 8 7 6 5 4 3 2 1

International Standard Book Number-13: 978-0-415-95563-8 (Softcover) 978-0-415-95562-1 (Hardcover)

Library of Congress Cataloging-in-Publication Data

Youth moves : identities and education in global perspective / edited by Nadine Dolby
and Fazal Rizvi.
    p. cm. -- (Critical youth studies)
Includes bibliographical references and index.
ISBN 978-0-415-95562-1 (hb) -- ISBN 978-0-415-95563-8 (pb)
    1. Youth--Social conditions. 2. Youth--Cross-cultural studies. 3. Transnationalism.
4. Popular culture. 5. Education and globalization. I. Dolby, Nadine, 1964- II. Rizvi,
Fazal, 1950-

HQ796.Y596 2007
305.23509'0511--dc22   2006102749

Visit the Taylor & Francis Web site at
http://www.taylorandfrancis.com

and the Routledge Web site at
http://www.routledge.com

Dedication

In Memory of Lynne Allen: friend, teacher, and inspiration. L'Chaim.

Contents

Series Editor Introduction

Youth Moves: Identity and Education in Global Perspective is a profoundly important intervention in contemporary debates around globalization and youth culture. More specifically, it complements and extends the concerns of both published and forthcoming books in the *Critical Youth Studies* series. Like other volumes in the series, *Youth Moves* puts the complex, lived realities of contemporary youth front-and-center. Deploying a range of theoretical frameworks and research methodologies, the editors and authors give us a complex picture of youth moving in and across shifting global terrains. In so doing, they challenge educators and researchers to meet youth on these terrains: to keep our own imaginations in motion as we strive to create educative institutions and curricula relevant to and for these new times.

Globalization has become something of a catchall term, describing the broad range of material, cultural, and technological shifts and dislocations that have marked the past several decades. These shifts and dislocations are registering in often disorientating and paradoxical ways. Nowhere is this more evident than in contemporary youth culture. Young people are growing up in a world increasingly marked by new, massive disparities in wealth, the worldwide circulation of (often rigidly fundamentalist) ideologies and belief systems, and a dizzying array of signs and symbolic resources dislodged from their traditional moorings, as well as a veritable explosion of new technologies. Youth are now trying to find their place in this world, moving across this terrain in ways we are only beginning to understand and appreciate.

Such a scholarly intervention has never been more timely or critical. As Arjun Appadurai argues in his *Fear of Small Numbers: An Essay on the Geography of Anger* (2006), the rise of violent fundamentalisms (including Islamic and Christian) around the world is largely a response to the anxieties of our now firmly globalized and interpenetrated world—or, as he writes, "the uncertainties about identity that global flows invariably produce." These violent fundamentalisms "may be seen as part of an emerging repertoire of efforts to produce previously unrequited levels of certainty about social identity, values, survival, and dignity" (2006, p. 7). Against this broad tide of fundamentalisms and false securities, the chapters collected in *Youth Moves* give us another version of how globalization is registering unique angles of vision from multiple points around the world today.

Taken together, the chapters have something of a kaleidoscopic effect, throwing into sharp relief the contingencies of globalization and its futures. We see this contingency starkly (sadly) highlighted in the discursive arc between Appadurai's 1996 book, *Modernity at Large: Cultural Dimensions of Globalization* and his aforementioned 2006 book, *Fear of Small Numbers*. The hugely influential *Modernity at Large* argued that various global "flows"—flows of people, ideas, images, technologies, and monies—mark our moment in both predictable and unpredictable ways. Although Appadurai left space for a more pessimistic reading of globalization, the book tended to highlight its enabling dimensions. Of course, the last decade has shown us another side of globalization. These global flows have not been met, on the whole, with cosmopolitan dispositions. Rather, they have been met with vicious fundamentalisms that aim for new and brutal kinds of clarities. A set of binaries now structure the beliefs and actions of many world actors—"us" vs. "them," "true believers" vs. "infidels," those "with us," vs. "against us." This quest for clarity is evidenced in much 21st century violence, from 9/11 to the invasion of Iraq.

All of this makes *Youth Moves* so terribly critical. The chapters in this volume highlight the ways young people are crafting new identities and social networks using a range of globally generated and proliferating resources. Young people are moving both literally and figuratively, crossing national borders with their bodies as well as imaginations, constructing new and unexpected kinds of identities. The chapters collected here do not only posit this movement as theory. They look at these practices with the kinds of empirical research methodologies that put us in touch with young people's everyday lived realities. Although the editors and authors are strategic and sober about this intervention, *Youth Moves* offers the reader a broadly ecumenical picture of young people's lives in the first part of the 21st century, from the ground up.

Greg Dimitriadis

Buffalo, NY

January 2007

References

Appadurai, A. 1996. *Modernity at large: Cultural dimensions of globalization.* Minnesota: University of Minnesota Press.

Appadurai, A. 2006. *Fear of small numbers: An essay on the geography of anger.* Durham, NC: Duke University Press.

Acknowledgments

This book was made possible through the support and generosity of many individuals and organizations. We would like to thank the graduate students enrolled in Nadine's seminar, "Youth, Identity, and Curriculum" for their assistance reading and commenting on the chapters in draft form. Thanks to Maricela Alvarado, Sybil Durand, Aliya Rahman, and Katie Wiesner. Special thanks to Aliya Rahman for editorial assistance.

We would also like to thank Jim Lehman, head of the Department of Curriculum and Instruction at Purdue University for publication assistance. Thanks also to Greg Dimitriadis for his enthusiasm and continued support for this work and this volume. As always, Catherine Bernard at Routledge has been a superb editor, and we thank her for her commitment to this project. We thank everyone who participated, and the authors whose essays appear in this collection.

Foreword

Writing the foreword is a really weird experience. I've prepared a few, and never quite know what to do. But I do know what to do.

Do I write it as a senior established scholar—with all the grandiose Eurocentric theory that that might imply, making sweeping metatheoretical statements about the various texts here, with authoritative, centered, and privileged position and voice, expressing age, patriarchy, and wisdom? Does doing so therefore bring honor and reputation, status and spin to the book and its peoples?

Do I write it as composite of ethnic, multiple, cultured and subcultured, gendered, sexualized identities—speaking narrative from a position in solidarity with these chapters?

Do I write it white or yellow, from Australia, from Asia, from margin, from center, from pacific, from city—or do I act as if I am something else: a senior white academic in a neutral western dislocated space and time, at once anywhere and nowhere? Or as expatriate traveling academic for hire, whose ideas circulate in the reputational ether and net of academic pose and prose.

Do I write it as old guy, or as someone who was once a kid, as a parent and grandparent, talking about my generation or this generation, as synchronic scientist speaking across time, as diachronic product of families and cultures, as storyteller telling it in the present tense?

And what differences might any of these textual choices make if you stopped to read it before, or after reading these writers' statements and stories about identity, about color, about other weird experiences of youth, new media, political economy, and whatever you want to call "self"?

Do I write it as noun, as canonical text form—a foreword before the real book—for editors, writers, colleagues, some known by reputation in the field, others unknown, of different academic generations, some of whom I know through face-to-face history, others through their texts only?

Do I write it for readers that I know, assume to know, or who I don't know from a bar of soap—but that the publisher could break down into an age/demographic mean with subpopulations? For readers who think they know me through sight, or perhaps they've just made up something in their heads from other texts?

Do I write it as the object of a preposition and a deictic—forward, pushing, or moving around these visions, narratives, statements, and writers' identities to another space and time? Or perhaps I should write the foreword as a "backward," reassembling them as coherent, as patterned, as singular out of mutiply sourced, placed, thought up and executed pieces.

I am stuck in the modality of the page. In and by writing. There is a necessary engagement with self, identity, writing forces upon us, as Bakhtin and Derrida suggested, a profound interiority. This is as much by textual convention, by historical choice and accident, as it might be through any technological affordances built into writing per se. Narrative affords particular relationships of self to others, ego/identity formation. Exposition declares distance, epistemological neutrality. Both are learned formations of the Western self, with different ontological and political, psychic and aesthetic investments. The choices around this particular "foreword"—entail building, selecting, and construing a particular version of self.

But then we couldn't SMS this text or talk it (though the authors might) or sing it or pluck it or rap it—or even telegraph it through a binary digital code transmitted as a program (though that's literally what is happening now to this text), squeezed onto a broadband and downloaded.

When we shift media, things begin to happen to selves. Though I write this on a laptop, it is still writing: an extension training in pens and pencils, blackboard and whiteboards. Keyboard alacrity and raw speed enable and engage particular cognitive paces, strategies—urgently closing the time/distance between what I can imagine, what I can think, and what I can get on the page. But it's still writing the "self" in one of the configurations noted above.

If I were to video a foreword and put it on YouTube it would enable an entirely different set of "selves" to be selected, assembled, generated and portrayed—planned and unplanned—and it would be taken as a different kind of statement on this book and its contents. Some we would recognize, others would test and stretch our available cultural resources and scripts. Yet others would seem simply incomprehensible.

That's what I think this book is about—from this reader at least. It's a basket of pages—worked through just as I've worked this through—about the relationships of historical moments and ages—multiple: those moments and ages of self, of reader, of text, of culture, of *zeit*, of *geist* all at once—of selves and identities, of modalities and technological means—acquired and invented, normalized and totally new. All plural, all mixed up in the historical moment. That's what identity, generation, history, place, and media do. It's called, for want of a better term, *textual culture*.

Allan Luke

Brisbane, Queensland, Australia

November 6, 2006

Introduction
Youth, Mobility, and Identity

NADINE DOLBY AND FAZAL RIZVI

I do not clearly remember her name, but I do remember her story. Tamara (that may have been her name) was sitting next to me (Nadine) on a flight from Johannesburg to Atlanta several years ago. Traveling with her mother, 10-year-old Tamara had only returned to South Africa from the United States 2 days earlier. She and her mother had spent 6 weeks in the United States on holiday and then returned to South Africa; only to receive a call that Tamara's grandfather was having emergency heart surgery, and they were to return immediately. Tamara was born in Canada of South African and Canadian parents, and had lived her short life in South Africa and the United States. Her parents had recently divorced, and her mother remarried to a Zimbabwean of British descent—adding potentially another two nations to the pile of passports and permanent resident visas in Tamara's drawer. During the night, I talked frequently to Tamara and her mother, who upon learning I was an educator, expressed dismay that Tamara's expensive private school in Cape Town required her to learn two local languages—Xhosa and Afrikaans—instead of the French, Spanish, or Chinese, which Tamara's mother had concluded would be much more useful to her daughter's future.

Tamara is perhaps iconic of Pico Iyer's (2000) "global soul" who lives everywhere and nowhere, who knows her way around Heathrow, O'Hare, and Hong Kong, but gets lost driving to a friend's house in her "hometown" because she is not familiar with the local roads. As James Clifford (1997) suggests, Tamara "dwells in travel" and she may have a clearer sense of self while in the air than while on the ground—more comfortable with liminal spaces than with the earth, which presents a dizzying array of conflicting affiliations and demands simple decisions about identity and identification, even as our lives increasingly defy such facile categorization.

As tempting as it is to hold up Tamara as the "poster girl" of *Youth Moves*, we know that most of us, at the beginning of the 21st century, have lives which are considerably more bounded than hers. Most of the world's inhabitants have no passports, no multiple permanent residence visas, and no idea what the inside of an international airport looks like. If they move internationally, they do so illegally or as refugees, and the maps they carry in their heads are of the most promising crossing points between Mexico and the United States or the best sea routes into Australia or Europe. Even those of us who are economically more secure rarely carry more than one passport and spend only a tiny fraction of our lives on planes. Tamara may be part of a borderless, global elite which "moves" with ease, but the reality of the intensification of globalization for most of us is more contradictory: capital moves easily, bodies which control capital move easily, but bodies which are more expendable or peripheral are still largely constrained. As one of us (Fazal) has written in reference to the analysis of international students in Australia,

> In contrast with the recent tendency in cultural analysis to avoid discussions of class, I argue, instead, that we cannot understand the everyday experiences of international students in Australia, and the uses they make of their education upon graduation, without also looking at how global conditions of mobility are both affected by, and are instrumental in producing and reproducing, class formation (2005, p. 84).

In his essay, "Tourists and Vagabonds," Zymaut Bauman (1998) has explored some of the ways in which mobility produces major social differentiations shaped by the emerging global cultural economies, which are, in turn, crucial for understanding new identities, new cultural tastes and desires, and new consumer practices. These economies are, of course, driven largely by the new information and communication technologies that make it possible for people not only to travel across vast distances but also to remain connected.

Increasingly, a large number of young people develop their identity within this context of mobility. Those who have a multiple and mobile sense of belonging view themselves as neither immigrants nor as tourists. They consider themselves to occupy an entirely different space. Unlike tourists, they are not interested in only a cursory look at its various physical and cultural objects and institutions. Nor do they regard themselves as immigrants. Both the concepts of tourism and immigration represent border-maintaining distinctions exerted around and by the nation-state. While it might be possible for states to maintain physical borders, cultural borders have become increasingly porous. James Clifford's idea of "traveling cultures" (1997) is designed to capture the fuzzy logic of this consequence of mobility and cultural interpenetration. Clifford prefers the word "travel'" to such terms as tourism, displacement, nomadism, pilgrimage, and migration because the notion of "traveling cultures" implies a two-way process, consisting of interactive dynamic relations, which suggests that cultural forms of travel can never be bound exclusively by national boundaries. Instead, people are able to imagine themselves as belonging to several places at once. Clifford uses the term "dwelling in travel" to refer to the experiences of mobility and movement through which people develop a range of new material, spatial practices that produce knowledge, stories, traditions, comportments, music, books, diaries, and other cultural expressions.

Physical mobility then is often accompanied by the circulation of a great deal of information as well as impressions and images across cultural spaces. In this sense, the international students Fazal studied are cultural mediators. They are in touch almost daily with friends and families through telephone and e-mail. As a student he interviewed remarked, somewhat cheekily, "Without us, Telstra (Australia's national telecommunication company) would have gone broke long ago!". "What do you talk about when you ring home?" he asked. "Oh, well, we discuss the weather, what we did that day, and sometimes my family wants my opinion about something or another."

This regular contact with "home" while in Australia suggests that the dislocation and displacement faced by international students has a particularly benign form, mediated not only by the compression of time and space but also, to an extent, by their class position. They remain engaged with developments at "home" and continue to participate in the decision-making processes relevant to family matters. This indicates that Clifford's phrase "dwelling in travel" is indeed apt to describe the experiences of these students. We should, however, be cautious about generalizing from this postmodern valorization of mobility and transnational dwelling. Traveling cultures are not available equally to everyone and are certainly inflected by gender and class considerations. As Avtar Brah (1996) has remarked, mobility can often be unsafe and insecure for many women. Women experience it differently, and its social consequences are unevenly distributed. Brah's reflections and others' suggest the need to understand how the materiality of class affects experiences of mobility and immobility. Thus, Clifford's notions of "traveling cultures" and "dwelling in travel" are helpful but only to a certain extent. Clifford insists that it is not only goods, people, and ideas that travel but cultures as well. But if they do, they do so, as we have noted, in a particular "classed" form, already impregnated by the cultural economies of globalization. In contrast with the recent tendency in cultural analysis to avoid discussions of class, we argue instead that we cannot understand the everyday experiences of young people without also looking at how global conditions of mobility are both affected by, and are instrumental in producing and reproducing, class formations.

Yet, we can think of movement, and specifically youth's movements, in other ways, which complicates the fact that for most of us, our only movement is between home, work, the mall, and school. For example, it is clear that these "places" we frequent are not stable and unchanging but, in fact, are always shifting. As Doreen Massey (1998), among others, points out, there is no rigid paradigm in which economies, cultures, and politics are first global, then national, then regional, then local. Instead, the different registers and scales intersect at all points: Our next door neighbor might have satellite television with a channel devoted to 24-hour news and commentary from Brazil, but no access to "local" news about the schools or work on the sewer lines. Wide swaths of prime oceanfront property in Cape Town are bought up by Europeans and Americans, so that the result of a national struggle for liberation is the opening up of local real estate to an international marketplace, and a neighborhood and a city are transformed in a matter of years. Such dynamics, of course, are not wholly new, as Massey (1998) observes in the British context;

> ... "Englishness" did not somehow grow out of the soil but rather is a complex product of all the people who over the centuries have settled that part of the British Isles, of all of their contacts and influences. The quintessential cup of tea could not be sipped without plantations in India, Opium Wars in China—and if you take sugar—a history of slavery in the Caribbean (p. 123).

For those on the receiving end of colonial practices, there was never an autonomous "local" or "national" context: culture, politics, and the economy were always international, always a site of interaction between a here and there, so much so that today the line between them is no longer clear, and "England" and "India" are deeply intertwined and largely inseparable in the human imaginations that constitute the spaces of modernity (Appadurai, 1996). Jamaica Kincaid (1988) similarly reflects on the illusion of disconnection which underpins modern practices of travel, such as tourism, in her home of Antigua. She writes:

> When you sit down to eat your delicious meal, it's better that you don't know that most of what you are eating came off a plane from Miami. And before it got on a plane in Miami, who knows where it came from? A good guess is that it came from a place like Antigua first, where it was grown dirt-cheap, went to Miami, and came back (p. 14).

Massey and Kincaid's reflections on the intrinsic connectedness of human communities might make us rethink how we bound "local" practices. For example, while it may be true that our neighbor is more concerned with the news from Brazil than the proposed sewer project in our community that will raise property taxes, the sewer project itself is also linked to global movements: our community needs to strengthen its infrastructure to serve the increasing number of immigrants pouring in from all over the world, and to be able to compete globally for businesses which have significant geographical mobility. Although historically these spaces of interaction were developed, contested, and negotiated over generations, today's interactions are driven by the "intensified and accelerated movement of people, images, ideas, technologies, and economic and cultural capital across national boundaries" (McCarthy, Giardina, Harewood, and Park, 2003, p. 454).

Youth, then, must move differently in the world today than they did in previous generations, as the sites in which they live are themselves transformed. Perhaps most significantly for this collection, schools and other educational institutions (e.g., colleges and universities) are both transformed internally within these new contexts, and are also no longer the sole—or even predominant—pedagogical site for youth. As Michael Apple, Jane Kenway, and Michael Singh (2005) discuss, these changes in policies, classroom practices, and the politics of education impact every facet of educational life, from the eternal question of "what to do Monday morning" (and today's answer—prepare for the standardized test); to the rapidly changing racial and ethnic composition of classrooms in urban, suburban, and rural settings; to the new images and commodities that enter classrooms and schools through the Internet; to policies which transform cities into "global cities" at the expense of minority children (Lipman, 2004); to the ever-present and often haunting question of what purposes schooling now serves in an economy which presents fewer and fewer job opportunities for youth of all backgrounds except the most privileged (Aronowitz, 2001; Aronowitz and DiFazio, 1994; Rifkin, 1995; Willis, 2003).

This book explores how youth "move" within these new geographies of modernity. When we write "move" we mean to signal the multiplicity of that term, and thus the multiplicities of possible movements. First, it is evident that some youth do literally move throughout the world with ease: Tamara's story represents the relatively borderless world which is available to a few (see, e.g., Ong, 1999). Others also move geographically, though under the more constrained circumstances and possibilities entailed in the movement of those who move for economic opportunity for their children, to escape political repression or because "home" is no longer available to them (e.g., Zlolniski, 2006). However, this movement—often examined through the lenses of immigration—is not simple movement from one place to another. Instead, the movement itself constitutes a new space of identification, of belonging, as communities are constituted within and of these transnational spaces (D'Aliseria, 2004; Levitt, 2001). Finally, there is a growing category of youth movement which is still largely uncharted—that of youth who move for educational purposes—the growing number of international students in Australia, Britain, the United States, South Africa, and throughout the world (Ninnes and Hellstén, 2005; Rizvi, 2005). These students' movements also create new networks (Castells, 2000), and circuits of identity. Even those youth who do not literally move throughout the world or a geographic region are undoubtedly caught up in the continual circulation of global culture, through the media, movies, fashion, the Internet—their identities are now inextricably linked to the currents of modernity that flow across the world at the speed of a mouse click (Suárez-Orozco and Qin-Hilliard, 2004).

In another way, we can also talk about "youth moves" in the context of how youth move not only within the conditions that they encounter but in the ways in which they are agents of change and *produce* the new conditions for their lives. The focus on youth's agency has a long history within the field of youth culture and is particularly relevant to education research and scholarship

(Dolby, 2003). As Paul Willis (1990) reminds us, we must take the worlds of youth seriously—their movements produce the terrain for the future. Thus, throughout this collection, we focus attention on how youth act and move to reshape their own lives, and the very ground on which they forge the possible movements and identities of generations yet to come.

New Times, New Identities

In this section, authors interrogate the global forces which saturate the "new times" in which youth are located (Dolby and Dimitriadis, 2004). Although schools and educational institutions—discussed above—are still a central component of youth's everyday lives, other sites are also both pedagogical and formative of the increasingly global terrain on which youth find themselves. Thus, here we take up discussion of some of these shifts, so as to provide a context for the essays to follow. We specifically discuss three sites that are critical to youth's present and future: work, technology, and the specter of consumer culture that has emerged in recent years as the lingua franca of youth globally.

One of the most frequently cited markers of the new times in which we live are the fundamental changes in the global economy over the past 30 years. As industrial production moves from the "First World" to the "Third World," large segments of working-class populations are left without the secure and steady jobs and futures that factory work—however monotonous and difficult—provided (Weis, 1990; 2004). Indeed, Paul Willis's landmark work (1981/1977) documenting how working class youth participate in the reproduction of their own class position may have been one of the final major studies of a working class in the First World that *had* jobs and a future to look towards. Instead, today, as Jane Kenway and Anna Kraack (2004) document, working-class male youth in Australia, for example, have to reinvent themselves to fit into the dictates of a new economy based on tourism, where job security is nonexistent and the future is unsure. More bleakly, Jean Anyon and Kathleen Nolan (2004) chart the rise of a new U.S. economy which has no need for African-American men, who find themselves schooled and prepared only for life in prison (see also Gilmore, 2006). But "new times" are not confined to the working-class and the poor, as middle-class jobs are also increasingly sent overseas, and employees are forced to train their replacements: almost always well-educated black and brown individuals who will be paid little money for long hours.

As Michael Buroway et al. (2000) demonstrate, such economic restructuring is intimately connected to new technological developments—often at dizzying speed—which make "global" corporations more possible. For example, corporations no longer need to be concerned with the quality of their local schools in order to provide an educated workforce for their backroom operations; instead, such monotonous chores can be electronically shipped overnight to

Ireland, India, or elsewhere, and the finished work back on a manager's desk in Toronto by the next morning. Indeed, technological developments evolve at such rapid speed that an essay one of us (Nadine) published in 2003 on popular culture and youth seems hopelessly outdated just four years later. The explosions in technology in the past few years—from YouTube, MySpace, and Facebook to IPods, Blackberries, and the ubiquitous cell phones—is increasingly providing a space for the creation of emergent cultures, identities, affiliations, and "new patriotisms" which could only be gestured towards in largely imaginary terms by scholars just a decade ago (Appadurai 1993, 1996; Levy and Stone, 2006; Mazzarella, 2005). As youth spend more and more of their time in on-line environments, the lines between "off" and "on" worlds blur, as technology now allows those with Internet access to go to school, shop, work, establish and maintain friendships, gamble, have sex, and even pray on-line (Ben-Zeev, 2004; Howard and Jones, 2004; "Overseas Indians turn to Web for festival prayers," 2006).

Finally, all of these developments intersect with the rise of a global consumer culture that provides a constant and insistent backdrop for daily life and becomes the ground for identity formation (Kenway and Bullen, 2001). Willis (2003) succinctly sums up this shift in his discussion of the "third wave" of modernity, as he writes,

> Even as their economic conditions of existence falter, most young working-class people in the U.K. would not thank you now for describing them as working-class. They find more passion and acceptable self-identity through music on MTV, wearing baseball caps and designer shoes, and socializing in fast-food joints than they do through traditional class-based cultural forms (p. 402).

Such conditions, which form the core of everyday life in industrialized societies and now penetrate every corner of the earth, are constitutive of the movement of youth.

In Chapter 1, "The global corporate curriculum and the young cyberflâneur as global citizen," Jane Kenway and Elizabeth Bullen focus their attention on the global consumer culture which so influences the "youth moves" that we chart throughout the book. Critiquing an approach that banishes consumer culture from the classroom and other pedagogical sites, Kenway and Bullen suggest that teaching global citizenship and awareness must involve a "hybrid blend of the playful and the earnest." They develop the concept of the youthful cyberflâneur, which they argue provides both a model for the new global citizen and is also a useful way to think about methodology and pedagogy.

Cameron McCarthy and Jennifer Logue ("Shoot the elephant: Antagonistic identities, neo-Marxist nostalgia and the remorselessly vanishing pasts") also take up the issue of methodology in their discussion of the foundational texts of cultural Marxism in the context of contemporary popular culture (Chapter 2).

McCarthy and Logue's essay is particularly relevant for this collection, as it interrogates a framework which has saturated scholarship in youth culture studies, most notably the seminal work of Paul Willis (1977/1981) and Dick Hebdige, 1979). Drawing on exemplars from two dominant cultural modes of production—film and literature—McCarthy and Logue demonstrate the limitations of these analyses for understanding the contemporary conditions of youth, specifically in relationship to class identities.

In the last chapter (3) in this first section, Catherine Beavis examines the new worlds of youth in "New textual worlds: Young people and computer games." Exploring one of the most prominent leisure activities for middle-class and elite youth worldwide, Beavis is concerned with studying not only the games themselves but the wider context of the communities and practices that surround them: She argues that what is critical is to understand how youth use these games, and the interplay between "texts, technologies, communities." As Beavis's chapter illuminates, any serious consideration of youthful movements in the 21st century must take into account the intertwined worlds of "on-" and "off-" line, despite the reality that only a relatively small portion of the world's youth actually have access to the on-line world.

Diasporic Youth: Rethinking Borders and Boundaries in the New Modernity

> If you ask me, the fact that they built a house back in the *bled* by surviving on rice and pasta every meal so they could send every penny to the builders, and now the mom's taking a vacuum cleaner, it means they're planning on staying there. Bet it didn't even cross the kids' minds. But the parents, they must have been thinking about it ever since the first day they arrived in France. Ever since the day they made the mistake of setting foot in this crappy country they thought would become theirs.
>
> **Faïza Guène,** *Kiffe Kiffe Tomorrow*

Doria, the main character in Guène's (2006/2004) acclaimed *Kiffe Kiffe Tomorrow,* is an immigrant teenager growing up in the Paris projects, who struggles to find her place in a society that seems to offer little hope for the future for the poor, black immigrants whose presence in France defines the postcolonial moment (Dimitriadis and McCarthy, 2001). While Doria's parents and those of her friends and classmates long for home, Doria and her generation know only France, despite the difficulties and hardships life there presents. For them, there is only forward movement into a decidedly hybrid future, one in which their identities are in perpetual translation, as they negotiate changing temporal and spatial registers (Hall, 2002). As JoAnn D'Alisera (2004) reflects on in her study of Sierra Leonean communities in the Washington, D.C., area, "These children, for their part, often describe themselves as simultaneously Sierra Leonean, Muslim, and American. In naming themselves, they more comfortably blur boundaries that their parents struggle to maintain in their own and in their children's lives (p. 126)." Although Sierra Leonean are, for the most part, refugees who cannot return to Sierra Leone, other diasporic communities are decidedly more fluid, with continual movement between geographical and virtual spaces, and the creation of communities that defy national boundaries (Ignacio, 2005; Levitt, 2001).

Such negotiations of self are not peripheral to the modern experience but are central to the very definition of industrialized societies throughout the world, as growing immigrant populations redefine both the relationship between the metropole and the periphery, and the very meaning and identity of the metropole itself. In France for example, recent uprisings by immigrant youth attracted international attention, as have attempts by European countries, the United States, and Australia to curtail the numbers of black and brown immigrants that so threaten the imagined heart of these "white" nations. Yet, as dozens of current novels (e.g., Guène, 2004/2006; Levy, 2004; Smith, 2000) ethnographic studies (e.g., Buroway et al., 2000; D'Alisera, 2004; Hall, 2002; Ignacio, 2005; Levitt, 2001; Stoller, 2002; Zlolniski, 2006), and demographic trends illustrate, these experiences are indicative of the new narratives of modernity, where human bonds and communities are saturated with the complexities of global movement, whether voluntary or imposed.

In Chapter 4, "Consuming Difference: Stylish hybridity, diasporic identity, and the politics of culture," Michael Giardina uses the popular and critically acclaimed recent film *Bend it Like Beckham* to explore issues of diasporic racial formation, culture, and identity in a world of movement. Giardina situates his analysis within the racially charged atmosphere of 21st century England, as British Asian communities actively challenge and resist their continued marginalization within English society. Giardina examines the multiple identities and sites that provide the context for youthful identity in these diasporic communities—in this case, Bengali, English, female, youth culture, rap, and political activism. Ultimately, Giardina notes the limitations of films such as *Bend it Like Beckham*, as they evade the difficult political questions stirred up by the diasporic identities of youth, and fail to challenge the racial order of contemporary England.

Continuing with the theme of diasporic youth identities, in Chapter 5 ("Diasporan Moves: African Canadian youth and identity formation"), Jennifer Kelly examines the lives of African-Canadian youth, and the ways in which they form youthful identities in relationship to the popular cultural forms emanating from the United States. Adopting a critical cultural studies framework, Kelly is concerned with how these youth make and give meaning to their everyday experiences as black youth in Alberta, Canada.

In Chapter 6 ("Popular culture and recognition: Narratives of youth and Latinidad"), the discussion of diasporic youth moves to the United States context, with a specific focus on Latina/o youth. As author Angharad Valdivia discusses, despite the explosion of literature about Latina celebrities, little is written about Latina/o youth, particularly middle-class youth. Valdivia notes that the transnational and hybrid nature of Latina/o youth identities and their relationship to media and popular culture is a significant—though undeveloped—area of research.

Finally, in Chapter 7 of the collection ("Mobile students in liquid modernity: Negotiating the politics of transnational identities") Parlo Singh and Catherine Doherty examine the experiences of Asian youth who enroll in Australian higher education institutions. Singh and Doherty explore an increasingly common but little studied phenomenon, examining how youth in these transitional spaces—these "contact zones"—make sense of their own shifting identities. The authors also analyze how these students' Australian teachers construct the students' identities, and the classed and raced nature of the interactions between the two groups.

Youth and the Global Context: Transforming Us Where We Live

In the final section of the book, we explore the lives and experiences of the majority of the world's youth—those for whom movement is not literal, but whose imaginations and identities are constituted within the currents of electronic global culture. Like the South African youth who wandered the corridors of his high school living his life as a Hollywood movie mogul, and his classmates who recreated last night's *Oprah Winfrey Show* every morning at tea break, the youth we discuss in this section are of multiple places simultaneously (Dolby, 2001). They are located in global communities both virtual and "real," and their very actions and identities unsettle the distinction between the two, as (at least for a global elite) much of their "real" life is virtual (Tobin, 1998). Youth in these rapidly globalizing societies also face ever-increasing pressure to excel and to be able to compete with their peers for a dwindling number of jobs in a tightening economy (Dolby and Dimitriadis, 2004). Whether they are "Generation Y" (South Africa), "Generation M" (Singapore), or "Generation Z" (United States), they are a generation whose identities are defined by brand loyalty, sometimes in combination with and sometimes in place of affinity to nation, race, class, or gender. Such moves undermine both conservative attempts to reinvent solid "national" identities such as in school curriculum in the United States, England, Singapore, and elsewhere, and a multicultural agenda which circles around a discourse of origins and eschews engagement with a "world of incompleteness, discontinuity, and multiplicity" (Dimitriadis and McCarthy, 2001, p. 117). This world is also increasingly dangerous and unstable: both in the "dangerous crosswords" George Lipsitz (1994) suggests are destabilizing to the presumed order of things, and the new dangers brought on by the polarizing discourses of "us" and "them," the "West" and the "rest," which are ever-prevalent in the post-September 11 world of surveillance, manufactured and orchestrated terror, and fear of the "other" sitting next to you on a plane or drinking tea at the next table in a café (Peters, 2005; Rizvi, 2004). It is these new realities that penetrate everyday life and consciousness at all levels, regardless of your movements across the globe.

In the first chapter of this section (Chapter 8), "The Children of Liberalization: Youth agency and globalization in India," Ritty Lukose examines how we might understand the agency of youth in the context of globalization. Looking specifically at the agency of young women in Kerala, India, in the context of beauty pageants, Lukose works within postcolonial and cultural studies frameworks to argue that we must integrate analysis that rests on the "power and culture that surrounds acts of resistance" with "attention to the conditions of possibility that produce these acts as resistant in the first place."

In Chapter 9 ("Youth Cultures of Consumption in Johannesburg"), we move to South Africa and Sarah Nuttall's exploration of the rise of "Y" culture in Johannesburg, the context for discussion of youth agency. Examining the rise of this emergent youth culture across multiple media and popular culture forms—including magazines, advertising, fashion, and music—Nuttall traces how the black body is repositioned within the first postapartheid generation. Moving beyond the resistance politics of the past, "Y" culture foregrounds the body as a site for the fashioning of self.

Peter Demerath and Jill Lynch (Chapter 10, "Identities for Neoliberal Times: Constructing enterprising selves in an American suburb") also examine how contemporary youth exhibit agency to construct identities, this time, within the context of the neoliberal politics and economics that saturate the lives of middle-class American youth. Drawing on ethnographic data, Demerath and Lynch investigate the "enterprising identities" produced by the youth in this affluent, predominantly white high school, and how these identities constitute new forms of self-discipline under neoliberalism.

In Chapter 11 ("Disciplining "Generation M": The paradox of creating a 'local' national identity in an era of 'global' flows"), Aaron Koh explores similar themes of youth culture and agency in the context of globalization in Singapore, and the ways in which such dynamics refract through the government's attempts to construct a solid national identity amid a thicket of cross-border flows. Koh maps the ruptures that appear within the liminal spaces, and how youth's performance of "elective belonging" interacts with the politics of attempting to stabilize national identity in educational sites.

"Marginalization, Identity Formation, and Empowerment: Youth's struggles for self and social justice" (Chapter 12) is the final essay in this collection. Here, author David Quijada returns us once again to the question of youth's agency, exploring how U.S. minority youth who participate in a summer diversity institute in California use "talking relationships" to understand both their marginalization and their privilege in U.S. society. Quijada reverses conventional pedagogical questions that ask what is "beneficial" for youth, instead suggesting that we focus on investigating youth's roles as active participants in the struggle for global social justice.

References

Anyon, J., and K. Nolan. 2004. Learning to do time: Willis's model of cultural reproduction in an era of postindustrialism, globalization, and mass incarceration. In *Learning to Labor in New Times,* ed. N. Dolby and G. Dimitriadis, 133–149. New York: Routledge.

Appadurai, A. 1993. Patriotism and its futures. *Public Culture 5,* 411–429.

Appadurai, A. 1996. *Modernity At Large: Cultural Dimensions of Globalization.* Minneapolis: University of Minnesota Press.

Apple, M., J. Kenway, and M. Singh, eds. 2005. *Globalizing Education: Policies, Pedagogies, and Politics.* New York: Peter Lang.

Aronowitz, S. 2001. *The Last Good Job in America: Work and Education in the New Global Technoculture.* Lanham, MD: Rowman and Littlefield.

Aronowitz, S., and DiFazio, W. 1994. *The Jobless Future: Sci-Tech and the Dogma of Work.* Minneapolis, MN: University of Minnesota Press.

Ben-Zeev, A. 2004. *Love Online: Emotions on the Internet.* Cambridge, U.K.: Cambridge University Press.

Bauman, Z. 1998. *Globalization: The Human Consequences.* New York: Columbia University Press.

Brah, A. 1996. *Cartographies of Diaspora: Contesting Identities.* New York: Routledge.

Buroway, M., J. Blum, S. George, Z. Gille, T. Gowan, L. Haney, M. Klawiter, S. Lopez, S. Riain, and M. Thayer. 2000. *Global Ethnography: Forces, Connections, and Imagination in a Postmodern World.* Berkeley, CA: University of California Press.

Castells, M. 2000. *The Rise of the Network Society.* 2nd ed. Oxford, U.K.: Blackwell.

Clifford, J. 1997. *Routes: Travel and Translation in the Late Twentieth Century.* Cambridge, MA: Harvard University Press.

D'Alisera, J. 2004. *An Imagined Geography: Sierra Leonean Muslims in America.* Philadelphia, PA: University of Pennsylvania Press.

Dimitriadis, G., and C. McCarthy. 2001. *Reading and Teaching the Postcolonial: From Baldwin to Basquiat and Beyond.* New York: Teachers College Press.

Dolby, N. 2001. *Constructing Race: Youth, Identity and Popular Culture in South Africa.* Albany, New York: State University of New York Press.

Dolby, N. 2003. Popular culture and democratic practice. *Harvard Educational Review* 73(3), 258–284.

Dolby, N., and G. Dimitriadis, eds. 2004. *Learning to Labor in New Times.* New York: Routledge.

Gilmore, R.W. 2006. *Golden Gulag: Prisons, Surplus, Crisis, and Opposition in Globalizing California.* Berkeley, CA: University of California Press.

Guène, F. 2006. *Kiffe Kiffe Tomorrow.* Orlando, FL: Harcourt Books. [Originally published 2004.]

Hall, K. 2002. *Lives in Translation: Sikh Youth as British Citizens.* Philadelphia, PA: University of Pennsylvania Press.

Hebdige, D. 1979. *Subculture: The Meaning of Style.* London: Methuen.

Howard, P., and S. Jones. 2004. *Society Online: the Internet in Context.* Thousand Oaks, CA: Sage.

Ignacio, E. 2005. *Building Diaspora: Filipino Community Formation on the Internet.* New Brunswick, NJ: Rutgers University Press.

Iyer, P. 2000. *The Global Soul: Jet-Lag, Shopping Malls and the Search for Home.* London: Bloomsbury.

Kenway, J., and A. Kraack. 2004. Reordering work and destabilizing masculinity. In *Learning to Labor in New Times,* ed. N. Dolby and G. Dimitriadis, 95–109. New York: Routledge.

Kincaid, J. 1988. *A Small Place.* New York: Farrar, Straus, and Giroux.

Levitt, P. 2001. *The Transnational Villagers.* Berkeley, CA: University of California Press.

Levy, A. 2005. *Small Island.* New York: Picador. [Originally published 2004.]

Levy, S., and B. Stone. 2006. The new wisdom of the Web. *Newsweek,* April 3, 46–53.

Lipman, P. 2004. *High Stakes Education.* New York: Routledge.

Lipsitz, G. 1994. *Dangerous Crossroads: Popular Music, Postmodernism and the Poetics of Place.* London: Verso.

Massey, D. 1998. The spatial construction of youth cultures. In *Cool Places: Geographies of Youth Cultures,* ed. T. Skeleton and G. Valentine, 121–129. London: Routledge.

Mazzarella, S. 2005. *Girl Wide Web: Girls, the Internet, and the Negotiation of Identity.* New York: Peter Lang.

McCarthy, C., M. Giardina, S. Harewood, and J. Park. 2003. Contesting culture: Identity and curriculum dilemmas in the age of globalization, postcolonialism, and multiplicity. *Harvard Educational Review 73*(3), 449–465.

Ninnes, P., and M. Hellstén. 2005. *Internationalizing Higher Education: Critical explorations of Pedagogy and Policy.* Hong Kong: University of Hong Kong, Comparative Education Research Centre.

Ong, A. 1999. *Flexible Citizenship: The Cultural Logics of Transnationality.* Durham, NC: Duke University Press.

Overseas Indians turn to Web for festival prayers 2006. Retrieved at cnn.com on October 10, 2006.

Peters, M., ed. 2005. *Education, Globalization, and the State in the Age of Terrorism.* Boulder, CO: Paradigm Publishers.

Rifkin, J. 1995. *The End of Work: The Decline of the Global Labor Force and the Dawn of the Post-Market Era.* New York: G.P. Putnam's Sons.

Rizvi, F. 2004. Debating globalization and education after September 11. *Comparative Education* 40(2), 157–171.

Rizvi, F. 2005. International education and the production of cosmopolitan identities. In *Globalization and Higher Education,* ed. A. Arimoto, F. Huang, and K. Yokoyama, 77–92. Hiroshima University: Research Institute for Higher Education, International Publications Series No. 9.

Smith, Z. 2000. *White Teeth.* New York: Random House.

Stoller, P. 2002. *Money Has No Smell: The Africanization of New York City.* Chicago, IL: University of Chicago Press.

Suárez-Orozco, M., and D. Qin-Hilliard. 2004. *Globalization: Culture and Education in the New Millennium.* Berkeley, CA: University of California Press.

Tobin, J. 1998. An American *Otaku* (or a boy's virtual life on the Net). In *Digital Diversions: Youth Culture in the Age of Multimedia,* ed. J. Sefton Green, 106–127. London: UCL Press.

Weis, L. 1990. *Working Class Without Work: High School Students in a De-Industrializing Economy.* New York: Routledge.

Weis, L. 2004. *Class Reunion: The Remaking of the American White Working Class.* New York: Routledge.

Willis, P. 1981. *Learning to Labor: How Working Class Kids Get Working Class Jobs.* New York: Columbia University Press. [Original work published 1977.]

Willis, P. 1990. *Common Culture.* Milton Keynes, U.K.: Open University Press.

Willis, P. 2003. Foot soldiers of modernity. *Harvard Educational Review* 73(3), 390–415.

Zlolniski, C. 2006. *Janitors, Street Vendors, and Activists: The Lives of Mexican Immigrants in Silicon Valley.* Berkeley, CA: University of California Press.

I
New Times, New Identities

1

The Global Corporate Curriculum and the Young Cyberflâneur as Global Citizen

JANE KENWAY AND ELIZABETH BULLEN

Contemporary youth are growing up in a rapidly changing and unpredictable world characterized by, among other factors, the unprecedented expansion of "transcontinental flows and patterns of social interaction," which have created complex and uneven forms of "interconnectedness" (Held and McGrew, 2002, p. 1). This has important implications for the young and their education. Our focus is on those forms of interconnectedness created by the global cultural economy, and more particularly global consumer–media culture. These are increasingly predicated on consumption (Best and Kellner, 2003). We begin with a discussion of these terms. We then explain how the global corporate curriculum for the young is part of the global cultural economy, showing how young people are located within it and pointing to its worrying silences. We explore what the corporate curriculum means for pedagogical projects associated with global citizenship, explaining the importance of developing a sense of critical agency in the young that goes beyond that made available by consumer–media culture (Kenway and Bullen, 2001). But we also identify the dangers of critically deconstructing children's pleasures in class and point to the importance of pedagogies for global citizenship that blend the playful and the earnest. The third section develops the case for an understanding of the young cyberflâneur as global citizen. Here we clarify the contours of the debates about the flâneur, justify our use of the term *cyberflâneur,* and offer examples of the young cyberflâneur as critical observer and as cultural producer.

The Global Cultural Economy

In this chapter, we consider globalization from a cultural studies perspective and focus particularly on global consumer culture. As a result of globalization, many cultural forms have become disembedded and deterritorialized, and the influence of global corporate capitalism has become increasingly pervasive as technological innovations have escalated the diffusion of consumer–media culture into almost every aspect of everyday life and across the globe. Consumerism is becoming normalized as a defining characteristic of the lifestyle of the so-called global North and South—the minority and majority world, respectively. Consumer–media culture is a central feature of what Arjun Appadurai calls the global cultural economy (1995) and is instrumental in the global movement of culture, information, images and desires and, overall, in the production of consumer society (Bauman, 1998).

Global Consumer–Media Culture

Markets and information and communication media together hold a powerful and privileged position in today's globalizing culture, society, and economy. An increasingly large proportion of contemporary market exchange activity involves cultural technologies, goods, and services (Kline, 1993) and experiential commodities such as cultural events, enterprise culture, the heritage industry, theme parks, commercialized sports, and other public spectacles (Lee, 1993). Indeed, consumption has so transformed the material landscape that it is possible to talk of the "aestheticization of everyday life" (Lash and Urry, 1994). Shopping complexes, malls, strips, and retail parks shape the character and functions of many urban landscapes and streetscapes around the globe. Consumerism as a way of life reaches many via globalized media, entertainment, travel, and sports industries. Some fear it will result in cultural homogenization on a global scale.

Cultural homogenization theses imply that cultural forms flow from the minority world to the majority world and that they are experienced in similar ways by differently located peoples. In contrast, fragmentation theses imply that we are somehow disconnected from the lives and concerns of others around the globe. However, as Michael Featherstone (1995) points out, "the binary logic which seeks to comprehend culture via the mutually exclusive terms of homogeneity/heterogeneity, integration/disintegration, unity/diversity, must be discarded" (p. 2). The operations of the global cultural economy need to be understood in terms of "disjunctive flows" of people, images, money, ideas and things (Appadurai, 1995). These have created global conditions of uncertainty, contingency, chaos, connectedness and disconnectedness—messy and unruly forms of "glocalization" (Robertson, 1995).

Mediascapes are among the five scapes of global cultural flow that Appadurai identifies in his exploration of global disjunctive flows. They encompass the images, narratives, and information created by the media, including advertising, and also their modes of delivery, for instance, magazines, television, and the Internet. Mediascapes blend fiction and reality; they profoundly mix the "world of commodities and the world of 'news' and politics" (Appadurai, 1995, p. 299). The experience or reception of mediascapes is not uniform; it is relative to a range of factors including the social, cultural, ethnic, ideological and historical location of social actors. It is inflected by geopolitical, institutional, and community groupings. According to Appadurai (1996),

> In the last two decades the deterriorialization of persons, images and ideas has taken on a new force…. More people throughout the world see their lives through the prisms of the possible lives offered by the mass media in all their forms. That is, fantasy is now a social practice, it enters, in a host of ways, into the fabrication of social lives…. The biographies of ordinary people are constructions (or fabrications) in which the imagination plays an important role… (p. 54).

Moreover, mediascapes not only provide a resource out of which social agents "script" their own "possible lives," but also the "imagined lives" of others living elsewhere.

Image and narrative elements circulated by media promote the "desire for acquisition and movement" (Appadurai, 1995, p. 299). They may exacerbate fear of the other, for instance, via representations of war and terrorism, or they may foster new forms of ethical community and solidarity, via such things as environmental awareness. Via its mediascapes, global consumer–media culture creates an attitude towards lifestyle and helps to build "communities of affect" (Hebdige, 1988, p. 90). The mediascapes of global consumer–media culture produce affective connections, longing and belonging, but also separation and distinction in Pierre Bourdieu's (1984) use of the term. Appadurai says we must be alert to "the fact that ordinary lives today are more often powered not by the given-ness of things, but by the possibilities that the media suggest are available" (1996, p. 52). He argues that mediascapes have created a fetishism of the consumer, by which he means that

> … the consumer has been transformed, through commodity flows (and the mediascapes, especially of advertising, that accompany them) into a sign, both in Baudrillard's sense of a simulacrum which only asymptomatically approaches the form of a real social agent; and in the sense of a mask for the real seat of agency, which is not the consumer but the producer and the many forces that constitute production…. *These images of agency [created by mediascapes] are increasingly distortions of the world of merchandising so subtle that the consumer is consistently helped to believe that he or she is an actor, where in fact he or she is at best a chooser* (1995, p. 307, our italics).

Mediascapes are fueled by desire—the desire of capital for profit and the desire of the consumer for pleasure and satisfaction. Lyotard (1984 [report, 1993]) terms this the "libidinal economy." The libidinal economy consists of social and market structures and dispositions that release, channel, and exploit desires and feelings (intensities), although never fully controlling them. These highly fluid intensities sustain the libidinal economy. Desire persists only as long as it remains unsatisfied. As a product is assimilated into the marketplace, it eventually generates less profit as its novelty and, thus, desirability diminishes. The result is product senility and aesthetic obsolescence, leading to the rapid turnover of style and fashion and the creation of an artificial sense of insufficiency. Satisfaction is anathema to the libidinal economy.

The Global Corporate Curriculum

The global consumer–media culture industries target young consumers particularly. As a consequence, a number of cultural studies scholars talk of the corporate curriculum and corporate pedagogues (e.g., Steinberg and Kincheloe, 1997). The corporate curriculum seeks to teach the young that consumption can assuage dissatisfaction and that consumption, identity, and pleasure are one, and reifies the general shift from a society of producers to a society of consumers. This society is, as Beck (2000) argues, individualized and normalized around consumption. It seeks to create a particular subjectivity based on the values associated with lifestyle commodity aesthetics rather than the work ethic or, indeed, ethical responsibility for others (Bauman, 1998, p. 31). How so?

Curriculum Carnivalesque and Jouissance

The corporate curriculum offers consumption to the young as a primary motivating force and cultural resource with which to construct their identities, set their priorities, and solve their problems. Further, it is about sensation; it is textually rich, entertaining, and engaging. Young people's culture, entertainment, and advertising have their own aesthetics. They are flashy, fast, frenetic, fantastic, and fun. Young people are encouraged to live only in the present, to delight in the impertinent and the forbidden, and to transgress adult codes. They are offered agential identities as pleasure-seeking, self-indulgent, autonomous, and rational decisionmakers, in effect, identities as adultlike youth. These features turn the orderly relationship between adults and the young, citizens and society, upside down. Bakhtin's (1968) concept of carnivalesque and Barthes' (1975) theorization of jouissance help to explain how this process works.

As we have argued elsewhere (Kenway and Bullen, 2001) the world where "kids rule" resembles the carnivalesque, which involves "a make-believe over-turning of the law and existing social norms" (Lechte, 1990, p. 105). The carnivalesque is characterized by "disorder, subversion, inversion, diversion, and perversion." It evokes a particular kind of pleasure, jouissance, which Barthes links to transgression of the social order. Jouissance is a surge of affect and involves a momentary loss of subjectivity (Grace and Tobin, 1997; Tobin, 1997). The carnivalesque is not necessarily as subversive as it appears, however. In this instance, its transgressions are highly regulated and are ultimately designed to reinforce the social status quo. The jouissance and the carnivalesque create acts to obscure this function.

The concepts of carnivalesque, jouissance and, indeed, hyperreality (Baudrillard, 1983) offer an explanation of the way children's consumer–media culture seeks *not* to operate at the level of rationality. As Lee (1993, p. 143) says of postmodern aesthetics, children's media culture "invites a fascination, rather than a contemplation, of its contents; it celebrates surfaces and exteriors rather than looking for or claiming to embody (modernist) depth." It also "transforms all cultural content into objects for immediate consumption rather than texts of contemplative reception or detached and intellectual interpretation." The jouissance that consumer–media culture evokes is designed to encourage young people to consume rather than interpret its texts. Indeed, as Appadurai says of mediascapes, consumer–media culture blurs the boundaries between data, information and knowledge and between entertainment and advertising.

Absences and Silences

Consumer–media culture seldom offers young people the pleasures of reflexive knowing or a sense of agency derived from recognizing how their meanings, identities, and affective investments and communities are produced. The potential pleasures of becoming informed and active citizens within the politics of consumption are usually overridden by the pleasures of fantasy. The corporate curriculum teaches no lessons about how consumption works, why consuming is equated with the good life, how advertising constructs their desires, identities and values, and why other values of citizenship get pushed to one side. Rather, it serves to distract, differentiate, and separate. In so doing, it conceals the interconnections between consumption and production, between pleasure and plenty and suffering and deprivation, which have evolved along with economic and cultural globalization.

Importantly, the global corporate curriculum screens from view the "night-time of the commodity"—the economic modes and practices associated with production and consumption. Lee (1993) explains:

> The ways in which commodities converge and collect in the market, their untarnished appearance as they emerge butterfly-like from the grubby chrysalis of production, the fact that they appear to speak only about themselves as objects and not about the social labor of their production is ultimately what constitutes the fetishism of commodities. The sphere of production is thus the night-time of the commodity: the mysterious economic dark side of social exploitation which is so effectively concealed in the dazzling glare of the market-place (p. 15).

Third World sweatshops, child labor, corporate greed, the corporate colonization of public space and the popular psyche, waste, and environmental damage—the corporate curriculum does not reveal any such practices.

Global Citizenship—Blending the Playful and the Earnest

An ethico-political engagement with consumer culture is vital and healthy for young people in schools. Indeed, in contemporary times, schools have a responsibility to teach about what it means to be scripted within the global corporate curriculum and how students might rescript themselves differently as young global citizens. This is easier said than done. The challenge is to help young people to see the downside of media–consumer culture, the contradictory tensions within the libidinal economy, without destroying their pleasures in it; to combine the critical and ethical in ways that are pleasurable and empowering. The aim is to create the possibility of an alternative subjectivity that enables them to challenge the dominance of consumption as a way of life and helps young people to find a range of other satisfying codes to live by. Schools can help the young to explore a sense of agency and citizenship beyond that made available through the media and consumption.

Several aspects of consumer culture can be recognized as integral to such a critical political engagement. On a global scale these include the following: the cultural dimensions of the economy (the use of material goods as communicators); the economy of cultural goods (the market principles of supply, demand, capital accumulation, competition, and monopolization); and the "nighttime of the commodity" (the concrete social-relations involved in the production of commodities). On a more personal scale such pedagogical engagement should recognize the wide range of affective intensities that consumer culture invokes. For schools and teachers, this means acknowledging both students' agency as producers of their own identities and their emotional or affective investment in, and consumption of, media culture and advertising images in the process of identity construction. The young are "vulnerably preoccupied with their self-image and 'issues of social impression management," (Cohen, 1998, p. 165). Media–consumer culture, likewise concerned with impression management, seeks to exploit this vulnerability and in so doing masks or mystifies its marketing intent.

In helping students to understand the processes involved in "why they want what they want" (Walkerdine, 1991, p. 89), teachers must work with and, just as importantly, through, their pleasures, investments and identities. Of course, gaining an understanding of the politics of consumption does not necessarily prepare students to re-envisage themselves as agents in the processes that they have come to recognize as political. If students are to become agents of whatever sort, schools must position them as agential and let them take pleasure in it. Unfortunately, the issues of agency and pleasure in the classroom are a source of ambivalence for some teachers and educational researchers and in many ways they conflict with the nature of schooling.

Teachers and schools need to *engage with the popular as the background that informs students' engagement with any pedagogical encounter"* (Sholle and Denski, 1995, p. 19, italics in original). This means recognizing that consumer–media culture exists as a competing pedagogy. It means recognizing young people's investment in it in terms of identity and peer-community building and acknowledging the pleasures and sense of agency they derive from it. Most of all, it means recognizing that the focus on identity, agency, pleasure and affective communities is what makes corporate pedagogies so successful.

To take a leaf from the corporate pedagogues' book does not mean turning education into entertainment or advertising. It means making the critical and the political pleasurable. There is a strand of anticorporate activism that models this sensibility. We refer to those modes of protest that politicize popular forms of entertainment. An example is the Reclaim the Streets Parties (RTS) involving music and stunts, costume and food, dancing, and games. They are, in fact, protests against the corporate colonization of public space. These parties turn the world upside down by making popular culture political, and politics popular. They partake of the carnivalesque, but in contrast to the top-down version promoted by corporate pedagogues, they work from the bottom-up. As Klein (2000) explains, RTS parties "mix the earnest predictability of politics with the amused irony of pop." Reconciling popular culture with "a genuine political concern for their communities and environments, RTS is just playful and ironic enough to finally make earnestness possible" (pp. 316–317).

Teaching global citizenship in the classroom requires a comparable hybrid blend of the playful and earnest. This means that consumer–media education must have critical and postcritical dimensions so that the earnestness of the critical is balanced with parody, play, and pleasure, and parody, play, and pleasure are understood as political. Clearly, this does not mean, as Bragg (2003) argues, that the teacher becomes a censorious authoritarian imposing an ethico-political agenda or as Frankham (2003) claims, that the pleasure of pleasure "is lost" because of critique (p. 519). As Appelbaum (2002) points out, the process of examining the "critical relationships among culture, knowledge, and power," is apt to be construed as ideological. However, the postcritical pedagogy we propose is reflexive and research-based, its emphasis is on the discovery and synthesis of information. It offers young people the critical resources to unpack their investment in consumer culture in ways that are not ideologically prescriptive but inevitably political, because consumer–media education is precisely concerned with the relationships of culture, knowledge, and power in global consumer culture.

The Young Cyberflâneur as Global Citizen

To assist with this pedagogical project, we have coined the notion of the youthful cyberflâneur (Kenway and Bullen, 2001). This concept builds on the critical and aesthetic features of the flâneur who first appeared in the literature of the 1840s—the gentleman stroller, a street reader, an observer of urban life and a window-shopper. His pleasures have been described as those of losing oneself in the streets of the metropolis, of "just looking" (Bowlby, 1985). However, the flâneur is doing more than just looking; he is a cultural critic and literary producer or visual artist. Typified by the poet and art critic Baudelaire, the flâneur's "object of inquiry is modernity itself" (Buck-Morss, 1991, p. 304). Today, the object of the young cyberflâneur's inquiry is the global cultural economy and he or she is not limited by territoriality or time. The young cyberflâneur uses information and communications technologies (ICTs) as tools for inquiry, and digital technologies for the production of visual and written commentary and critique. The youthful cyberflâneur, we shall argue, provides a model for the young global citizen, and also a metaphor for a methodology and pedagogy. Of course, we are conscious that there are young flâneurs in the majority and minority world who do not have ready, adequate, or ongoing access to ICTs. However, our focus here, in the first instance, is on those who do.

The Flâneur—a Contested Concept

We acknowledge that the historical and critical background of the flâneur makes our appropriation potentially contentious. Not least among the obstacles is the gendering of the flâneur as masculine. There is a body of criticism, for instance, which focuses on the link between flânerie and the male gaze or the excluded feminine flâneuse (Bowlby, 1985; Walkowitz, 1992; Wolff, 1985). We do not underestimate the significance of the gendering of the flâneur as masculine, or the impossibility of the flâneuse in the nineteenth century— although Friedberg (1994) argues, that, on the contrary, the emergence of shopping arcades made feminine flânerie possible because it allowed women to roam the city alone. However, to argue the impossibility of a postmodern flâneuse on the grounds of historical precedence which confines women to the private sphere is the equivalent of arguing that women should be excluded from professions for the same reason. Moreover, the use of technology radically alters, if not obliterates, the relevance of the gendered body. Like cinema before it, ICTs permit a form of virtual flânerie that is available to women and girls. To paraphrase Friedberg (1994, p. 38), they permit a new form of subjectivity which is decorporealized.

More problematic, however, is the literature that suggests a fundamental analytical incompatibility between the flâneur and reflexive citizenship. Initially the flâneur was regarded as "a solitary onlooker" who "stands wholly outside production" (Wilson, 1992, p. 95), who looks beyond the lure of pleasure to see that consumption is often accompanied by disappointment and exploitation. However, in the literature including and following Benjamin (1982, 1997) the flâneur falls under the spell of the commodity; indeed, is equated with the consumer. Nixon (1997, p. 334), for instance, regards the flâneur as "an allegorical representation of the new relationship between the display of commodities and consumers" and, thus, is as a figure for "a new spectatorial consumer subjectivity." The pleasures of window-shopping are the pleasures of looking at oneself reflected in the midst of this spectacle and are, by implication, narcissistic. When not the idle consumer of postmodern cultural experience, the flâneur is depicted as a purveyor of global consumer culture (Buck-Morss, 1986; Buck-Morss, 1991; McLaren and Hammer, 1995); a veritable creator of Baudrillard's simulacra or Appadurai's mediascapes.

On the other hand, those conceptualizations that emphasize the flâneur as an outside observer frequently lead to presumptions of voyeurism, idle sensationalism, and political disengagement:

> To the perfect spectator, the impassioned observer, it is an immense joy to make his domicile among numbers, amidst fluctuation and movement, amidst the fugitive and infinite. To be away from home, and yet to feel at home; to behold the world, to be in the midst of the world and yet remain hidden from the world—these are some of the minor pleasures of such independent, impassioned and impartial spirits (Baudelaire, 1986, p. 34, quoted in Friedberg, 1994).

Baudelaire, of course, has come to be regarded as the prototypical flâneur. According to Jenks (1995), the conflation between Baudelaire (the man) and the flâneur (the concept) has tended to consolidate the disreputability of this figure. The Baudelairean flâneur may be a poet and critic, but he is also the dandy, dilettante, and decadent—not a model for global citizenship to which schools are likely to subscribe.

The flâneur, then, is an ambivalent figure, but it is precisely for this reason that it is so apt for our purpose. Jenks's (1995) explanation of the polarization of critical understandings of the flâneur, in particular its degradation, is illuminating. He argues that the dominant strand of negative critique "emerges, most typically, from a moral–political position … that is resistant to the pleasures that stem from: aesthetic excess; abstract expression; and the aestheticization of social life itself" (Jenks, 1995, p. 147). Possibly pedagogies that permit such pleasure will also be met with conservative resistance. However, it is our view that young people's proximity to consumer culture and its mediascapes and the opportunity to take pleasure therein actually permits the young cyberflâneur to "see." We admit this is rather paradoxical. For the young cyberflâneur is not simply a consumer of the commodity or of commodified experience. He or she is not the badaud—"the mere gaper who becomes intoxicated by the urban scene to the extent that he forgets him (or herself)" (Featherstone, 1998, p. 914). On the contrary, the flâneur is typified by reflexivity, by what Matthew Arnold called "disinterested interest" in the objects of (post)modernity. Jenks (1995) writes:

> The wry and sardonic potential built into the flâneur enables resistance to the commodity form and also penetration into its mode of justification, precisely through its unerring scrutiny. Its disinterested

interest burns deep into the assumed necessity of consumption and it consequently demotivates the distinction between "wants" and "needs" (p. 148).

Featherstone (1998, p. 913) argues that the flâneur's aesthetic sensibility, which oscillates between involvement and detachment, "is no natural gift or inherited skill, but entails a pedagogy." It involves a "hermeneutic of seeing." To paraphrase Featherstone (1998), the task is to see the city anew, to make the familiar strange and the strange familiar. Ultimately Jenks (1995) concludes:

> The flâneur, though grounded in everyday life, is an analytic form, a narrative device, an attitude towards knowledge and its social context. It is an image of movement through the social spaces of modernity…. The flâneur is a multilayered palimpsest that allows us to "move" from real products of modernity like commodification and leisured patriarchy, through the practical organization of space and its negotiation by the inhabitants of a city, to a critical appreciation of the state of modernity and its erosion into the post—and onwards to a reflexive understanding… (p. 148).

The Young Cyberflâneur as Critical Observer

The nineteenth-century flâneur strolled the streets of Paris, its cafés and arcades, parks and theatres, boulevards and hidden alleys, and saw its glittering surface and its seamier underside. The young cyberflâneur explores the virtual geographies to which the ICTs give them ingress. Like the material metropolis, the virtual cosmopolis (Featherstone, 1998) is not without its dangers and discomforts. Unquestionably, there are places where the young cyberflâneur should not stray. There is perhaps a danger "that youth will become excessively immersed in a glittering world of high-tech experience and lose its social connectedness and ability to communicate and relate concretely to other people" (Best and Kellner, 2003, p. 88). We also need to ask whether an authentic flânerie is possible when the images viewed are simulations produced using such technologies as photography (Sontag), cinema, television, and the Internet. Bauman (1992) suggests not. He says:

> Baudrillard tied the flâneur to the armchair in front of the TV set. The stroller does not stroll any more. It is the TV images, TV commercials, the goods and joys they advertise who now stroll, and run, and flow in front of the hypnotized view (pp. 154–155).

Is it really possible, therefore, to go behind mediascapes, behind the simulations and simulacra of hyperreality, using a computer screen?

We believe that of all the means of virtual flânerie, cyberspace is the most consonant with the essence of flânerie. Like the nineteenth-century flâneur, the young cyberflâneur passes through the spectacle of the virtual cosmopolis incognito but can also engage with the crowd and the commodity via its interactive features. Whereas cinema and television and photography situate the spectator as a passive consumer of images or text located in linear time and space, the World Wide Web offers multiple entry and exit points, trails, and traces. The young cyberflâneur may not have physical mobility, but as Featherstone (1998, p. 921) suggests, in cyberspace "instantaneous connections are possible which render physical spatial differences irrelevant." As a tool for inquiry, the Internet offers young people the freedom and agency to look at and beyond the surface gloss of global consumer culture and to discover what lies hidden. This is a form of detective work and, according to Benjamin (1997, p. 41), "No matter what trail the flâneur may follow, every one will lead him to a crime."

Through the networks of the World Wide Web, the young cyberflâneur is able to make connections between the theatrical spectacle of the virtual Rialto or mall and the sweatshops and shantytowns of Latin America, Indonesia, China, Vietnam, the Philippines, and other free-trade zones. He or she can make connections between the products consumed and those who produce them, between the fetishism of the consumer described above, and the fetishism of production, and thus the cultural and economic aspects of the global cultural economy. As Appadurai (1995) explains,

> To the extent that various kinds of free-trade zones have become the models for production at large, especially of high-tech commodities, production has itself become a fetish, masking not only social relations as such, but the relations of production, which are increasingly transnational. The locality… becomes a fetish which disguises the globally dispersed forces that actually drive production (pp. 306–307).

In that production, fetishism and the fetishism of the consumer (and the illusion of agency it fosters) are mutually supportive, to unmask one is to assist in the unmasking of the other. Such unmasking assists young people to make more authentic and informed choices about how to live an ethical–political life, to imagine other possible lives.

Tracing the travels of things across time and space, watching to see who uses what and with what effects, self-conscious adolescents become conscious of the self and the other on a global scale. They watch themselves, their peers, and previous generations using cultural goods to communicate, and they identify the masquerades and simulacra involved. They also discover other secrets, such as "the nighttime of the commodity." The reflexivity they develop involves shattering the illusion of reality by making the codes of production transparent and questioning the ideological nature of the messages and the social relationships they construct. Take some examples. Activist Web sites such as McSpotlight (http://www.mcspotlight.org/), Whirled Bank (http://www.whirledbank.org/), and Global Arcade (http://www.globalarcade.org/home.html), offer young cyberflâneurs political/parody insights and opportunities. Indeed, there are many activist websites on which the "trails" to recent manifestations of "crime" in Benjamin's (1997, p. 41) terms can be found. It does not take much virtual strolling to see the links between commodification, commercialization, and corporatization and such things as environmental degradation, animal cruelty, and human rights violations.

The Young Cyberflâneur as Cultural Producer

The flâneur is not, of course, merely a spectator or virtual tourist, but also a critic, and this critical facility can be expressed through aesthetic means. As Featherstone (1998) explains, flânerie is a method of reading the streets (or texts), and it is also a method of producing and constructing texts. Nevertheless, the interest of many cultural theorists has tended to focus on the spectatorial aspects of flânerie at the expense of the process of reflection and expression in aesthetic forms. The young cyberflâneur can use multimedia formats (image and text, audio and video, hypertext and hyperlinks) and postmodern design methods (pastiche, bricolage, parody, montage) and genres (advertising, design, journalism, filmmaking) to reflect upon and articulate their critique. Indeed, we suggest that advertising and design are prime sites for this sort of work. As Soar (2002, p. 570) points out, they "are readily distinguishable from other economic institutions because of their declared expertise in creating specifically cultural forms of communication which mediate between, or more properly, *articulate*, the realms of production and consumption" (emphasis in original). The young cyberflâneur uses these genres and forms to contest dominant ideologies and express alternative perspectives—for example, to expose corporate greed and call on corporations to be good global citizens and to conduct their affairs ethically. Indeed, traditional literary and visual arts media, the genres of the archetypal flâneur, are apt for this purpose, too.

Culture jamming is an example of the sort of global citizenship a young cyberflâneur might enjoy. It involves the practice of parodying advertisements; it "mixes art, media, parody, and the outsider stance" (Klein, 2000, p. 283) of the flâneur. The principles of culture offer a paradigm for young people to make their own media, using the same tools and techniques as the media and to take pleasure in doing so. Multimedia technologies allow students to create parodies as flashy, fun and visually arresting as their own media and consumer culture. At the same time, because parody manipulates and mocks elements of genre, form, language, image, and structure, it demands a consideration of the function of each of these in the parodic target, thus revealing "the deeper truth hiding beneath the layers of advertising euphemisms" of the original corporate strategy (Klein, 2000, p. 282). E-zines provide a further opportunity for producing texts and for joining others who are doing various sorts of life politics online. Cybergirl Web sites are an example of this, being designed to transgress societal expectation and disrupt the stereotyping of women and technology. These are hybrids which have hijacked elements of media–consumer culture to blend politics with pleasure. In doing so, they offer girls and young women opportunities to enjoy the very objects they subvert. They provide a forum for the dissemination of knowledge which young women might consider boring or irrelevant as a topic of conventional classroom instruction. The Cybergirl Web site (http://www.cybergirl.com/), for instance, offers technological advice in ways which are feisty, subversive, politicized, alternative, celebratory, impassioned, fun, chic, and sexy. E-zines offer opportunities for information sharing and for creativity and self-expression. They provide a forum within which young people can distribute their voices and views in ways that they enjoy; they can blend the playful and earnest. Their message is "Do it yourselves" (DIY) rather than passively waiting for someone to do it for/to you.

To propose these Web sites as models for a pedagogy is not to assume, as Frankham believes we do (2003, p. 518), that there are not already cybergirls—and cyberboys—in classrooms and that, as she goes on to deduce, students are currently capable only of "naïve 'readings' of consumer–media culture." It is not to suggest, as Bragg (2003, p. 525) does when she comments on the comparison we draw in *Consuming Children* between youth-initiated e-zines and online newspapers produced at school, that the classroom constituency be expected to conform with an understanding of a minority of activist youth who reflect our own "projections and ambitions." Rather, it is to suggest that culture produced by youth for youth is much more fun, feisty, colorful, subversive, celebratory—and, yes, political—than school newspapers produced as much for teachers as fellow students. These youthful cyber-activities are presented as bases of pedagogical approaches, not, as negative judgments on the young people we teach. By appropriating popular cultural forms such as e-zines and culture jamming, youthful cyberflâneur as global citizen activities offer more agency and edge than traditional critical pedagogies. They offer popular paradigms for young people to make their own media, using the same tools as the media uses but to promote their own ideas and to "police their own desires" (Klein, 2000, p. 293). They help to develop a strong sense of agency by allowing young people to produce their own culture and their own cultural criticism in their own voices. Although using the tools and resources of global consumer culture, the young cyberflâneur is not involved in commodification. Rather, he or she can take pleasure in this process, but retain a critical distance. It is through this critical distance that the young cyberflâneur discovers the hidden connections between consumption and production in the global cultural economy and finds new opportunities for forging connections.

Conclusion

Via the pleasurable intensities of the libidinal economy, the carnivalesque and jouissance, global consumer–media culture integrates and segregates young people. Further, it seeks to construct a self-gratifying but ultimately perpetually dissatisfied and superficial consumerist subjectivity among today's youth. It conceals beneath its seductive skin the insidious and exploitative processes of its production and consumption. Overall, it is at odds with critical and civic values. We have offered the figure of the youthful cyberflâneur as the basis for a postcritical pedagogy that brings together the pleasures of agency with a critical global political sensibility. This is a model for the young global citizen as both a critical observer and as a cultural producer. We have argued that consumer–media culture can be used pedagogically to provide the young with the resources to reflect upon consumption as a way of life and as a personal practice. Such reflections have the potential to bring into view the global web of interconnections with those who are excluded or exploited by global consumer culture. In so doing, they provide opportunities for highly contemporary forms of youthful global citizenship.

References

Appadurai, A. 1995. Disjuncture and difference in the global cultural economy. In *Global Culture: Nationalism, Globalization, and Modernity*, ed. M. Featherstone, 295–310. London and Thousand Oaks, CA: Sage Publications.

Appadurai, A. 1996. *Modernity at Large: Cultural Dimensions of Globalization*. Minneapolis, MN: University of Minnesota Press.

Appelbaum, P. 2002. Review of consuming children: education-entertainment advertising. *Education Review*, online at http://edrev.asu.edu/reviews/rev193.htm (accessed October 14, 2003).

Bakhtin, M. 1968. *Rabelais and His World*. Trans. H. Iswolsky. Cambridge, MA: MIT Press.

Barthes, R. 1975. *The Pleasure of the Text*. Trans. R. Miller. New York: Hill and Wang.

Baudelaire, C. 1986. *My Heart Laid Bare and Other Prose Writings*. London: Soho Book Company.

Baudrillard, J. 1983. *Simulations*. Trans. P. Foss, P. Patton, and P. Beitchman. New York: Semiotext(e).

Bauman, Z. 1992. *Intimations of Postmodernity*. London and New York: Routledge.

Bauman, Z. 1998. *Globalization: The Human Consequences*. Cambridge, U.K.: Polity Press.

Beck, U. 2000. *What Is Globalization?* Trans. P. Camiller. Malden, MA: Polity Press.

Benjamin, W. 1982. *Gesammelte Schriften*. Ed. R. Tiedemann and H. Schweppenhäuser. Frankfurt: Suhrkamp Verlag.

Benjamin, W. 1997. *Charles Baudelaire: A Lyric Poet in the Era of High Capitalism*. Trans. H. Zohn. London and New York: Verso.

Best, S., and D. Kellner. 2003. Contemporary youth and the postmodern adventure. *The Review of Education, Pedagogy and Cultural Studies* 25: 75–93.

Bourdieu, P. 1984. *Distinction: A Social Critique of the Judgement of Taste.* Trans. R. Nice. London: Routledge and Kegan Paul.

Bowlby, R. 1985. *Just Looking: Consumer Culture in Dreiser, Gissing and Zola.* London: Methuen.

Bragg, S. 2003. Review symposium 1. *British Journal of Sociology of Education* 24: 522–526.

Buck-Morss, S. 1986. The flâneur, the sandwichman and the whore: the politics of loitering. *New German Critique* 39: 99–140.

Buck-Morss, S. 1991. *The Dialectics of Seeing: Walter Benjamin and the Arcades Project.* Cambridge, MA: MIT Press.

Cohen, P. 1998. On teaching arts and 'race' in the classroom. In *Teaching Popular Culture: Beyond Radical Pedagogy,* ed. D. Buckingham, 153–176. London: UCL Press.

Featherstone, M. 1995. An introduction. In *Global Culture: Nationalism, Globalization, and Modernity,* ed. M. Featherstone, 1–14. London and Thousand Oaks, CA: Sage Publications.

Featherstone, M. 1998. The flâneur, the city and virtual public life. *Urban Studies* 35: 909–925.

Frankham, J. 2003. Review symposium 1. *British Journal of Sociology of Education* 24: 517–522.

Friedberg, A. 1994. *Window Shopping: Cinema and the Postmodern.* Berkeley, CA and Los Angeles: University of California Press.

Grace, D.J., and J. Tobin. 1997. Carnival in the classroom: elementary students making videos. In *Making a Place for Pleasure in Early Childhood Education,* ed. J. Tobin, 159–187. New Haven, CT: Yale University Press.

Hebdige, D. 1988. *Hiding in the Light: On Images and Things.* London: Routledge Comedia.

Held, D., and A. McGrew. 2002. *Globalization/Anti-Globalization.* Cambridge, U.K.: Polity.

Jenks, C. 1995. Watching your step: the history and practice of the flâneur. In *Visual Culture,* ed. C. Jenks, 142–160. London and New York: Routledge.

Kenway, J., and E. Bullen. 2001. *Consuming Children: Education-Entertainment Advertising.* Buckingham and Philadelphia, PA: Open University Press.

Klein, N. 2000. *No Logo.* London: Flamingo.

Kline, S. 1993. *Out of the Garden: Toys and Children's Culture in the Age of TV Marketing.* London: Verso.

Lash, S., and J. Urry. 1994. *Economies of Signs and Space.* London: Sage Publications.

Lechte, J. 1990. *Julia Kristeva.* London: Routledge.

Lee, M.J. 1993. *Consumer Culture Reborn: The Cultural Politics of Consumption.* London: Routledge.

Lyotard, J.F. 1984 [repr. 1993]. *The Postmodern Condition: A Report on Knowledge.* Trans. G. Bennington and B. Massumi. Minneapolis, MN: University of Minnesota Press.

McLaren, P., and R. Hammer. 1995. Media knowledges, warrior citizenry, and postmodern literacies. In *Rethinking Media Literacy: A Critical Pedagogy of Representation,* ed. P. McLaren, R. Hammer, D. Sholle, and S. Reille, 171–204. New York: Peter Lang.

Nixon, S. 1997. Exhibiting masculinity. In *Representation: Cultural Representations and Signifying Practices,* ed. S. Hall, 291–336. London: Sage Publications.

Robertson, R. 1995. Glocalization: Time-space and homogeneity-heterogeneity. In *Global Modernities,* ed. M. Featherstone, S. Lash, and R. Robertson, 25–44. London and Thousand Oaks, CA: Sage Publications.

Sholle, D., and S. Denski. 1995. Critical media literacy: reading, remapping, rewriting. In *Rethinking Media Literacy: A Critical Pedagogy of Representation,* ed. P. McLaren, R. Hammer, D. Sholle, and S. Reille, 7–31. New York: Peter Lang.

Soar, M. 2002. The first things first manifesto and the politics of culture jamming: Towards a cultural economy of graphic design and advertising. *Cultural Studies* 16: 570–592.

Steinberg, S., and J. Kincheloe. 1997. Introduction: no more secrets—kinderculture, information saturation, and the postmodern childhood. In *Kinderculture: The Corporate Construction of Childhood,* ed. S. Steinberg and J. Kincheloe, 1–30. Boulder, CO: Westview Press.

Tobin, J. 1997. Introduction: the missing discourse of pleasure and desire. In *Making a Place for Pleasure in Early Childhood Education,* ed. J. Tobin, 1–37. New Haven, CT: Yale University Press.

Walkerdine, V. 1991. *Schoolgirl Fictions.* London and New York: Verso.

Walkowitz, J. 1992. *City of Dreadful Delight: Narratives of Sexual Danger in Late Victorian London.* Chicago: University of Chicago Press.

Wilson, E. 1992. The invisible flâneur. *New Left Review,* 191: 90–110.

Wolff, J. 1985. The invisible flâneuse. *Theory, Culture and Society* 2: 37–46.

2

Shoot the Elephant
Antagonistic Identities, Neo-Marxist Nostalgia and the Remorselessly Vanishing Pasts[1]

CAMERON MCCARTHY AND JENNIFER LOGUE

Say Cockney fire shooter. We bus' gun
Cockney say tea leaf. We just say sticks man
You know dem have a wedge while we have corn
Say Cockney "Be my first son." We just say Gwaan!

—Paul Gilroy, *There Ain't No Black in the Union Jack* (p. 196)

The problematic of a word or concept consists of the theoretical or ideological framework within which that word or concept can be used to establish, determine and discuss a particular range of issues and a particular kind of problem.

—Althusser and Balibar, 1968, quoted in Dick Hebdige, *Subculture: The Meaning of Style* (p. 142)

Introduction

Could a cockney translation of cultural Marxism, its overall perceptual, conceptual, and linguistic apparatus, provide insight into the basis on which to imagine and build networks of affiliation across race, class, gender, and national divides? What does a conversation between aspects of contemporary popular culture and scholarly discourses of cultural Marxism reveal? And why is it important to ask?

Illuminating the way discourses of resistance function to reinforce aspects of the very power structures they aim to and claim to subvert, we subject the analytic apparatus of cultural Marxism to scrutiny. Reading it contrapuntally (Logue, 2005) through the lenses of cinematic and literary representation (restoring an absently present cockney translation?), we begin to see how the units of analysis in the discourse of cultural/historical materialist revolution are incapable of encapsulating the dynamics of power at work in past and present social and global relations. Juxtaposing analysis of the nostalgic and unified nationalist structure of feeling with which the neo-Marxist discourse in postwar Britain is silently aligned to the problematization of tradition we see in cinematic and literary representation an opportunity to (re)examine the conceptual tensions and categorical contradictions existent within this discourse of resistance, the terms of which, as commonly deployed, seem to undermine the possibility of adequately diagnosing the (new but reminiscent of old) dynamics of power and resistance it portends.

The tendency to at once universalize and pathologize particularity in a manner disavowed allows terms such as *tradition, culture, class, power, privilege,* and so forth to be deployed as though they weren't each of them riddled with complexity, contradiction, and antagonistic genealogical formation—an age-old strategy in the struggle for domination. The persistent assignment of particularism and atavism to the vast wastes of the third world begins with Karl Marx himself as well as Max Weber and Émile Durkheim in their particular staged model of historical evolution of human societies, and it continues in contemporary thinking in the attribution of the same scarlet letter to the new social movements and the rejection of identity politics in the writings of Marxist scholars such as Todd Gitlin (1995). This essay bucks this trend, restoring a corrective valence to the whole enterprise of the analysis of culture. We read all of this against the troubling of tradition and the past in recent films on the working class subject such as *Billy Elliot* (2000) and *The Full Monty* (1997) as well as George Orwell's discourse on tradition, power, and privilege in his essay, "Shooting an Elephant" (1946/1981). Here, in the latter, the "ear'oled" working class subject now operates on colonial secondment overseas. In reading back and forth between Birmingham and Burma, a new light is shed on recombinant particularism (*There Ain't No Black in the Union Jack!*) that the analytic framework of cultural Marxism seems to have foreclosed. For to understand British cultural studies is in part to understand that Matthew Arnold's project still survives in the hearts and minds of men and women at home, and even overseas in the empire, as C. L. R. James argues in *Beyond a Boundary* (1983).

Examining the status of tradition and the past within cultural Marxism as a way of clearing a path to the future, looking particularly at the work of historical recuperation within Marxist cultural humanism and its tendencies towards the universalization of the particular, a sharp light of attention is focused on British cultural studies, its anxiety of influence, and its graven desire for plenitude and fullness of understanding of the socially and materially constructed demarcations of the modern world. One is reminded here of the definition of culture and cultural studies advanced by John Fiske in his essay "British Cultural Studies and Television." "Cultural studies," argues Fiske, "is concerned with the generation and circulation of meanings in industrial societies (the study of nonindustrial societies may require a different theoretical base...)" (Fiske, 1987, p. 254). Cultural studies' search for the vanishing point, the origins of consciousness and general mythologization and valorization of the industrial working class subject is nestled within a peculiar narrative and play of national endowment, affiliation, and ethnic and localist distinctiveness in its founding arguments and concerns. Of course, similar arguments could be made about the nationalist canalization of tradition and the localist focus of the urban sociological ethnographies coming out of the Chicago school inspired by Robert Park and his students, right down to Howard Becker and the deviance research that influenced cultural studies proponents' pathbreaking ethnographies as Michael Burawoy has argued (see Burawoy et al., 2000).

This valorization of the traditions of the industrial working class has had several consequences (beyond the mistaking of spitballs for revolution) not always adequately accessed or diagnosed to date—one being the disavowal of particularism no different in structure and tone than what could be found in the patterned variables and structural functionalism over all in the work of mainstream social scientists such as Talcott Parsons. Of course, an integral feature of the reverence for working class traditions is the methodological overlay of field-bound ethnographic rules and the visual culture documentary impulses that flow from Bronislaw Malinowski, Evans-Pritchard, Radcliffe Brown, and Margaret Mead and monumentalist classical anthropology into the critical sciences in education and elsewhere, paralleling the rise of visual culture as a whole in silent and sound film, television and radio broadcasting, and the like. As an aside, it is to be remembered that in the 1920s and 1930s it was naturalistic ethnographic research not quantitative survey analysis that was the dominant research paradigm in the social sciences. The dominance of survey and market research would come later when Paul Lazersfeld crossed the open seas of the Atlantic from Austria and joined Robert Merton at Columbia University in New York. But that is a matter for another time.

Interrogating the foundational assumptions and technical terms deployed in the discourses of cultural Marxism, we foreground the epistemological, ethical, and political implications of not investigating what it is these conceptual tools enable us to open up and what it is they foreclose. Does the concept of "class," for example, as deployed within cultural studies research properly capture the contradictions experienced by category members in their everyday, lived existence and their class trajectories as they intersect with the new social subjects of the modern world—the diasporic "Pakis" and "West Indians" of British urban ethnographic lore (carriers of class histories of a different order)? How are the class affiliation and performative practices of Willis's "ear'oles" to be understood within this paradigm, particularly when these putative class members no longer seek to align themselves with the traditions which theorists of the working class describe? Is the working class concept equipped to theorize the collective formation of agents with shared interests as members of interpretive communities comprised of individuals that may or may not share the same relation to the means of production? Should it be? What follows is a critical conversation between foundational texts of cultural Marxism and forms of popular culture to illuminate some of these complexities captured on the big screen and in the ill-fated peregrinations of the working class/lower middle class subject in modern literature (our example, here, being George Orwell's tale of an "uneducated" colonial police officer's fateful encounter with the "native" agro-proletariat in the Burmese context as British imperial rule there waits to exhale). An effort at (re)historicizing the "tradition" of cultural Marxism, uncovering its inherent ethnocentricism, provides the framework for a brief discourse analysis of the deployment of terms like class, power, and privilege held together by notions of culture and tradition that are problematically monolingual and monotoned. Reading these discourses, texts and conceptual tools contrapuntally through the lenses of cinematic and literary representation magnifies the need to reconfigure language, perception, and desire so that the conversation and transnational hybridity that is culture can take place and be grappled with collectively.

Demystifying the Demystifiers

A central task of this essay then is to demystify the demystifiers on the problem of tradition and particularism which the classical sociologists had assured us would diminish with the advance of capitalism. The tendency to shunt particularism off to the periphery is therefore consistent with this core form of thinking. The ethnographic impulse that underlies cultural Marxism fuses action and interpretation, experience and text, worlding the world from the metropolitan center into its visible hierarchies of class and culture. Standing at the center of this panopticon, the whole social field spreads out before the Marxist observer like a vast unscrolling map. This cartographer of the modern world measures and weighs its social distinctions with the finality of a puritan and with the fervor of what Rey Chow calls "the protestant ethnic" (Chow, 2002). In the cultural Marxist's elective epiphany, the third world subject would virtually perish (*There Ain't No Black in the Union Jack*). But in this disavowal, particularism returned like a plague of innocence. Read on its own terms as a quest for scientificity, cultural Marxism divines class from the entrails of the social present and past, and ethnicity disappears. Read against the grain as a reluctant form of autobiography, the root book of cultural Marxism reveals its protagonist dressed in his solipsistic bright suit of ethnic privilege. And here, by this strategy, ethnic particularism appears. It is this deep-bodied ethnocentrism, paradoxically attached to the generalizations and transhistorical statements about the industrial working class and human societies associated with the theorizing of critical social scientists, that Horace Miner satirizes in his classic essay "Body Ritual among the Nacirema" (Nacirema spelled backwards, of course, is "American.") Here, Miner talks about the mouth rites of the Nacirema, in the process exposing the classic norms underlying the cultural description that constituted the leit-motif of culturalist scholars writing about others:

> The daily body ritual performed by everyone includes a mouth rite. Despite the fact that these people are so punctilious about the care of the mouth, this rite involves a practice which strikes the uninitiated stranger as revolting. It was reported to me that the ritual consists of inserting a small bundle of hog hairs into the mouth, along with certain magical powders, and then moving the bundle in a highly formalized series of gestures (Miner, 1956, p. 503).

The everyday practice of brushing the teeth is elevated to the realm of magic. The magician, the social observer and his besotted humanism, are defamiliarized here. And the anthropological gaze of the West upon the third world subject is turned back on power for an evanescent moment full of illumination.

When we look, too, at the writings and founding motives of cultural studies, we find a similar hidden subject within the text that attaches itself to the working class and hides its own anxieties and its professional updraft. When we look at the work of Richard Hoggart, Raymond Williams, E.P. Thompson, or later Paul Willis and Dick Hebdige, we find an ethnographic Marxism alloyed to a visceral nationalism, an ethnic particularism and wish fulfillment which it denies. How else can we read the intellectual history of Williams's (1966) *Culture and Society, 1780–1950* but as a formidable and unrelenting recuperation of the Leavisian moral sensibility and purpose of British cultural form—the dream of the whole way of life as the encoding and decoding of national ethos in the British industrial novel and literary works? Burke, Cobbett, Southey, Owen, Bentham, Coleridge, Carlyle, Gaskell, Disraeli, Dickens, Arnold, Ruskin, Richards, Leavis, Orwell!!! If ever there was an assertion of national canon, a court of appeal, the breaking out of particular cultural sensibility linked to national distinctiveness, this was one. How else is one to read Richard Hoggart's (1958) *The Uses of Literacy* with its characteristic mourning of the loss of the English working class way of life—its rampant nostalgia for a translucent past then in imminent dissolution? How else are we to read the brilliant E.P. Thompson, who, at the end of *The Making of the English Working Class* (1980), gives the disclaimer that he was not competent to speak for any other working class than the English … not even the Scots or the Welsh? How else are we to read Paul Willis and his lads of Hammertown Boys school who reduce the postcolonial other to the metonymic "Pakis" and "Jamaicans"? This great cauterizing reflex, this severe backward glance, was born in fact in the context of a general crisis of the relevance or irrelevance (depending on your ideological persuasion) of Western Marxism as the Soviets marched into Hungary in the 1950s and later Czechoslovakia in the 1960s (Dworkin, 1997). In this rude awakening from methodological slumber, British Marxist historians would disconnect from the work of international socialism, the CP, and found its own distinctive theories of the origin of the British working class in the revival of working class radical traditions (Dworkin, 1997; Hall, 1980). This working class construct, for the subcultural theorists of resistance at Birmingham, was defined around a militancy of style, distinctive accoutrements and dress, argot, and the like. This characteristically muscular construct, as Angela McRobbie (1997) would note, folded the working class into a singular, homogenous structure, powerful against its class adversaries, its semiotic chora set against the "ear'oles" and contemptuous and disdainful of the periphery. The power within this framework almost operated like a blunt instrument that was directed toward the working classes and applied, in turn, like the clubbed foot of an elephant by the working class against its ethnic rivals and latecomers from the third world (e.g., Sisyphus pushing against his enemies, and all costermongers pushing rotten apples, as V.S. Naipaul would say of the donned dwellers of Oxbridge).

In its radical ethnocentrism, cultural Marxism closed off the white working class from its racially minoritized Other—orientalizing the latter, whether they were from Asia or the Caribbean, as metonymic attachments (the Pakis or the Jamaicans). A deadly consequence of this is that the working class subject and the nature of power were not presented in a sufficiently complex or nuanced way. Indeed, it would be left to the filmic culture and the literary culture to present more complicated views of class power and class subjects. Films such as *Educating Rita* (1983), *The Full Monty* (1997), *Billy Elliot* (2000), *Sammy and Rosy Get Laid* (1987), and *My Beautiful Laundrette* (1985) exemplify some of this complexity. While in the literary world, Wilson Harris's *Carnival* (1985), Samuel Selvon's *The Lonely Londoners* (1956), Kazuo Ishiguro's *The Remains of the Day* (1989), George Lamming's *The Emigrants* (1954/1994) and *Water with Berries* (1971), and V.S. Naipaul's *The Mimic Men* (1967) and *Half A Life* (2001) seem to do a better job at grappling with dynamics of power than the scholarly discourses we have been discussing. But before we turn to the filmic and literary culture for insight, let us try and spell out a little more thoroughly the nature of the conceptual tensions that stem from this radical ethnocentrism.

Conceptual Calamity and Lexical Lapse: Who Fills in the Gaps?

The lack of unity and fluidity found within different lived realities within nations and around the globe are not/can not be contained in the concepts we have with which to articulate them—concepts such as "the" working class which has been the animating and organizing category deployed in much contemporary "neo-Marxist" analysis. Crucial aspects of what it means to be a socio-/discursively constructed subject differentially positioned in a nebulous network of power relations are overlooked when definitions of culture, class, and power involve a nationalist monologue at the expense of intercultural dialogue and exchange. Language, here, is of primary importance, for not only does it serve to articulate and delimit a set of criteria for establishing whether or not one belongs to a given tradition or, rather, where one belongs in relation to it, it often seems to reinforce the very social structures it is invoked to subvert.

Historicizing the concept of class, for example, reveals not only that common contemporary usage of the term too often fails to adequately absorb and embrace crucial distinctions and complex variations found with in "it." However, it is also the case that "class" is then disembedded from its proclaimed tradition thereby eliding paradoxical implications of forms of resistance achieved by revolutionary discourses past and present. How, for example, is the Marxian distinction between *Klasse en sich* (class in itself) and *Klasse fuer sich* (class for itself) placed within the work of cultural Marxism? Marx theorized "class in itself" to signify those who share a common location with regard to their relations to the means of production and "class for itself" to pertain to members of a group who consciously recognize their shared predicament and common interests, actualizing their needs and desires through networks of communication and resistance by organizing around their shared conflict with the opposing class. The two contending classes here, for contemporary Marxism, included the proletariat, destined to become *class for itself* and the bourgeoisie, incapable of formulating class consciousness beyond the pursuit of individual self-interest. What was less spelled out, however, were the dynamics, shifts, and conflicts found within *class in itself*. For when one tries to figure out how factors of race, gender, and sexuality figure into the operationalization of definition of the proletariat/"working class" *in itself,* one may be inclined to suggest that there were numerous formations and reformations of *class for itself* within the "working class" and that these variations on the theme were of less urgency for Marx (and later neo-Marxists) to articulate. Continuing in this vein, early postwar cultural studies theorists failed to track the dynamic patterns of migration, dislocation, and rearticulation that had begun to feed into the class experience of working class subjects in England and that brought new elements, new potential conscripts, to membership within the industrial working class. They had failed to adequately assess the changing map of spatial relations and the interior realities of British urban life itself as part of a broad scale set of effects brought on by late-capital—effects that were now stalking modern industrial societies. It seems that, here, the seeds of an under-theorized dynamic involving the mis(sed)diagnosis of the impact of networks of global communication, movement, and migration of economic and cultural capital and the amplification of representations and images had been consolidated. What was nurtured instead was an ethnic and nationalist myopia planted firmly in the soil of an agrarian England transcoded onto the urban setting. The nurturing work of much of the historical recuperation of British radical traditions such as that of E.P. Thompson or Raymond Williams always, then, had a backward glance—an eternalist sense of *le temps perdu, los pasos perdidos*. Time and space essentially stood still. And, for instance, Willis would find in the Hammertown Boys School in *Learning to Labor* (1981) that the progeny of the working class grew from seedlings that were planted by their fathers on the shop floor. This backward glance—a nostalgia for the past, a nostalgia perplexed by the present—rendered problematic the entire analytical apparatus of the cultural studies discourse on class and change. In affirming the class essence of the industrial proletariat, this nostalgia has a particular methodological effect concerning class analysis as deployed within cultural studies: a tendency to gloss over contradiction, variation, and multiplicity.

Is this affirmation of traditional essence and the indivisibility of the working class in a sense what Dick Hebdige accomplished by writing of reggae and punk as seemingly equivalent subcultures in *Subculture: The Meaning of Style* (Hebdige, 1979). Rather than emphasizing these formations and modes of resistance as mutually constitutive, reggae figures in as an expression that culminates in the response of the punks. Neither is reggae considered counter-cultural or as more than an articulation of style, despite the fact that Hebdige cites its having created its own language, religion, and vision of the future. Are we to understand the white and black factions described herein as manifestations of *class for itself* contained within the *"working class"*? How are the lived realities and cultural achievements of the diaspora/black Britain subsumed by this move? Does it contribute to the idea that tradition and culture can be claimed as the moorings of an ethnically invisible yet distinctive group that remains forever threatened by that which it codes as deviant?

And what happens if we take seriously Michel Foucault's assertion that the concept of class struggle evolved out of (was extracted/de-historicized from) the discourse of race war/race struggle? Foucault's (2002) genealogy of the discourse of history reveals that racism is imbricated in revolutionary thought coming from the moment when the discourse of race struggle was being transformed into revolutionary discourse, where the state functions no longer as an instrument that one race uses against another: the state becomes the protector of the integrity, the superiority, and the purity of the race. Foucault reminds us that the concept of class struggle is found first in the discourse of the French historians—in the works of Augustin Thierry, Guizot, John Wade, and others. Thierry is defined as the father of the "class struggle," used to replace the notion of "race struggle." The effort to recode race struggle into class struggle is read as a manifestation of the shift in focus on race as existing whenever one writes the history of two groups that do not have the same language, to the term *race* becoming pinned to a biological meaning. This shift in race as linguistic difference to race as biological is what will become actual racism. This racism, according to Foucault, takes over and reconverts the form and function of the discourse of history, which was hitherto a discourse on race struggle/race war. Racism is born then of the shift in historical discourse, once reporting on the theme of historical war with its battles, invasions, victories, and defeats, to the recording of history with a new postevolutionist theme of the struggle for existence by a society that is biologically monist, but which is (needs to be) threatened by a certain number of heterogeneous elements it deems not essential to it (Foucault, 2002). Racism, then, at its inception, becomes manifest in the idea that foreigners have infiltrated society, which is to be safeguarded from deviants who serve to foreground class conflict by being coded as factors that complicate it.

Foreclosing examination of its own origins, disembedding the discourse of class conflict from the discourse of race struggle impairs analysis of the complex organization of hierarchical social relations and resistance to them. Not only does the term *class* commonly function as though it were a static category with an invisible ethnically particular tradition, but it fails to connote the actual strategies through which social subjects forge collective oppositional identities from the grounded pragmatics of cultural hybridities. Rather than attending to the centrality of sexual orientation, gender, and ethnic affiliation in cultural formations and transformations, in creating networks of communication and association, these categories are too often treated as complications contained within the already established organized relations to the means of production. And while the insights and methodological breakthroughs of cultural Marxism are important, like the emphasis on the popular imaginary, style, and other forms of often overlooked resistance, might the struggles and forms of active resistance of what cultural Marxism lauds as the "working class" be better described as strategies developed by those differentially positioned in a complex web of power relations? It seems as though some of these overlooked dynamics of power and resistance are better captured in the very popular culture that cultural Marxism sought to interpret, but while cultural Marxism begins to analyze popular culture, does it really converse with it?

It is both in *The Full Monty* and *Billy Elliot* that we see the working class, the "foot soldiers of modernity" as Willis (2005, p. 461) calls them, metamorphosing in the transitional light of globalization, and the tragic programs of deindustrialization and postfordism that radically transform the labor market and labor process from hard to soft, from materiality to immateriality, from the decaying manufacture of the metropole to the export processing zones overseas in Asia, Latin America, and the Caribbean, from hard industry to flexible information, from the working class cast in the center of history to the mass appearance of the proletarianized, working cognitariat (Jencks, 1996; Klein, 2000). Do the terms of the cultural studies working class discourse on resistance traditions capture such complexity? And, how are these complexities of tradition, class, and power addressed in the filmic and literary culture?

Leaping out of the Lexicon: Cinematic and Literary Representation

> *Billy Elliot's dad:* Ballet????
> *Billy Elliott:* What's wrong with ballet?
> *Dad:* What's wrong with BALLET????
> *Billy:* It is perfectly normal...
> *Dad:* Perfectly NORMAL???... For girls, not for lads, Billy... Lads do
> football or boxing or wrestling... not frigging ballet!
> *Billy:* What lads do?... Wrestling?... I don't see what's wrong with...
> *Dad:* Yes, you do!!!
> *Billy:* No, I don't!!!
> *Dad:* Yes, you bloody do!!!... Who you think I am?
> *Billy:* What are you trying to say, Dad...?
>
> —From *Billy Elliot*

Contemporary filmic representations offer complex and nuanced accounts of the transforming circumstances of working class lived and commodified existence, revealing fault lines of contradiction and multiplicity. Indeed, the vaunted traditions and the folkways of the past so celebrated in the cultural studies ethnographic portrayal of the proletariat from Hoggart to Willis and Hebdige now hang like proverbial dead weights upon the new working class subject. As Billy (Jamie Bell) of the film *Billy Elliot* (2000) demonstrates, the shop floor and the coal mines belong to a distant past and now exist as strait-jackets constraining the desires of youth. Billy, instead, chooses a future in the Royal Ballet, in dance, rather than in the Victorian role of male provider of the coal mines and the deunionizing labor of North Durham, England. And in the end, when his late comer dad arrives at Billy's performance, he gets to see his son leap, soar, literally and metaphorically, out of the terms of existence that fashioned his life. There is no possibility of return to the past, just the flatlining of traditions and ephemeral revision of hierarchy of cultural distance.

And while Billy's doing ballet demonstrates the falling and collapsing—the ephemerality of—tradition, as well as the ability and desire to leap out of it with passion and grace into creative self transformation, what does our youthful subject have in common with that weary and worn-out working class subject featured in the spotlight of much media in the mainstream as well as with the scholarly and political discourses of the radical left? It portrays the young white (presumably straight?) "working class" male as triumphant; the battle scars, struggles, and defeats of the racially and reproductively marginalized Others (always present even in their absence) are subsumed in the spotlight of his victory over those forces that constrain and oppress *him*. We can see here how the construct of the working class constricts those who find themselves in it and casts out those who provide the other side of the boundary line, for it is not just the capitalists that constrain him and over whom he seeks to triumph; there are no more lines drawn in the sand.

Providing for him an unnamed but central aspect of his coauthored identity, Debbie Wilkinson (Nicola Blackwell), the daughter of his dance teacher, his potential friend (or rather girlfriend) could have had a voice and purpose of life beyond becoming his worshipping subject seeking to possess him for herself at all costs. This one visible female counterpart is vanquished in the representation. Rather than being portrayed as a potential ally with agency, she is pitted against him, so they remain alienated from each other as well as the structures that define and code them. Moreover, the way whiteness functions (for anyone possessing it) as property, providing a special but spectacularly hidden ethnic particularity, cultural capital, and symbolic power that translates into material profit remains unexplored. The depiction of the "traditional" masculinist working-class subject united against an identifiable enemy with similarly positioned Others is indeed challenged here, opening the door for analysis of the underground economies of national identity, sexual orientation, and ethnic affiliation.

In a somewhat different way, but with similar intensity of the uprooting of the past and tradition, Gurinder Chadha's *Bend it Like Beckham* (2002) is yet another refreshing depiction of the flatlining of tradition, but this time the star of the show is a young Asian girl, Jesminder. Jess is the youngest daughter in a rather orthodox Sikh family living in Britain who struggles to participate in family tradition while at the same time, pursuing her dream to "bend it like Beckham." She is a wonderful football (soccer) player who feels that she may be destined to only kick the ball around in parks when no one is looking, but manages to get picked up by the Hounslow Harriers women's team, where she is soon to become a star—until her parents find out and ban her from playing. Her mother scolds her, "Who'd want a girl who plays football all day but can't make chapattis?" However, her father eventually comes around, preferring his daughter's happiness to the confines of "tradition," and we are presented with wonderful depictions of his daughter's ability to participate fully in seemingly separate traditions laid out side by side.

Again we see the notions of the past and the "tradition" of the "working class" challenged when the six unemployed steel workers of *The Full Monty* (1997) form a male striptease act, literally defrocking and leaving nothing but their Poulantzian number plates on their backs. The "Full Monties" of Sheffield literally search for, and then abandon, their iron-mongering past in the decayed industrial rubble of the once-thriving, manufacturing city of Sheffield—shelving their overalls and dungarees for the regular beat as male strippers. Going a few years back in filmic representation, we must not forget the telling sentiment: "We're not English, we're Londoners" explained by Sammy in *Sammy and Rosie Get Laid* (1987) after numerous depictions of what might have made Hoggart turn in his grave: Sammy is depicted doing eight different things simultaneously, eating fast food, watching the news, listening to the radio, flipping through a porno magazine, sipping beer and indulging in a line or two of cocaine while conversing with his father trying to unwind. We have here a depiction of the shifting and fragmented nature of coauthored identities' disidentification with the ethnic particularity of the "nation" and its culture, even as one seemingly indulges in what it has to offer. An alternative representation of desire, romantic/domestic partnerships are pursued here as well as the building of alliance across class (as conceived or portrayed in its strictly material sense) lines. The confines of compulsory heterosexuality and notions of ethnic purity and distinction are subverted as alliances and love affairs transpire between members who are differentially placed within the categories of race, class, and sexuality. Depictions of interracial and homo-erotic desires are indeed a sight for sore eyes in this film and in the depictions of love and desire outside the confines of heteronormativity in *My Beautiful Laundrette*, which is we can't forget the space owned by "Pakis," who are white working-class jonnys, employers, and lovers.

And with an eye to the under-theorized pathologies of imperial domination, we get a glimpse in these films also of the perils of privilege lived out by its perpetrators. There's Ravi, Sammy's father, whose involvement in British imperialism leads him to commit suicide after he finds that relocating to Britain fails to drive brutal memories from his mind, memories of how, perhaps, his own involvement in maintaining his notion of tradition contributed to its demise. Notably, the wealth and riches he received from his affiliation with the colonizers provided neither luxury nor peace of mind, alienating him from his family who cried—but did they mourn his death? The very privilege promised by tradition seems to have driven him to take his own life, not celebrate it. But where is the guilt or the consciousness of the white colonialist? Though not depicted here, the film helps to demonstrate that thinking of class merely in terms of one's relationship to the mode of production does not allow for the building of alliances outside shared relationships to the means of material production (often more a product of the abstract "in itself" formulations of neo-Marxist scholars). The film thus offers an excellent example of what networks of affiliation and interpretative communities could look like.

Oppositely privileged individuals both alienated from their assigned class/social function are portrayed in film, demonstrating once again the way in which crucial aspects of lived social relations form and reform with those who may or may not share the same relationship to the means of production. As Paulo Freire would be inclined to point out, both "oppressor/oppressed" are alienated, dehumanized in relations that prize hierarchy and cultural/traditional superiority as we see in the lives of white working class Rita of *Educating Rita* (1983) and her professor and fleeting mentor (Frank). Both are disillusioned by the promises of becoming offered in dominant ideologies, aspiring to cross over the confines of their class distinctions. We get a sense of the ways in which identity is not a finished product one is bestowed with at birth but a project always in process, an ongoing, ever-changing conversation and exchange with Others. Filmic representations such as these depict the world of change driven by consumer durables. The logic of mobile privatization that made Hoggart so uncomfortable has followed a relentless line to the disembedding of the lads. All that is left is resentment as Lois Weis so effectively underscores in *The Working Class without Work* (1990) and Michelle Fine and Weis do in *The Unknown City* (1998). And the incursions and the blowback of Empire, cell phones or mobiles, smart TVs and remotes, the musical language of hip-hop or bhangra or dance hall now course through and mark the new constantly disembedding territory of the Hammertown boys, the "lads"—a flower, an orchid, a rhizome blooms viscously in defiance of the Grim Reaper of urban space.

Depictions of Tradition in the Literary Imagination

Then he said, "On my travels I visited an Indian tribe known as the Hopi. I could not understand them, but in their company they had an old European man, Spanish, I think, though he spoke English to us. He said he had been captured by the tribe and now lived as one of them. I offered him passage home but he laughed in my face. I asked if their language had some similarity to Spanish and he laughed again and said, fantastically, that their language has no grammar in the way we recognize it. Most bizarre of all, they have no tenses for past, present, and future. They do not sense time in that way. For them, time is one. The old man said it was impossible to learn their language without learning their world. I asked him how long it had taken him and he said that question had no meaning." After this we continued in silence.

(Winterson, 1989)

Like cinematic representations, the literary imagination troubles notions of tradition, power and privilege, revealing those dynamics of power and privilege that seem to be foreclosed in scholarly discourses of working class resistance. Orwell, for example, presents the working class ear'ole or lower-middle-class actor "divided to the vein" conflicted to the bones, as Derek Walcott (1986) says of his identity struggle in *Far Cry from Africa* (p. 17). As Uma Kothari (2005) has told us, many of the colonial bureaucrats who went out to the colonies were often of working class or "ear'oled" backgrounds, sponsored up to the public school, Eton or Harrow or whatever and deployed to the imperial periphery with all their hang-ups. Read against this phalanx of national assertion, George Orwell's *Shooting an Elephant* (1946/1981) presents a picture of the lower-middle-class subject operating overseas, confronting the periphery inhabitant on his native soil, in a different light… more internally divided, more complexly linked to England and Empire, more uncertain about self and role in the elaboration of Britishness. The ethnographic lens now puts the Western actor under the microscope. And Orwell portrays the everyday negotiation of class and power in the Imperial outpost of Burma through the mediation of modernizing energies and subaltern subversions ("the weapons of the weak"), the anticipation of the waning of Empire and the dubiousness of civilizing missions abroad. The story draws on Orwell's experience as a colonial officer, and it concerns the angst of an environmentally conscious, uncertain British police officer who, egged on by a crowd of natives to shoot a rogue elephant, compromises his own agency and his hegemonic subjectivity. The narrator/police officer does not want to shoot the elephant, but he feels compelled to by the Burmese agro-proletarians and peasants, before whom he does not wish to appear indecisive or cowardly. The situation and events that Orwell describes underscore the hostility between the administrators of the British Empire and their "native" subjects. But, at another level, it is a deep examination of power. It foregrounds what the anthropologist, James Scott, calls the "weapons of the weak" (Scott, 1985). Here, the native is not the butt of Paki jokes for the lads or the source of black cultural economy of symbols for the Punks.

Orwell problematizes power and the agency of so-called dominant subjects, carefully depicting the colonial situation as one in which the "subjection of the ruled also involves the subjugation of the ruler," showing us how "subjects of colonies controlled rulers as much as they were controlled by them" (Nandy, 1983, p. 39). Plagued by divided consciousness, unable to act in accordance with his own volition, the protagonist is tormented by guilt, hatred, and fear, and forced to suffer the felt contradictions of his precarious position "in the utter silence that is imposed on every Englishman in the East" (Orwell, 1946/1981, pp. 148–149). Having decided long ago that "imperialism is an evil thing," this colonial official claims to be on the side of the Burmese population but feels "stuck between the hatred of the empire" and "rage against" the villagers who try to make his job so utterly impossible. One part of the official, we are told, views British rule as "an unbreakable tyranny" clamping him down while the other part of him feels that the "greatest joy in the world would be to drive a bayonet into a Buddhist priest's guts" (Orwell, 1946/1981, p. 149). These feelings, we are told, are the "normal by-products of imperialism" (Orwell, 1946/1981, p. 149). And, while it is certain that the torment and suffering of those on the other side of the foul smelling "lock-ups" could never be equivocated, the dominant subject in Orwell's narration is clearly not enjoying the promise his "privilege" provides.

Challenging simplistic notions of the ways in which power operates and who creates and belongs to the "British" tradition, on the most telling event of the day in question we learn that the colonial official is far from being decisive, all-powerful, fully authoritarian, or in control. Rather, he feels like an "absurd puppet," a "hollow, posing dummy" unable to do that which he most desires. Having been ordered to find a work elephant that was wreaking havoc about the town in which he was posted, the subject in question follows his orders, armed and ready to serve and protect. He sets off to pursue the rogue elephant but is met with resistance from the villagers who claim neither to have seen the elephant nor even to have heard of its havoc, though clearly standing right there in its midst. This noncooperation on the part of the "helpless" unarmed Burmese population was yet another "normal" element of daily life one counts on as a colonial official, he adds. After almost giving up on his search, thinking the whole thing to be "a pack of lies" (p. 150), the narrator finally stumbles upon the large beast's most recent victim; the official spots the elephant up ahead in the distance and halts momentarily in his steps and reports, "As soon as I saw the elephant I knew with perfect certainty that I ought not to shoot him" (p. 151); moreover, he adds, "I did not in the least want to shoot him" (p. 152). He decides that the best thing to do is to keep an eye for a while to ensure the elephant did not turn savage again, and go home for the day. But then he sees the crowd:

> I looked at the sea of yellow faces above the garish clothes—faces all happy and excited over this bit of fun, all certain that the elephant was going to be shot. They were watching me as they would watch a conjurer about to perform a trick. They did not like me, but with the magical rifle in my hands I was momentarily worth watching. And suddenly I realized that I should have to shoot the elephant after all. The people expected it of me and I had got to do it; I could feel their two thousand wills pressing me forward, irresistibly. And it was at this moment, as I stood there with the rifle in my hands, that I first grasped the hollowness, the futility of the white man's dominion in the East. Here was I, the white man with his gun, standing in front of the unarmed native crowd—seemingly the leading actor of the piece; but in reality I was only an absurd puppet pushed to and fro by the will of those yellow faces behind. I perceived in this moment that when the white man turns tyrant it is his own freedom that he destroys. He becomes a sort of hollow, posing dummy, the conventionalized figure of a sahib. For it is the condition of his rule that he shall spend his life in trying to impress the "natives," and so in every crisis he has got to do what the "natives" expect of him. He wears a mask, and his face grows to fit it. I had got to shoot the elephant.

(Orwell, 1946/1981, pp. 152)

No simple matter for the official in question who repeatedly insists, "I did not want to shoot the elephant" (p. 153), and knowing with perfect certainty what he *ought* to do, he looks again at the crowd and he reflects that there "was only one alternative" (p. 154). He loads the cartridges into the rifle and fires. A slow and agonizing death tortures the struggling gasping elephant while the official is tormented by the sight and the need to keep shooting continuing to fail to put the beautiful, gasping, living being out of the misery he'd inflicted upon it.

The privileged subject here cast is condemned to conform to a tightly scripted code of conduct with which he does not identify. Three metaphors from the story, the gun, the gaze, and the mask (Logue, 2004) serve as useful devices with which to depict what Cesaire (1972) termed the "boomerang effects of domination." The gun symbolizes the moment of usurpation as one in which his imposed superiority coerces him to be what he has forced the Other to see him as. Paradoxically, the instrument through which he performs his fantasy of superiority becomes the vehicle through which he suffers his own agentic demise. Unable to affirm his freedom, the dominant subject finds himself sentenced to an unending struggle for status and justification symbolized through the inescapable look of the Other. This gaze represents the instability and precariousness of his usurpation, his becoming a victim of his own unconscious— riddled with guilt, internal fears, and anxieties. In the desperate attempt to shield against this hideous onslaught of unruly emotion and external threat, he projects them onto the Other who now constitutes that which he most needs to defend himself against. The mask signifies the onset of his own dehumanization, for in wearing it, he can only reach for the gun. A self-destructive vicious circle is begun. The "posture of absolute domination" (Theweleit, 1989), adopted by Orwell's "hollow, posing dummy" (p. 152), and the processes through which he brings about his own destruction, help to illuminate the way culture is a conversation, not what belongs to an ethnically superior tradition. How are these tensions grappled with in neo-Marxist cultural analysis?

What do the imminent deaths of the elephant, Sammy's father (*Sammy and Rosie Get Laid*), and the hopes "traditional" parents (*Billy Elliott*) have for their children signify? Could it be that with the death of the subject lies the death of tradition, an imperial tradition on the wane? Billy Elliot's grandma with Alzheimer's stands in her dreamlike silence in the face of the scrambled riddle of past attachments, past associations, and feeling. Do our perceptual and linguistic apparatuses allow for the articulation of the complexities of lived social relations and networks of affiliation?

Conclusion: Transforming Contexts, Transforming Traditions, Transforming Identities

No olvides que lo que llamamos hoy realidad fue imaginación ayer. ("Do not forget that what we call today reality was merely imagination yesterday.")

José Saramago, *El Hombre Duplicado*, 2002

The real Marxist must not be a good Marxist. His function is to put orthodoxy and codified certainties into crisis. His duty is to break the rules.

Pier Paolo Pasolini, quoted in *Petkovic*, 1997

It seems cultural studies analysis in its treatment of class has been overtaken by events. The perceptual/conceptual/linguistic apparatus of sociocultural analysis on the whole is now unable to diagnose the global predicament we are in, seemingly reinforcing the very structures we seek to subvert. Our entire perceptual, conceptual, and linguistic apparatus is in need of overhaul as we come to recognize the rise of networked societies in which traditions, affiliations, and "cultures," subcultural or not, are now disembedded from the moorings of the final property of any group. There has been a flattening out of cultures and traditions integrated into global expansion of markets and flexible models of production of capital pursuing new sites of value in ever-increasing alienated contexts. We have reached a stage in this new millennium where the old "conflict" versus "consensus" metaphors, "your traditions versus mine" do not seem to apply. Instead of models based on conflict and resistance, increasingly social groups are being defined by overwhelming patterns of transnational hybridities and new forms of association and affiliation that seem to flash on the surface of life rather than to plunge deeper down into some kind of neo-Marxist substructure. This new model of power could now be called "integration." It does not have a negative pole. It is what Foucault describes as a "productive" not "repressive" model of power. It articulates difference into ever more extensive systems of association, flatlining the edges of culture into a pastiche of marketable identities, tastes, neuroses, and needs processed through the universalization of the enterprise ethic. It lays traditions down side by side, layering them in ever new ephemeral patterns and intensities; whole elements and associations given in one place can be now instantaneously found in another. Paul Willis's nationally and geographically inscribed "lads" are now being replaced by Jenny Kelly's Afro-Canadian youth who are patching together their identities from the surfeit of signs and symbols crossing the border in the electronic relays of U.S. television, popular music, and cyber culture (Kelly, 2004). Postapartheid South African youth now assign more value to markers of taste—Levis and Gap jeans, Nikes or Adidas, rap or rave—than ancestry and place in their elaboration of the new criteria of ethnic affiliation (Dolby, 2001). All these developments are turning the old materialism versus idealism debate on its head. It is the frenetic application of forms of existence, forms of life, the dynamic circulation of and strategic deployment of style, the application of social aesthetics that now govern political rationalities and corporate mobilization in our times. The new representational technologies are the new centers of public instruction providing the forum for the work of the imagination of the great masses of the people to order their pasts and present and plot their futures. They are creating instant traditions and nostalgia of the present in which our pasts are disembedded and separated out as abstract value into new semiotic systems and techniques of persuasion, new forms of ecumenical clothing that quote Che, Mao, Fidel, and Marx, and "revolution" in the banality of commodified life. The publicizing of one brand of dish-washing liquid as having "revolutionary" effects is just one good example of the brazen rearticulation of terms and traditions in the brave new world in which we live. Who now owns the terms that define the authentic traditions of radicalism that inform our works? Who now has final purchase on the terms *resistance, revolution, democracy, participation,* and *empowerment?* The massive work of textual production is blooming in a crucible of opposites—socially extended projects producing the cultural citizen in the new international division of labor, in which the state may not be a first or the final referent. Naomi Klein (2000) reminds us ultimately of this radical disembedding. Spadina Avenue, the garment district of Toronto of the 1930s, is now in postindustrial limbo and a center of a masquerading consumerist heaven. Its transformation to its new millennial identity of warehouse flowering apartments, Sugar Mounting, retro candy, edible jewelry, and dispensing of London Fog coats owes its genesis to the cruel juxtaposition with Jakarta and the flight of its garment industry to Indonesia. And while there is not much need for overcoats on the equator, "increasingly," according to Klein, "Canadians get through their cold winters not with clothing manufactured by the tenacious seamstresses on Spadina Avenue but by young Asian women working in hot climates.... In 1997, Canada imported $11.7 million of its anoraks and ski jackets from Indonesia..." (2000, p. xvi).

The outlines of this new global context have precipitated a crisis of language in neo-Marxist scholarly efforts to grasp the central dynamics of contemporary societies, bearing on the question of "tradition" and the centering term *culture.* The latter developments have led to a depreciation of the value and insightfulness of neo-Marxist analysis in our time—old metaphors associated with class, economy, state ("production," "reproduction," "resistance," "the labor/capital contradiction,") are all worn down by the transformations of the past decades in which the saturation of economic and political practices in aesthetic mediations has proceeded full scale (Klein, 2000). The scale and referent for most all of these organizing terms of analysis had been set and bounded at the nation, defined in the localist anthropological/ethnographic terms of *traditions, ritual,* and *culture* understood on the localizing plain of community, ethnic group, society, etc. The new circumstances associated with postfordist capital—the new international division of labor, movement, and migration, and the amplification of images and the work of the imagination of the great masses of the people, the great masses of our times, driven forward by computerization, the Internet, popular culture, and so forth—have cut open particular traditions, spilling the entrails of so much fluttering fish around the world. New working units for understanding modern life are needed. Maybe not the nation, not the state, not society, but the "Globus," the Global City, and ultimately the Globe itself, may be the new unit of analysis, the new referent, with its nodes and networks of affiliation where traditions are attenuated, even as the public sphere and the life world have become more susceptible to refeudalization, sectarianism, and fundamentalism.

Note

1 An earlier version of this essay appeared in *JCT: Journal of Curriculum Theorizing 22*(2): 7–24. Summer 2006.

References

Burawoy, M., J.A. Blum, S. George, Z. Gille, T. Gowan, L. Haney, M. Klawiter, S.H. Lopez, S.O. Riain, and M. Thayer. 2000. *Global Ethnography: Forces, Connections, and Imaginations in a Postmodern World.* Berkeley, CA: University of California Press.

Cesaire, A. 1972. *Discourse on Colonialism.* Trans. J. Pinkham. New York: Monthly Review Press.

Chow, R. 2002. *The Protestant Ethnic and the Spirit of Capitalism.* New York: Columbia University Press.

Dolby, N. 2001. *Constructing Race: Youth, Identity, and Popular Culture in South Africa.* Albany, NY: State University of New York Press.

Dworkin, D. 1997. *Cultural Marxism in Postwar Britain.* Durham, NC: Duke University Press.

Fine, M., and L. Weis, 1998. *The Unknown City.* Boston: Beacon Press.

Fiske, J. 1987. British cultural studies and television. In *Channels of Discourse,* ed. R. Allen. Chapel Hill, NC: The University of North Carolina Press.

Foucault, M. 2002. *Society Must Be Defended: Lectures at the College de France, 1975–1976.* New York: Picador.

Gitlin, T. 1995. The rise of identity politics: An examination and critique. In *Higher Education Under Fire,* ed. M. Berube and C. Nelson, 305–325. New York: Routledge.

Hall, S. 1980. Cultural studies: Two paradigms. *Media, Culture and Society 2,* 57–72.

Harris, W. 1985. *Carnival.* London: Faber and Faber.

Hebdige, D. 1979. *Subculture: The Meaning of Style.* London: Methuen.

Hoggart, R. 1958. *The Uses of Literacy.* Harmondsworth U.K.: Penguin Books.

James, C.L.R. 1983. *Beyond a Boundary.* New York: Pantheon.

Jencks, C. 1996. *What Is Post-Modernism?* 4th ed. New York: St. Martin's Press.

Ishiguro, K. 1989. *The Remains of the Day.* New York: Vintage.

Kelly, J. 2004. *Borrowed Identities.* New York: Peter Lang.

Klein, N. 2000. *No Logo.* New York: Picador.

Kothari, U. 2005. Authority and expertise: The professionalisation of international development and the ordering of dissent. *Antipode 37*(2), 425–446.

Lamming, G. 1954/1994 *The Emigrants.* Ann Arbor, MI: University of Michigan Press.

Lamming, G. 1971. *Water with Berries.* London: Logman.

Logue, J. 2004. Agentic ambiguity and the politics of privilege: Recognition versus reevaluation of privilege in social justice education. MA thesis, Toronto: University of Toronto.

Logue, J. 2005. Deconstructing privilege: A contrapuntal approach. In *Philosophy of Education,* ed. K. Howe, 371–379. Urbana, IL: Philosophy of Education Society.

McRobbie, A. 1997. More! New sexualities in girls and women's magazines. In *Back to Reality?—Social Experience and Cultural Studies,* ed. A. McRobbie, 190–209. New York: Manchester University Press.

Miner, H. 1956. Body ritual among the Nacirema. *American Anthropologist 58,* 503–507.

Naipaul, V.S. 1967. *The Mimic Men.* London: André Deutsch.

Naipaul, V.S. 2001. *Half a Life*. New York: Vintage.

Nandy, A. 1983. *The Intimate Enemy: Loss and Recovery of Self under Colonialism*. New York: Oxford University Press.

Orwell, G. 1946/1981. Shooting an elephant. In *A Collection of Essays*, ed. G. Orwell, 148–156. New York: Harcourt.

Petkovic, N. 1997. Re-writing the myth, rereading the life: The universalizing game in Pier Paolo Pasolini's Edipo Re. *American Imago* 54(1), 39–68

Saramago, J. 2002. *El hombre duplicado*. Miami, FL: Santillana USA Publishing Company.

Scott, J. 1985. *Weapons of the Weak: Everyday Forms of Peasant Resistance*. New Haven, CT: Yale University Press.

Selvon, S. 1956. *The Lonely Londoners*. London: Logman.

Theweleit, K. 1989. *Male Fantasies Volume 2: Male Bodies: Psychoanalyzing the White Terror*. Cambridge, U.K.: Polity Press.

Thompson, E.P. 1980. *The Making of the English Working Class*. Harmondsworth, U.K: Penguin Books.

Walcott, D. 1986. Far cry from Africa. In *Collected Poems, 1948–1984*, ed. D. Walcott. New York: Noonday Press.

Weis, L. 1990. *Working Class without Work*. New York: Routledge.

Williams, R. 1966. *Culture and Society, 1780–1950*. New York: Harper and Row.

Willis, P. 1981. *Learning to Labor*. New York: Columbia University Press.

Willis, P. 2005. Afterword: Foot soldiers of modernity: The dialectics of consumption and the 21st century school. In *Race, Identity and Representation in Education*, ed. C. McCarthy, W. Crichlow, G. Dimitriadis, and N. Dolby, 461–479. New York: Routledge.

Winterson, J. 1989. *Sexing the Cherry*. New York: Grove Press.

3

New Textual Worlds

Young People and Computer Games

CATHERINE BEAVIS

Imagine an entire 3D world online, complete with forests, cities, and seas. Now imagine it populated with others from across the globe who gather in virtual inns and taverns, gossiping about the most popular guild or comparing notes on the best hunting spots. Imagine yourself in a heated battle for the local castle, live opponents from all over collaborating or competing with you. Imagine a place where you can be the brave hero, the kingdom rogue, or the village sage, developing a reputation for yourself that is known from Peoria to Peking. Now imagine that you could come home from school or work, drop your book bag on the ground, log in, and enter that world any day, any time, anywhere. Welcome to the world of Massively Multiplayer online gaming (Steinkuehler, 2004, p. 1).

Steinkuehler's account of life within the online universe of Massively Multiplayer games provides a glimpse of the attractiveness of such worlds, their close proximity to more mundane, everyday off-line "reality," and their anytime-anywhere availability and appeal. Massively Multiplayer online games (MMOGs) or Massively Multiplayer online role-play games (MMORPGs) are the most dramatic examples of the popularity and spread of video or computer games, not just among young people but with players of every age. Notable because of their persistent virtual worlds (that is, worlds that continue to exist even when the player is not online), their complex narrative scenarios, settings and iconography, their often-entrancing aesthetics and their scale, their most striking features, arguably, are the ways in which they work as social spaces for all manner of activities, and their blurring of boundaries and potential overlap between the "real" and the "virtual" and off-line "realities."[1] They create their own allegiances and communities, muddy and complicated distinctions between on- and off-line spaces, actions, and identities, and create contexts for sociality, challenge and debate of many kinds.

As new media and digital culture take an increasingly central place in young people's lives, computer games come to epitomize the ways in which contemporary identities, expectations, and understandings about the world may be shaped and influenced by their engagement with the online world. They provide sites in which to explore intersections and overlaps between on- and off-line worlds, the socially situated nature of game play and game playing practices, the ways in which adolescents are positioned within global culture, and the implications of young people's immersion in digital popular culture for contemporary youth culture and education.

The Scale of Play

The pervasiveness and popularity of online culture, epitomized in computer games, can be glimpsed in figures showing computer games and related software sales exceeding those of the Hollywood box office, in the convergence of media forms and the reach of companies spanning film and games, and in figures on young people's uses of computers and of leisure time.

Figures on the popularity of computer games are breathtaking, with games sales exceeding Hollywood box office and player numbers running into the millions for the most popular multiplayer games worldwide. Price Waterhouse Coopers estimates that in 2002 the global electronic games market was worth $40.8 billion, surpassing box office receipts of $39.6 billion (Australian Film, Television and Radio School, 2006). In the U.S., in 2002, over 200 million games were sold, with an annual income close to $7 billion. European sales for 2002 were $5.5 billion with $3.5 billion of that from the U.K. (Buckingham, 2006, p. 1). In Australia, 2005 figures for combined sales of console, computer, and edutainment games were AUS$589.4 million, with the vast majority of these being console games: console games, AUS$468.1; computer games, AUS$114.1; and edutainment, AUS$7.2 (Australian Film Commission, 2006).

Asian figures reflect the enormity of games' popularity and the place of countries like Korea and Japan at the forefront of games development, alongside huge disparities of access across the region, and the likely further expansion of currently less networked areas as countries like China rapidly industrialize: China is estimated to have 25–35 million players currently online, with predictions of growth to 80 million by 2010 (Australian Film Commission, 2006). In Korea, where computer gaming both at home and in Internet cafés is one of the most common and popular forms of entertainment (Lee and Choudrie, 2002), the games industry is described in governmental documents as "the core of the industry of cultural content" which will "become the central industry that will complete the IT revolution due to the combination of content and high technologies" (Ministry of Culture and Tourism, 2004, p. 6). Korean games sales for 2003 were $626 million, with a further $1409 million taken through online games played in Internet cafés (Ministry of Culture and Tourism, 2004, p. 6). The Korean game *Lineage II*, the second most popular Massively Multiplayer game in the world, had over 2.25 million subscribers in the first half of 2005, with servers based in Asia, Europe, and America (Wikipedia, 2006). *World of Warcraft*, the most popular Massively Multiplayer game in North America and the most popular American game worldwide in 2006, is estimated to have almost 7 million players, (2006).

As these figures also show, computer games take a number of forms—stand-alone and online, console and personal computer-based, leisure and edutainment games. So, too, do the ways they are accessed and used. Sites for game play, and the kinds of interactions and communities associated with them, also vary, with Internet cafés providing an important venue for particular styles of game play, interactions, and concentrations of gaming communities in addition to more private or self-contained locations such as the home. For the purposes of this chapter, "computer games" is taken to include games played on both consoles and personal computers, and to refer to leisure-based rather than edutainment games. It focuses on online multiplayer games, in particular Massively Multiplayer Online Role Play Games (MMORPGs) with particular attention to young players, although "youth" itself is a complex and commodified phenomenon only partly coterminous with chronological age (Buckingham, 2000, 2006).

A rounded picture of the growth and popularity of computer games and their take-up by young people needs to take account of this diversity and as far as possible reflect more nuanced information, including hours and patterns of use. Competitive market pressures means that while detailed breakdowns of sales figures and profiles exist, access to specific figures about hours and penetration is difficult and costly to obtain. U.K. and European figures from the late 1990s put children's hours of play at between 25 to 45 minutes per day (Livingstone and Bovill, Roberts, and Foehr as cited in Buckingham, 2006, p. 2). As David Buckingham (2006) notes, we might reasonably expect figures such as these to have increased significantly since that time.

In Australia, playing computer games was one of the top three leisure activities for young people aged between 5 and 14 in 2003 (71%), together with watching television or videos (98%), and reading for pleasure (75%). Figures for computer game playing differed according to gender, with 82% of boys and 59% of girls participating in game playing in their leisure time (Australian Bureau of Statistics, 2003). In 2004, over 84% of 7- to 17-year-old Australians owned a computer game console (Australian Film, Television and Radio School, 2006). Of Australian games players, 45% were age 18 or under, 36% were aged 18 to 25, and 19% were aged over 36—figures which reflect more general trends showing both the concentration of game players among young people but also that game playing is not limited to those under 18. Of Australian households 35% had a dedicated console system, and 2.5 million played console games (Australian Film, Television and Radio School, 2006). More males than females play computer games but a significant number of women play, with 72% of game players male and 28% female.

Australian figures for game playing that put the median age of game player in their 20s are consistent with the profile of game players elsewhere in the world. The American Entertainment Software Association gives the average age of players as 33, with 31% of players under 18, 62% of game players male, and 38% female (Entertainment Software Association, 2006). A 2004 Korean study found that 75% of the survey group aged between 9 and 49 had "at least tried" playing games, and that games were one of their top three leisure time activities, along with watching TV and accessing the Internet. Perhaps the most striking feature of the Korean research is the almost universal participation in games playing by the youngest group surveyed, with 87% of those aged 20 to 24 and 95% of respondents aged 9 to 19 self-describing as "currently playing games" (Ministry of Culture and Tourism, 2004, p. 40).

Figures like these show that computer games are by no means the marginal or quirky phenomenon that until recently they have been portrayed to be. At the same time, as games become increasingly immersive and attractive, game playing is becoming ever more visible and mainstream as generations of game players grow older and games become increasingly normalized. Despite media panics to the contrary, game playing is not largely confined to children and adolescents. What is clear is that game playing is enormously popular with young people, generally as part of a network of other social and cultural activities (Australian Bureau of Statistics, 2003; Entertainment Software Association, 2006). As multiplayer forms of gaming (massive or otherwise) continue to grow in popularity in terms both of numbers of users and hours played, young people's engagement with it warrants close attention. We need to learn more about the kinds of meanings and relationships that are made, the ways young people negotiate these texts and spaces, and the ways on- and off-line worlds combine and merge. This includes attention to the forms of semiosis and textual worlds young people engage in as they play, forms of representation and the ways others' representations are interpreted, negotiations undertaken as they connect with other players, and the ways these things play out and cross over in on- and off-line worlds, where connections may be with both local and global communities, and across age and gender divides.

The Literacy Practices of Gaming

Online games immerse young people in highly complex and engaging worlds in which literacy and communicative practices are significantly reconfigured and extended by the contexts in which they occur. As "networked semiotic domains" (Gee, 2001) games are sites for learning that link meaning making, knowledge, and identity. By "semiotic domain," Gee explains, "I mean any set of practices that recruits one or more modalities (e.g., oral or written language, images, equations, symbols, sounds, gestures, graphs, artifacts, etc.) to communicate distinctive types of meanings" (Gee, 2003, p.18). Games present challenging tasks and environments, where problems may be solved by a single player or collectively with other members of the in-game community or related affinity groups. This means learning becomes both individual and collaborative, and knowledge socially and materially distributed. Games model socially and materially distributed forms of knowledge and cognition, and provide rich environments within which players are constructed as active and agential, with opportunities for trial and error, consequences and rewards, and increasing authority and expertise as they progress through the game.

As multimodal and interactive texts, computer games embody new forms of literacy or meaning making, in what Kress characterizes as the "changed communicational landscape" (Kress, 2000) of the present day, where the logic of the image rather than the logic of the word becomes the organizing framework of meaning making. The screen is the "contemporary canvas" where "a new constellation of resources for meaning making is taking shape" (Kress, 2002, p. 137). Games also provide representative instances of literacy as design. Design is a crucial concept in contemporary understandings of multimodal literacies, and in research that looks at the ways in which young people interact with and use the resources and opportunities offered by digital culture. It is central to expanded definitions of literacy that reflect the move from word to image, page to screen, as the dominant media form. Design refers both to the multiple modalities and affordances of contemporary media and forms of literacy and to the active use people make of the semiotic resources available to them in new ways, to create new meanings including textual constructions and representations of self. Design is "transformative and innovative" (Lam, 2000, p. 461) and "not only a matter of deploying existing representational resources according to conventions, but also a dynamic process of adopting and reshaping existing resources in different measures to create new meanings and ways of representing reality" (p. 461). The use of "design," in conjunction with sociolinguistic and poststructural notions of discourse, provides a powerful lens for exploring relations between language/semiotic resources and identity, and has continued to provide one of the most useful theoretical frameworks for researching young people's engagement with online media and digital literacies.

Game playing is primarily a textually mediated activity and especially so in games with more than one player, where the game is played against (or with) other people rather than the machine. Language—in game-typed chat and speech through purpose-built microphones and technology, discussions in Web sites surrounding the game, response to written options, and instructions—plays an important part in how games are played, in combination with other elements of design (image, sound, color, gesture, movement, and so on) and with more technologically enabled actions such as the use of the cursor or mouse. Language plays a central role in the construction and representation of self, including the creation and use of avatars through which players play, in the formation of relationships, the management of game play, and the negotiation of issues of ethics and values within and outside the world of the game. Thomas (2004) describes the heavy reliance on textuality in constructing identity in the digital world, where:

> The performance of identity is divorced from a direct interaction with ... cues from the physical, and instead relies upon the texts we create in the virtual worlds we inhabit. These texts are multiple layers through which we mediate the self and include the words we speak, the graphical images we adopt as avatars to represent us, and the codes and other linguistic variations on language we use to create a full digital presence (p. 358).

Thomas's analysis of adolescent cybergirls' representation of self within the online world of "the palace," links talk, image, and identity, through online avatars and spoken/written exchange. She argues that the palace works as

> ... a new site for the consumption of a body culture, where the girls are making conscious decisions about the presentation of the idealized feminine body. On the palace, a substantial amount of talk surrounded avatars, appearance, and the body. Talk was also replete with written cues and symbols to reflect movements, expressions and emotions of the body .... To be adept at creating and modifying avatars, and to have command of the words that shape the self in this space, is to possess power. For girls who are disenfranchised in other everyday practices, the palace, coupled with expertise in digital literacies, provides a site for empowerment, relative freedom, originality, exploration, and reinvention (p.380).

As textual practice, computer game playing shares with other literacy occasions real-world social and cultural contexts and ideologies, purposes and effects. As Thomas's example suggests, game play is not just about literacy, text and play, but is also situated, highly social, and linked to the negotiation and construction of identity. This is the case even with stand-alone games, but much more so with multiplayer online games.

A related framework for analysis that also foregrounds the textually mediated nature of games and the ways they work as communities of practice is Gee's ("big D") *Discourse theory.* Gee defines discourse as "a socially accepted association among ways of using language, of thinking and of acting that can be used to identify oneself as a member of a socially meaningful group or social network" (Gee, 1992, p.3). From this, he posits a notion of discourses which describes the centrality of language to social organization and identity:

> Discourses are ways in which people coordinate and are coordinated by language, other people, objects, times, and places so as to take on particular socially recognizable identities.... Operating within Discourse,

we align ourselves and get aligned by words, deeds, values, thoughts, beliefs, things, places, and times, so as to recognize and get recognized as a person of a certain type (Gee, 1994, p. 5).

Steinkuehler (in press) describes the ways in which games work as discourse communities of this kind:

A "big D" Discourse is the social and material practices of a given group of people associated around a set of shared interest, goals and/or activities (e.g., gamers within a particular MMOG community). These practices include shared discursive resources such as word choice and grammar ... shared textual practices ... customary practices for social interaction ... characteristic ways to coordinate and be coordinated by material resources ... shared folk theories ... appreciative systems ... and epistemologies .... Such practices function as the observable means by which individuals display their membership within a given Discourse community and others recognize them as such.

Massively Multiplayer Online Role Play Games (MMORPGs)

As they play MMORPGs, players interact with both the world of the game and with other players through fictional characters or avatars, tailored in accordance with the rules and conventions of the game. Avatars enable players to take up specific roles within the game narrative—join clans, fight, heal, and so on. In the process, they need to interact with other players in ways that enable and rely on communication, representations, and negotiation. Game playing necessitates collaboration for the action to progress. Players are presented with complex problems and situations often relying on joint knowledge, scaffolding, and interaction. Issues of values, ethics, or morality may be debated both within the game and well beyond the in-game world to surrounding forums and chat sites, and on out into players' "real world" lives.

MMORPGs vary considerably in the kinds of textual worlds they create, but most draw on the ambience and characteristics of fantasy, remediating earlier iterations of epic narrative traditions, most notably those of Tolkien (Bolter and Grusin, 2000), and most are subscription based, requiring players to buy the game to get started then pay a monthly fee to play. Typical features include:

- Traditional Dungeons and Dragons style game play, including quests, monsters, and loot.
- A system for character development, usually involving levels and experience points.
- An economy based on the trade of items such as weapons and armor, and a regular currency.
- Guilds or clans, which are organizations of players, whether or not the game actively supports them.

- Game moderators or Game masters (frequently abbreviated to GM) which are sometimes-compensated individuals in charge of supervising the world.

(Wikipedia, 2006)

Social Networks and Game Play

These games have become a particular focus for research on the social and cognitive dimensions of game play with other players, within the flexible but rule-governed spaces of play, with the literate and social practices in which players are engaged in and around play, and with crossovers and boundary blurring between on- and off-line spaces, identities, and relationships. Communal play, distributed knowledge networks, and relationships establish strong bonds and allegiances among players, inside the world of the game. In one of the few quantitative studies of MMORPGs, Yee (2006) devised a framework to analyze reasons for and enjoyment of game play amongst the 30,000 participants in his survey. Drawing on Bartle's earlier taxonomy, Yee offered respondents five categories—achievement, relationship, immersion, escapism, and manipulation (Yee, 2006). Yee's analysis showed stereotypical gender differences between male and female players, together with some differences according to age, with men "significantly more likely" to be motivated by achievement and manipulation factors and women by factors surrounding relationships (p. 2).

Among the youngest group of players, the overwhelmingly male group (96%) of those under 18, the overlap between on- and off-line worlds, and the intensity of salience of their in-game experience was very strongly marked, more so than for any other cohort. Yee notes,

> The data on motivations show that male teenagers tend to objectify the environment and other users for their own personal gain. Out of all cohorts, users under 18 are most likely to feel that the friendships they formed online were comparable or better than their real life friendships, and were most likely to self report that the most positively or negatively salient experience they have had in the past month as having occurred in the MMORPG environment, rather than in real life. This is also the group that felt they had learnt the most about leadership skills from the MMORPG environment (pp. 35–36).

Yee (2006) argues that "the architecture of these environments facilitate relationship formation and are windows into and catalysts in existing relationships in the material world" (p. 8). If this is the case, and players are also drawn from a wide age range and demographic, it is likely that young players are interacting and forming close bonds with a group united by the culture of the game which is likely to be more diverse than groups necessarily similar to those they might engage with in real life. Young players' emotional investment in online game play, and the potential for crossover between "real world" choices, judgments, and behavior in their in- and out-of-game worlds, provide a glimpse of the ways in which digital culture flows across on-and off-line divides, shaping concepts of values, community, and identity that may include, but likely extend well beyond, those experienced in their immediate and physically everyday localities.

In their study of the Massively Multiplayer game *Everquest* (EQ), Jakobsson and Taylor (2003) present a nuanced account of the centrality of social networks to game play, and the ways in which off-line mores and affiliations shape participation both within and against rules set down by the makers of the game. Jakobsson describes his expectations that as a new player he would progress in much the way the manual outlines, beginning with lowly quests during which he would largely fight alone, developing his character until it was sufficiently skilled to be attractive as a team member to other players. "Secretly, he nursed a vision of finally revealing himself to the community once he had become truly powerful, similar to the ways Gandalf returns in the second book (or should we say film?) of Tolkien's Middle-earth trilogy" (p. 81). Instead, he is inducted into the game at a high level by an experienced player, Taylor, who introduces him as "a RL [real life] friend" to influential players—"not only very nice but also very useful people to know"—and gives him a range of money and other items that enable him to operate at higher levels very rapidly. As Jakobsson begins to recognize the centrality of social networks inside the game, he realizes that the game works somewhat differently than the way the manual portrayed. Powerful friends, made possible by out-of-game connections, make a big difference to what the game offers and how he is able to play, "instead of having Gandalf as a role model, he would be better off trying to think as Tony Soprano, a present day mafia boss in New Jersey from the American TV show *The Sopranos*" (p. 81). Although technique, strategy, and skill are important to some degree, Jakobsson and Taylor argue that sociality is central to in-game success, "The production of social networks and the circulation of social capital proves to be one of the most important aspects in EQ" (p. 88).

Jakobsson and Taylor draw on common knowledge features of the Mafia, as portrayed in popular culture, to frame their discussion of social networking within the game—trust, honor, favors, reputation, and so forth—"the deep connections, the social rituals, the insider/outsider status, the exchange of favors, and the general reliance on others" (p. 81–82). In doing so, they also demonstrate ways in which players exert control that may be quite at odds with the rules and guidelines laid down by makers of the game. Instances include the endowment of unearned weapons and cash ("twinking") such as Jakobsson receives, the importation or substitution of extra characters when a crisis arises (e.g., bringing in an outside cleric played in a different context to heal a party in distress), calling on off-line connections between players to solve a problem, engaging in "out of character" (OOC) comments, and the sharing of player accounts. On a darker note, they suggest that the Mafia comparison foregrounds the ways in which it is also necessary to have the right connections, and that failure to do so may result in being "locked out." Mirroring between in- and out-of-game worlds also means that familiar "real world" issues to do with access, opportunity, and equity can exist also in worlds like these.

Learning as Social Practice: The Kind of Person You Want to Be

Jakobsson and Taylor's study shows the degree to which the in-game world "regularly bleeds over into the physical world and vice versa" and the impossibility of "the idea that one can separately and distinctly inhabit ooc- and in-character space" (p. 81). Steinkuehler (2004) and Thomas (2004), in their ethnographic analyses of *Lineage* and *The Palace,* the online graphical chat environments discussed earlier, provide instances of in-game conversations and communities that closely approximate in-character play in content and tone, but show the same overlaps and flows between in- and out-of-game characters and worlds. The central point of their analyses, however, is to show how games function as social sites and virtual communities of practice, where learning is scaffolded and socially enabled, and where high valuation is placed on "the kind of person 'you are'" much as Jakobsson and Taylor emphasized this with respect to the importance of reputation and trust. Steinkuehler provides examples of the ways in which an inexperienced character, JellyBean, played by the researcher, is inducted into the strategies and ethics around mithril gathering by a more experienced passerby, Myrondonia. Myrondonia has heard JellyBean's cries for help as she escapes from a monster in the forest. She takes JellyBean with her on a mithril hunt and, in so doing, models and explicitly teaches important elements of the game, including how to find and harvest mithril (dropped by monsters and zombies) but also how to leave opportunities for other players to gather mithril by not following these players when they are nearby. In doing so, she "apprentices JellyBean into a highly valued and routinely engaged in practice in all the classic ways":

> She engages JellyBean in *joint participation* in a meaningful activity with a mutually understood and valued goal. She scaffolds her students by modeling successful performance, focusing her attention on key material, social, and contextual aspects that are crucial to its success (such as attending first to the incoming and attacking zombies, second to the busy work of collecting one's mithril), entrusting more and more control over the ongoing actions to the apprenticeship, and allowing numerous opportunities for practice and situated feedback…. Information is given "just in time," always in the context of goal-driven activity

that it's actually useful for—and made meaningful by—and always at a time when it can immediately be put to use (Steinkuehler, 2004, np; emphasis in original).

Although the emphasis here is on situated pedagogy or instruction (JellyBean is told what to attend to, how and where to move her mouse, and when to click her cursor to kill zombies and gather the mithril they leave), learning how to perform the skills necessary to harvest mithril is only part of what is going on. Myrondonia is also inducting JellyBean into the ethics and values of the game, teaching her about both social practice and identity—desirable ways of being in this world (being friendly to other elves, responding to cries for help, and displaying courtesy by avoiding hunting in areas others have identified)—how to become the kind of person a good player/elf should be:

> The two continue their way to the end of the corridor. An unknown elf named IrisArker passes by.

Myrondonia: Another rule.
JellyBean   : Yes?
IrisArker   : ^_^ [Smiley face gesture while walking by]
Myrondonia: If you see someone go one way, go the other.
Myrondonia: Hi. [To IrisArker]
Myrondonia: We are all here for mithril.

Commerce, War, Politics, Society, and Culture

Where Steinkuehler foregrounds the existence of a parallel and persistent world ever ready to welcome players, providing the lure of both membership and escape, these worlds are also seen as parallel sites for more prosaic dimensions of everyday life activities. Edward Castronova (2005) describes the online gaming world as

> … a universe that hosts massive flows of real human intercourse—information, commerce, war, politics, society, and culture… places where thousands of users interact with one another in the guise of video game characters on a persistent basis: many hours a day, every day, all year round. As such, these places are like real cities and fairy-tale cities at the same time, and some of the numbers they are producing might surprise you (Castronova, 2005, p. 1).

The figures he goes on to provide include hours per week spent by typical users (20–30), the current number of users at the time of writing (10 million "at a minimum"), in-game currencies trading against the dollar on eBay "at rates higher than those of real Earth currencies including the yen and the Korean won," annual figures for the sale of money and virtual items ($30 million in the

United States, $100 million globally), and accounts of real world arrests and successful lawsuits, where people have lost virtual items because of hacks and poor server security (Castronova, 2005, p. 2). Games, Castronova observes, have become places where "anthropologists see new cultures, entrepreneurs see new markets, lawyers see new precedents, and social and political experts see new pressures and looming crises" (Castronova, 2005, p. 3).

Such social spaces encompass play, but more than this, provide sites for the cultural production of identities and relationships, and the negotiation of a wide range of matters—ethical, judicial, and interpersonal—with links in/from and back out to the "real" world. Games are becoming "an important host of ordinary human affairs," Castronova argues, with real world overlaps and consequences, and "subtle and not so subtle effects of this behavior at the societal level in real Earth countries" (Castronova, 2005, p. 2).

Conclusion

A significant body of studies of computer games within education focuses on the models they provide of distributed knowledge and learning, and the possibilities game structures and engines provide for designing well-resourced learning environments that utilize, games' affordances to provide rich learning and curriculum. However, as Steinkuehler (2004) and others warn, we need to better understand what contemporary informal learning environments do well or badly before rushing to emulate them uncritically. Crucial in this are understandings of not just the games and game environments themselves, but also the practices and communities surrounding them. Fine-grained and extensive studies of game players and their communities are essential if we are to achieve this. While the attention paid to the possibilities and affordances of digital media contains much promise for education, particularly with respect to the kinds of learning online texts and sites facilitate, and the multimodal forms of meaning making they present, it is essential that research focuses not just on the sites or the technology but also on the practices, understandings, and identities they invite and the dynamic relationship between these. We need to attend to the texts and spaces of digital media but also to the uses people make of them, as well as to the interplay between these texts, technologies, and communities and the ways people live their lives.

Note

1 This common form of terminology presents a clumsy and problematic distinction that suggests clear boundaries between the two, and that the off-line world is "more real" than life online. For the most part, in this chapter I refer to on-and off-line worlds to avoid the artificiality of these distinctions, and the attribution of qualities in one area to the exclusion of the other.

References

Australian Bureau of Statistics. 2003. Children's participation in cultural and leisure activities, Australian Bureau of Statistics. Retrieved October 5 from http://www.abs.gov.au/AUSSTATS/abs@.nsf/ProductsbyTopic/0B14D86E14A1215ECA2569D70080031C?OpenDocument.

Australian Film Commission. 2006. Retrieved September 20, 2006, from http://www.afc.gov.au/GTP/index.html.

Australian Film, Television and Radio School. Laboratory of Advanced Media Production 2006. Retrieved August 16, 2006 from http://www.lamp.edu.au/wiki/index.php?title=DIGITAL_DISTRIBUTION_TRENDS_ANALYSIS_AND_BUSINESS#Game_Usage_Worldwide.

Bolter, J., and R. Grusin. 2000. *Remediation: Understanding New Media*. Cambridge MA: MIT Press.

Buckingham, D. 2000. *After the Death of Childhood: Growing up in the Age of Electronic Media*. Cambridge, U.K. : Polity Press.

Buckingham, D. 2006. Studying computer games. In *Computer Games: Text, Narrative, Play*, ed. D. Carr, D. Buckingham, A. Burn, and G. Schott, 1–13. Cambridge, U.K.: Polity Press.

Castronova, E. 2005. *Synthetic Worlds: The Business and Culture of Online Games*. Chicago: University of Chicago Press.

Entertainment Software Association. 2006. Game player data. Retrieved October 3, 2006, from http://www.theesa.com/facts/gamer_data.php.

Gee, J.P. 1992. *The Social Mind: Language, Ideology and Social Practice*, New York: Bergin and Garvey.

Gee, J.P. 1994. Learning and reading: The situated sociocultural mind. In *Realising the Future*, ed. Australian Association for the Teaching of English, 7–39. Perth Australia: Australian Association for the Teaching of English.

Gee, J.P. 2001. Learning in semiotic domains: a social and situated account. Paper presented at Literacy and Language in Local and Global Settings: New Directions for Research and Teaching. Conference of the International Association for Applied Linguistics, Capetown, South Africa, November 13–17.

Gee, J.P. 2003. *What Video Games Have to Teach Us about Language and Literacy*. New York: Palgrave Macmillan.

Jakobsson, M., and T.L. Taylor. 2003. The Sopranos meets Everquest: Social networking in massively multiplayer online games. *Digital Arts and Culture, Melbourne Conference*, 81–90. Retrieved September 28, 2006, from http://citeseer.ist.psu.edu/jakobsson03sopranos.html.

Kress, G. 2000. A curriculum for the future. *Cambridge Journal of Education* 30(1), 133–145.

Kress, G. 2002. Interpretation or design: From the world told to the world shown. In *Art, Narrative and Childhood*, ed. M. Styles and E. Bearne, 137–154. Stoke-on-Trent: Trentham Books.

Lam, W.S.E. 2000. L2 literacy and the design of the self: A case study of a teenager writing on the Internet. *TESOL Quarterly* 34(3), 457–482.

Lee, H., and J. Choudrie. 2002. *Investigating Broadband Development in South Korea*. London: DTI/Brunel University.

Ministry of Culture and Tourism, Korea Game Development and Promotion Institute. 2004. *The Rise of Korean Games: Guide to Korean Game Industry and Culture* Seoul: Korea Game Development and Promotion Institute.

Scheisel, S. 2006. Online game, made in U.S., seizes the globe. *The New York Times,* September 5, section A, p. 1.

Steinkuehler, C.A. 2004. Learning in massively multiplayer online games. In *Proceedings of the Sixth International Conference of the Learning Sciences,* ed. Y.B. Kafai, W.A. Sandoval, N. Enyedy, A.S. Nixon, and F. Herrera, 521–528. Mahwah, NJ: Erlbaum. Retrieved July 19, 2006 at http://website.education.wisc.edu/steinkuehler/papers/SteinkuehlerICLS2004.pdf .

Steinkuehler, C.A. In press. Cognition and literacy in massively multiplayer online games. In *Handbook of Research on New Literacies,* ed. D. Leu, J. Coiro, M. Knobel, and C. Lankshear, Mahwah, NJ: Erlbaum.

Thomas, A. 2004. Digital literacies of the cybergirl. *E-Learning* 2(3), 358–382.

Wikipedia. 2006. MMORPG. Retrieved October 3, 2006, from http://en.wikipedia.org/wiki/Mmorpg.

Yee, N. 2006. The demographics, motivations and derived experiences of users of massively-multiuser online graphical environments. Retrieved September 20, 2006 from http://www.nickyee.com/daedalus/archives/001539.php.

II
Diasporic Youth

Rethinking Borders and Boundaries
in the New Modernity

4

Consuming Difference

Stylish Hybridity, Diasporic Identity, and the Politics of Youth Culture[1]

MICHAEL D. GIARDINA

There's not one single valid identity, but many varied and perfectly compatible identities.

—Catalan student, *L'Auberge Espagnole*

The Doctor: How come I've never seen you people before?

Okwe: Because we are the people you do not see. We are the ones who drive your cabs. We clean your rooms. And suck your cocks.

— *Dirty Pretty Things*

Proem

Summer 2002, on a flight from London to New York. I'm returning from a conference in Finland and a few weeks of travel through Europe, and the last thing on my mind is thinking critically about anything other than a few hours sleep. Lazily flipping through the in-flight magazine (in which there is a noticeable post-9/11 focus on "travel safety" and "airport security"), I come across a listing for a film billed as "a feel-good story about girls' sports" with the catchy title of *Bend it Like Beckham* (an obvious reference to global sport celebrity David Beckham and his penchant for "bending" the ball around defenders on free kicks). Vaguely intrigued (*Have I heard about this film before?* I think to myself, wondering when drinks will be served), I navigate the digital controls of Virgin Atlantic's in-seat entertainment console and punch up the listings for the "On Demand" movie feature. Absentmindedly watching the film once through—missing bits and pieces of it here or there because of the surprisingly tasty in-flight meal of faux chicken tikka masala and the invariable chat with the person sitting next to me about the relative merits of George Orwell's (1933) *Down and Out in Paris and London* versus Anthony Bourdain's (2001) *Kitchen Confidential*—it finally cuts through my jet-lag addled fog that there is a major cultural intervention taking place in the film with respect to "British Asian" identity politics and diasporic migration as read over and against girls' youth sport. (*I just wish it hadn't taken me so long to "get" it.*)

69

The central purpose of this chapter brings critical reflection to bear on our present historical conjuncture characterized by emerging dynamics associated with diasporic racial formation and representation and their broader articulations to the twinned narratives of culture and identity in a globalizing world. Specifically, this chapter focuses to a great extent on the 2002 independent British film *Bend it Like Beckham*, which portends to privilege the voices of "British Asians" in a narrative of girls' sporting empowerment, participation, and multicultural inclusivity. Additionally, I discuss within and alongside the *Beckham* film the complex, conflictual, and continually shifting identity performances revealed in films that challenge such "easy" multicultural fare, such as *England Is Mine* and *Dirty Pretty Things*. Although popularly considered as a progressive, multicultural text by a vast majority of moviegoers and film critics alike for its (alleged) "realistic" portrayal of Asian culture, I argue that *Bend it Like Beckham* revels in and reveals its liminal positioning within and against the hyphenated spatial histories of British colonialism and Asian diaspora as it remains grounded in, and privileges, the very same racial order it alleges to challenge. In this vein, I see it operating in a pedagogical sense as it works, on one level, to reinscribe and perpetuate essentialist notions of British Asian culture in Britain while, on another, it inaugurates a process of bringing a *particular* iteration of "Asian" (popular) culture and identity into "mainstream" (read: Western) public spaces.

I begin by setting the stage for the racialized context in which the aforementioned films were released in the U.K., paying specific attention to developments in popular British culture that I have elsewhere (Giardina, 2003) referred to as a growing trend of stylish hybridity. Next, I discuss the performative nature of racialized identity, especially as it speaks to and is implicated in the "selling" of hybridity to a popular/mainstream (youth) audience. I then move to interrogate the film, excavating the overarching transnational identity and male patriarchal hegemony, and unmasking underlying neonationalistic, essentializing, and masculinist tropes that continue to circulate in contemporary, multicultural Britain via the circuitry of popular culture.

Situating Hybrid Identities

During the summer of 2001, the cities of Oldham, Bradford, and Burnley in northwest England experienced Britain's most devastating racially charged uprisings in the last 20 years. This time, however, the aggrieved communities were Asian, not black, and shattered the myth that a prevailing multiculturalism had displaced Britain's historical racial tensions during Prime Minister Tony Blair's tenure. The most violent incident occurred when a peaceful anti-Nazi League protest meeting held in Bradford's Centenary Square was interrupted by far-right National Front supporters. Allegedly, National Front supporters, many of whom had gathered at a local pub, incited the uprising by confronting and then shouting racial slurs at the 500 (mainly Asian) protestors. The youths' response was widely reported as "instant and violent" (Harris, 2002). Bradford was set alight as Asians, whites, and police engaged in contentious struggles, many becoming violent and out of control. According to published reports, nearly 1000 police officers were deployed to "restore order"—an irony not lost on local residents. Although a multicultural city, the relationship between police and Muslim, Hindu, and Sikh communities has grown increasingly strained over the past few years, mainly because of the perception that the (primarily white) police force is out of touch with the needs and concerns of Bradford's some 100,000 minority residents (one fifth of Bradford's total population). In the months following the uprisings, British newspaper columns, editorials, and investigative reports endeavored to "get to the heart of the matter."

Yet herein lies the crux of the problem when attempting to address Britain's British Asian population (and any of the so-called "problems" associated with it): The assumption that the British Asian community is homogeneous and can thus be discussed as one singular racial or ethnic division grossly ignores significant diversity between and among ethnic minority groups. And, moreover, even focusing on a seemingly "specific" formation grouped under any sort of 'British Asian" tag brings with it untold levels of difference and differentiation: the culturally hybrid individual is "already open to two worlds [or more] and is constructed within the national and international, political and cultural systems of colonialism and neo-colonialsm …[so that] to be hybrid is to understand the question as well as to represent the pressure of such historical placement" (Sangari, 1987, pp. 180–181). Burhan Wazir (2001) is thus correct in his assertion that the British Asian tag is itself *inherently* misleading, calling it "a patronising, polyglot term that unfairly gathers together various sects of Muslims, Indians, Sikhs, Kashmiris, Sri Lankans, and Bangladeshis" (p. 16). Complicating matters, as Gurinder Chadha's (1989) documentary *I'm British But* maintained, is that Asian youth in south London variously self-reflexively identify themselves as "British," "Asian," and "British Asian," depending upon the situation. (That is, young girls might adopt an historically stereotypical Asian identity when they are with their "white" friends, for example, while simultaneously combining it with a post-traditional view of being Asian in Britain when they are with their British Asian friends.) Tariq Modood and his colleagues (1997) go one step further, observing the ever-present conflictions between "British" and "English" identification vis-à-vis "Asians":

> While it seems that Asians in Scotland, like other Scots, are thinking of themselves in terms of Scottishness rather than Britishness… in England, where the whole issue of English identity is full of complexity and ambivalences, of implicit superiority and suspicion of nationalism, "English" has been treated by the new Britons as a closed ethnicity rather than an open nationality. Hence, while many Asians have come

to think of themselves as hyphenated Brits, few yet think of themselves as English (1997, p. 77).

Additionally, while even a general "Asian" delimitation may be considered essentialist by some, Chris Barker (1997) makes an insightful contribution by confessing that, although it "might be deemed problematic insofar as it homogenizes diverse cultures and identities," it remains the most prevalent marker that many youthful British Asians *themselves* deploy in defining—however fleetingly—their own shifting identities (p. 617). His research on televisual depictions of British Asians is useful in teasing out these conflicts, for it reveals that, even on a general level, a multilayered schism exists between Asians born in Britain and those who have emigrated from South Asia. Interviewing a representative sample of female British Asian youths about popular portrayals of their imagined collectivity (or what Karen Qureshi [2006] might refer to as a "trans-boundary communicative space"), he reports that, for the most part, his research participants "see themselves as Asian yet distance themselves from aspects of tradition by virtue of their participation in other domains of British culture. They are both in and out of British society and Asian culture" (p. 611).

This trend is likewise mirrored within the sporting arena. With respect to the context of "British South Asians" and sport, Sanjiev Johal (2001) reminds us that "most discussions concerning race, racism, and sport in Britain have largely tended to concentrate the dialectic within a black, African-Caribbean discourse" to the extent that what does exist in the literature vis-à-vis South Asians is couched almost entirely in the "institutionalized domains of sport and leisure" (p. 154). Johal's work on South Asians and their experiences with football in Britain is enlightening insofar as it reveals the ground-level conditions for which South Asian football and South Asian footballers have historically "been denied recognition, development, and access by and to the predominantly white-controlled world of British football" (ibid., p. 154). Additionally, and though somewhat problematic for not directly contesting the British Asian tag itself, Daniel Burdsey's (2006) essay on sport and diasporic national identities within English sporting contexts is worth mentioning for it suggests that representational divisions exist between the sporting worlds of cricket (where fans/athletes are more likely to identify with a desire to play for or support their various national teams such as Bangladesh or Pakistan) and football (where support of the English side is more pronounced).[2] A comment from one of his research participants illustrates this point, especially with respect to the younger generation,

My son certainly says to me at times, "Dad, what am I?" And I say to him, "Obviously, by parents, you're Indian—because we're both Indian—but by your right of birth, you know, you're English." So he's already said to me, "If I ever play football, Dad, can I play for England or India?" And

I said, "Who do you want to play for?" He said, "England," so I said, "There you are, you know, it's *your* choice" (Burdsey, 2006, p. 19).

As for the inverse, Pnina Werbner (1997) points out that, for example, "it is in the field of sport, through support of the [Pakistan] national team, that young British Pakistanis express their love of both cricket and the home country, along with their sense of alienation and disaffection from British society" (p. 101).

What this may suggest is that, given the intensification of diasporic flows of cultural and economic capital—aided most significantly by deepening patterns of aestheticization in popular culture as foregrounded in new modes of transnational advertising (e.g., what Silk and Andrews [2001] refer to as "Cultural Toyotism") and new forms of electronic mediation (e.g., the Internet, WiFi, wireless PDAs, etc.)—the new millennial nation-state now more than ever comprises an increasingly fluid population where practices of identity construction are no longer bound by physical borders of nation-state formations (see Silk, 2001). Rather, practices favoring "flexibility, mobility, and repositioning in relation to markets, governments, and cultural regimes" (Ong, 1999, p. 6) have become commonplace, no longer the sole preserve of cosmopolitan *flâneurs*. Indeed, more and more people define themselves "in terms of multiple national attachments and feel at ease with subjectivities that encompass plural and fluid cultural identities" (Caglar, 1997, p. 169). Generally speaking, this can be seen in individuals—particularly youth—who strategically and situationally patch together their identities from an international array of global television, popular music, and techno-culture so as to actively manipulate global configurations of cultural difference, racial hierarchy, and citizenship (cf. Kelly, 2004). This form of cultural hybridity, filled with gaps and fissures cascading across the landscape of identity practices, "defines the combined and uneven cultural logic of the way so-called Western 'modernity' has impacted the rest of the world ever since the onset of Europe's globalization project" (Hall, 2000, p. 226).

To wit, it is precisely this presence of "gaps and fissures" that helps to "maintain a stance of openness, a resistance to the closure and fixity perpetuated in narratives of pure or essential identity" (Stoddard and Cornwall, 1999, p. 333). Luis F. Mirón and Jonathan X. Inda (2000) refer to this destabilization of normative subjective embodiment as establishing a "deconstituting potentiality in the process of reiteration, making the subject the site for the perpetual possibility of a certain resignifying process, the site for the proliferation of certain effects that undermine the power of normalization" (p. 95). In discursive-performative terms, (hybrid) identities such as those located within the British Asian diaspora are thus not "already accomplished facts, but are rather performances which are never complete, always in process, and always constituted within, not outside, representation" (Barker, 1997, p. 615). To conceive of a performative (British Asian) subject (for example), then, "calls attention to those constitutive instabilities that contest the naturalizing effects of discourse" (Mirón and Inda, 2000, p. 95).

Significantly, at a time when such hybrid, hyphenated and/or flexible identities have become commonplace—though simultaneously celebrated and derided within various segments of mainstream society—hybridity, diaspora, and postcoloniality have become not only fashionable political terms, they have also (and especially) become extremely fashionable *marketing* and *advertising* terms (cf. Hutnyk, 2000). Although often intentionally appropriated for positive, identity-affirming reasons that acknowledge "the ways in which identities have been and continue to be transformed through relocation, cross-cultural exchange, and interaction" (Gillespie, 1995, p. 7, which I have no quarrel with), such terms have increasingly been deployed within popular British culture as a means of politically and financially capitalizing on the multicultural fervor currently dominating mainstream discourse. As John Hutnyk (2000) has written, "Difference *within the system* is now the condition and stimulus of the market—this necessarily comes with an illusion of equality, of many differences, and, in the bastardized versions of chaos politics which results, the image is of 'crossed' cultural forms merely competing for a fair share" (p. 119; italic emphasis in original). On a global scale, Douglas Kellner (1995) sums up the playing field thusly,

> Difference sells. Capitalism must constantly multiply markets, styles, fads, and artifacts to keep absorbing consumers into its practices and lifestyles. The mere valorization of "difference" as a mark of opposition can help market new styles and artifacts if the difference in question and its effects are not adequately appraised. It can also promote a form of identity politics in which each group affirms its own specificity and limits politics to the group's own interests, thus overlooking common forces of oppression. Such difference or identity politics aids "divide and conquer" strategies, which ultimately serve the interest of the powers that be (p. 40).

This has resulted in an explosion of commercially inspired inflections of border crossing racial, sexual, and gendered identities moving to the forefront—rather than into the shadows—of popular cultural sites.

Such popularized movements have generated a growing trend of what I have elsewhere (see Giardina, 2003) termed *stylish hybridity*, or, an influx of performative representations of hyphenated persons and cultural (mis)translations occupying leading spaces in mainstream media (television, film, music, and sport). Koushik Banerjea's (2000) astute observation on musical iterations of this phenomenon is worth quoting at length,

> In the rush to embrace a brave new millennium where "Cool Britannia" once more rules the airwaves, we are being asked to suspend our usual disbelief. We might still be riven by endemic racism and class division,

but on the dance floor, at least, we can still come together as a nation. When the lights dip and Talvin trips we're all "One Nation Under a Groove." Or so the story goes.... Marked by the ready appropriation of *bindis*, *saris*, incense, and the more narcoleptic aspects of Ravi Shankar, these are spaces which offer a primarily middle-class constituency a sanitized encounter with an imagined Asian 'other.' This allows white folk to rub shoulders with a carefully constructed exotica and for the perpetuation of a myth of multiculture.... For such a constituency they perform the function of interlocutors who make knowable the heart of an imaginary darkness (p. 66).

Thus, and while purporting to be positive, progressive artifacts subverting the status quo, the majority of these popular iterations commonly wash over and efface harsh realities witnessed in the everyday interactions between and among diverse segments of a population. One of the end results of this turn, Stuart Hall (2000) points out, is the depoliticization of the transgressive potentiality of the message that leaves us (only) with a commercialized multicultural vision that "assumes that if the diversity of individuals from different communities is recognized in the marketplace, then the problems of cultural differences will be (dis)solved through private consumption, without any need for a redistribution of power and resources" (p. 210). Such kernels of utopian fantasy—commonly held notions of what, for example, Afro-Carribeans or South Asians are "like"—are continually invented and inscribed, reinvented and reinscribed, within mediated representations that have emptied out any hint of reality beyond that which is staged or performed. More to the point, multiple performances of racial and ethnic identity in popular culture—located in the era of New Labour and revealed most noticeably within the affective dis/placement of multicultural Britishness—have re/produced and reified the idea that stylized culture (in this case, elements of Asian or British Asian) should be read as "authentic" representations of reality. Therefore, understanding the contextual politics of racial representation governing British culture in the contemporary moment is key for deciphering its "popular" racial order because nothing can stand outside of representation; that is, the apparatus of representation is itself always already ideological and, through that, always already performative. This kind of "managed" cultural hybridity can be better revealed by a close exploration of how various incarnations of British Asian identity have been produced and finessed in contemporary popular cultural formations.[3] Ergo, *Bend it Like Beckham*.

Blending it like Chadha?

Against the backdrop of the aforementioned conjunctural histories (as well as the booming commercial success of the Bollywood film industry throughout the world more generally), *Bend it Like Beckham* marks Gurinder Chadha's formal movement from progressive BBC documentarist and filmmaker to the mainstream. Her two previous feature-length films, *Bhaji on the Beach* (1992) and *What's Cooking?* (2000), received positive reviews from film critics, but neither was a commercial hit. Unlike her previous films, however, the low-budget *Bend it Like Beckham* was poised from the start to become an instant hit. Significantly, London's *Daily Telegraph* called *Bend it Like Beckham* the next best British film after *Bridget Jones's Diary* to come out in years, and over 400 cinemas featured it on its opening weekend (a number normally reserved for such Hollywood blockbusters as *Lord of the Rings* or the latest *James Bond* installment). Moreover, it was strategically released a few weeks prior to the start of the 2002 Fédération Internationale de Football Association (FIFA) World Cup. Says Chadha, "Football is like religion in England and with the World Cup coming, names like Beckham, Shearer, and Cole will acquire the status of demigods, I wanted to *cash in* on this hysteria which sweeps both British and Asian fans" (quoted in Marwah, 2002; italics my emphasis.)

Chadha's plot weaves together seemingly divergent narratives of race, ethnicity, class, gender, and sexuality into one coherent story line. Eighteen-year-old Jesminder "Jess" Bhamra is an East African Sikh who lives in Southall, West London. A predominantly Sikh community, Southall is widely regarded as the epicenter of Britain's Punjabi culture. Her father works at nearby Heathrow Airport, while her mother tends to the family's needs at home. Together, they raise Jess and her older sister, Pinky, in a strict environment that stresses the importance of their conservative Punjabi culture and traditional values. The Anglicized Jess, however, dreams of playing alongside Manchester United's David Beckham and having her performance appraised on TV by presenters Gary Lineker, Alan Hansen, and John Barnes. Playing pick up games in the park with neighborhood boys is the closest she gets to organized football, though, until she is "discovered" one day by Jules, the star footballer from a middle-class background who invites Jess to join the local women's club, the Hounslow Harriers.

Jess's parents have other ideas: they foresee her attending university, marrying a "proper" Indian boy, and becoming a lawyer. Football is clearly not their version of Jess's future. They view it as decidedly unladylike and see it as symptomatic of a corrupt British modernity that, in this case, is drawing their daughter's attention away from learning how to make a proper Punjabi dinner, searching for a husband, and respecting one's elders. Once they learn of Jess playing for the Harriers, they ban her from playing, citing both its gendered "inappropriateness" and counter cultural appeal. Conversely, Jules is encouraged by her father to play, and we are shown several scenes with him helping her work on her skills in the backyard of their house. Her mother, though, becomes frustrated with Jules's "tomboyish" behavior, viewing her interest in football as "improper" for a teenage girl. "There's a reason that Sporty Spice is the only one of 'em without a fella," she tells Jules. Melodramatic effect is added to the narrative when Jules's mother suspects that

Jess and Jules are romantically involved. In the end, the all-important match that will be watched by a scout for an American university coincides with Jess's sister Pinky's traditional Indian wedding. Instead of resolving in crises, Chadha gets to have things both ways as Jess plays in the final and attends the wedding, facilitated by her father's acquiescence to his daughter's wishes.

The film's title functions on two levels. On the one hand, it refers to all-world football star David Beckham's physical skill of "bending" the ball around defenders on shots on goal. This connection to the game of football itself is important in establishing the film's mainstream appeal; it announces to the casual viewer that this is not a movie solely about "Asians" but rather one about football and those who play it. At the same time, the title turns on itself, hailing the viewer to associate with Beckham's penchant for bending the rules (i.e., as read through his celebrityhood). This theme of bending (but never outright breaking) rules and traditions underlies the film, as director Chadha attempts the dual task of weaving and interlacing the struggles Jess faces at home and within her Punjabi community with that of Jules's struggle to gain acceptance as a female footballer within the larger framework of male sporting hegemony. In so doing, Chadha has already coded the resolution to the upcoming crises as one that privileges the very system Jess and Jules (and Chadha herself) are struggling against.[4]

However, although publicly advocating for a political consciousness that seeks to subvert the racist stereotypes left over from such early cultural endeavors as *The King and I* and offering the possibility of representing "Asianness" in a positive light, Chadha's ultimate failure shows through insofar as both youngsters—Jess and Jules—end up conforming to the mores and values of Prime Minister Tony Blair's mythical Cool Britannia. Correlatively, this failure reduces the solution to the problems of cultural difference to simply "getting out," as both girls leave Britain for the so-called greener pastures of the collegiate soccer fields in the United States. Although Chadha has been an outspoken exponent of multiculturalism for many years, her aesthetic is not the radical or militant aesthetic of, for example, the black arts movement of the 1960s and 1970s in the United States (see Karenga, 1997). Rather, much like Jess's mediated Britishness, Chadha's multiculturalism "is a conservative aesthetic that *appears* radical" (Denzin, 2002, p. 156; my emphasis).

Further, and offering up in its totality a representational manifesto of what it means to "be British" (or, even, "British Asian") in the new world order of multicultural London, *Bend it Like Beckham*'s originary narrative erases political and ethical considerations that mark history as a site of struggle, producing what Henry Giroux (1995) has called "a filmic version of popular culture" (p. 57), one that effaces the everyday hardships and struggles of daily life in favor of, in this case, a reformulated, faux progressive New Labour vision of race, gender, and class relations. Such a configuration, then, operates in tandem with a transnationally mediated public sphere that produces "technologies of truth and identification that serve to transform concrete individuals into cultural citizens whose lines of loyalty and affiliation now exceed the territory and social geography of the nation-state" (McCarthy, 2002, pp. 5–6). Within the frame of *Bend it Like Beckham*, the representation(s) of (British)-Asianness in popular British culture ultimately become(s) that of multiply re/inscribed re-membrances of performatively represented identity. In this regard, the active deployment of a fictionalized past drawn from traditional notions of Empire "becomes a vehicle for rationalizing the authoritarian, normalizing tenden-cies of the dominant culture that carry through to the present" (Giroux, 1995, p. 47). It is of no surprise, then, that we see the Runnymede Trust's (2000) report titled *The Future of Multi-Ethnic Britain* concluding, "Britishness, as much as Englishness, has systematic, largely unspoken, racial connotations... [where] the idea of a multicultural post-nation remains an empty promise" (p. 38–39). "Cool Britannia" it may be, as long as racial inclusivity matches with the official pedagogies of the state.

Black British playwright Grant Buchanan Marshall—currently a leading activist voice in the London theatrical scene—is one of many outspoken critics of such "easy" multiculturalism of the kind displayed in *BILB*, stating: "Racism is not *really* tackled by writers in Britain. You get mixed-race couples floating in the background or even right in the front, but the realities of what these people must be going through is left well alone" (quoted in Alibhai-Brown, 2002). Although centering the viewer's gaze on "positive" representations of marginalized human group actors, the status quo is not challenged in any substantial way. Carrington (2001) posits that this celebration of such superfi-ciality within late capitalism has "increasingly emptied out and appropriated [these signifiers] solely in terms of the stylized elements" that we have come to expect from minority representations. In these instances, tropes such as "multicultural" and "hybrid" have become reconfigured "through a prolifera-tion of images and practices into a normalized, non-politically charged dis-course that assume[s] that ethnic minority communities [are] homogenous and somehow representative of an authentic and unified culture" (Giardina and Metz, 2001, p. 210).[5]

This whitewashing of (cultural) hybridity has further materialized itself in official government policy machinations. As Rupa Huq (2003) chronicles, the late-1990s witnessed "Britons originating from the former British India... attain[ing] a greater degree of visibility than ever... [and] by the 1997 U.K. General Election, being courted by all sides of the political spectrum" (p. 31). It was at this time that the Blair government's "Cool Britannia" national brand-ing campaign was launched. Stressing in part the multiethnic composition of the nation, the campaign framed Britain—and London, in particular—as a site of "periphery-to-center reversals and ex-imperial transformation" (Wilson, 2003, p. 45). The overall goal of this campaign, as noted by June Edmunds and Bryan S. Turner (2001), was to "shed the impression of Britain as staid, cold, and pompous... instead, promoting a vision of Britain as a 'modern-minded country' with a more positive outlook towards Europe" (p. 85). In so doing, focus was directed especially toward a normalization of multiculturalism/hybridity (e.g., British Asian, Afro-Caribbean, etc.) *while at the same time* contradictorily exoticizing various groups so as to portray Britain as an "outward-looking, diverse, creative hub in an increasingly open, global economy" (Leonard, 1997). Thus, even as it was gaining new cultural currency, the South Asian diaspora was being cast as a site of "mystery, aroma, color, exotica, even when [appearing] in the midst of Britain" (Huq, 2003, p. 120). This outward normalization of British South Asians in popular cultural formations (of which Cool Britannia is, as well, most certainly of) should not be overlooked, as (oppositional) popular culture has the potential to play a major role in reversing (negative and or stereotypically held) opinions of the Asian community in Britain.

Encouragingly, however, there are some very visible challenges to this paradigm at the ground level of such interactions, especially in the form of what we might call postcolonial/diasporic artists, writers, and painters who, like Jean Michel Basquiat or Gordon Bennett, rework and reorder the ruins left by colonial relations to "foreground the complex human condition produced in the wake of colonization and its subsequent struggles of resistance against colonial and neocolonial domination" (McCarthy, Giardina, Harewood, and Park, 2003, p. 460). Instructive of a rigorous approach to the complex interrelations of South Asian, British, and black identities offered by such culture works, Gayatri Gopinath (1995) intones that reading bhangra music, for example, as a performative postcolonial text would

> ... allow for a far more complicated understanding of diaspora, in that it demands a radical reworking of the hierarchical relation between diaspora and the nation. Bhangra, a transnational performance of culture and community, reveals the processes by which multiple diasporas intersect both with one another and with the national spaces that they are continuously negotiating and challenging [6] (p. 304).

Gardner and Shukur (1994) enlighten us further with the words of a young bhangra singer, who notes that

> ... I rap in Bengali and English. I rap on everything from love to politics. I've always been into rapping... it was rebellious, the lyrics were sensational. I could relate to that, I could identify with it. Like living in the ghetto and that... it's from the heart. It's "I'm Bengali, I'm Asian, I'm a woman, and I'm living here" (p. 161).

This young woman's cultural pedagogy of multiple figurations and identities thus encompass—at once and as a part of—a variety of sites including Bengali, English, female, youth culture, rap, and performative political activism, as she becomes "involved in shifting identifications and in enacting a hybrid identity constituted from multiplying global resources" (Barker, 1997, p. 615). Numerous progressive-minded films have recently unmasked these complex identity performances. The Dogma 95 dogumentary [sic] *England Is Mine*, notes Ben Carrington (2001), reveals cultural dislocations between what it means to "be" English and/or "be" British—especially with respect to Britain's Asian population—and further challenge essentialist representations and blur the lines between local and national (and national and transnational) identification. Here, director Joseph Bullman follows an intensely nationalist English football [soccer] fan to Japan for the 2002 FIFA World Cup. While there, the self-described skinhead and National Front supporter befriends a Japanese woman and several Muslims, experiences a "new world" outside his closely sequestered home environ, and is challenged to reconsider his own comfortable understandings of "Englishness" and how he is implicated in perpetuating it. Likewise, Stephen Frears's 2002 film, *Dirty Pretty Things*, was positioned as a lightning thrust into the heart of global capitalist relations from the point of view of those who work to invisibly sustain it. Frears's London is presented *not* as a United Colors of Benetton Mecca but rather as a "globalized Babel, a fluorescent-lit service economy of sweatshops, hospitals, and hotel bathrooms that could just as easily be in Paris or Hamburg or New York" (O'Herir, 2003, p. 1). The leading figures driving his complex story line have been systematically and without care reshaped by the horrors wrought by neoliberalism run wild. The main characters—a mixed bag of diasporically floating Turks, Russians, and Spaniards (i.e., "people who move, often in great swarms in order to create collective 'home' around them wherever they happen to land" [Werbner, 1997, p. 12])—all survive day-to-day in the cracks carved by their own sweat and tears in the icy-cold wall of neglect towering over them as they live in constant fear of being deported; theirs is a ghost-world life separate from the freedoms of juridical citizenship represented by the (white) immigration officials lurking around every corner. The sunny-side up disposition of the semi-assimilated-into-a-racist-British-modernity Bhamra family from *Bend it Like Beckham* is nowhere to be found here in the cruel underbelly of the famed imperial capital, where long-standing colonialist perceptions, racial prejudices, and economic disparity remain as stumbling blocks for recent *émigrés* (especially those without financial capital).[7]

Coda

For all of the problems endemic to *Bend it Like Beckham* (and other movies in its vein), it would be a mistake to dismiss it totally out of hand. A British colleague reminded me with the following note after reading an earlier version of this chapter:

> To be honest what struck me the most about your article on *Bend it Like Beckham* [was] the sensitivity to the cultural specificity of the situation in England—the reading was spot-on. The only thing I would say—and

no doubt you're aware of this—is that despite the problems with the narrative and the kind of easy multiculturalism produced, the fact that such a film can be made, produced and gain fairly widespread audiences is a huge shift. I watched the film [when it was released] in a packed cinema in [city name withheld] full of mainly white teenagers and they loved it—the film doesn't really engage with racism, as you note, but within the realm of the popular, progressive texts have to start from where the audience is. This isn't a cop-out in arguing against difficult work that challenges audiences, just that I think some of our critical readings (I've often thought this about bell hooks's work) overlooks the intangible shifts that take place at the level of the everyday that we (as cultural critics) often miss and only "recognise" a decade later.

And my colleague is right (at least, in a certain respect). Since its debut in April 2002, interest in girls' football has skyrocketed, and new girls' leagues are starting up all over the country. Most notably, (British) Asian girls and women are signing up for leagues in higher numbers than ever. In that sense, Chadha and her writing crew are to be congratulated for attempting to challenge long-standing colonial and patriarchal narratives of dominance and subordination, both within Britain specifically and sport more generally (and I do not say that in a patronizing manner, as some have accused).

Presenting us with positive portrayals of strong, empowered young women seemingly beating the odds to attain their goals is, most assuredly, a step in the right direction. However, as Norman K. Denzin (2002) reminds us, it is not sufficient for cultural producers to simply offer examples of warm and fuzzy race and gender relations: "It is time to move away from the search for an essentialist (and good) black or brown [or Asian] subject" (p. 185). We must be strident in our quest to think through what terms like democracy, multiculturalism, and equality mean in a society that tactually—and honestly—confronts difference and doesn't code "normal" with "white" or "heterosexual." And we must acknowledge the promise of multiple subjectivities and diverse cultural traditions. Too much is at stake to do otherwise.

Notes

1 This chapter revisits and reworks arguments contained in Giardina 2003 and Giardina 2005. I thank Norman K. Denzin, David L. Andrews, Michael L. Silk, and C.L. Cole for comments on an earlier draft of this chapter. Special thanks to Elizabeth S. Pittelkow for thought-provoking conversations about life, the universe, and everything in between.

2 To be fair to Burdsey, he took this up in his excellent later (2007) book, *British Asians and Football: Culture, Identity, Exclusion* (London: Routledge).

3 In the popular television soap *EastEnders*, for example, one of the recent [c. 2002] story lines revolves around a British-Asian boy named Anish trying out for a local football club. Adding to the "intrigue," his British-Asian mother Nita is engaged to Robbie, who is white. The football story line is part of a larger plot which sees Robbie spending too much time with Anish (coaching/teaching him at football) and neglecting Nita, who has started spending some "quality" time with Gus (a black Briton of Caribbean descent).

Though a strong, empowered character, Nita works as a manager in a mini mart, thus perpetuating an ongoing stereotype that all "Asians" work in corner shops. Here, we see quite clearly the superficiality of commercially inspired inflections of race draped in front of—*not behind*—the veil of neoliberal capitalism (the new avatar of colonialism). In full view for all to see (rather than placed in the background as a minor or supporting character), this pseudo-celebration of an essentializing Asian subject(ivity) denegates its very purpose—celebrating a multicultural pluralism (but doesn't cost any viewers to do so).

4 For an extensive critique of the film and its multilayered story lines, especially as relating to gender, see Giardina, 2003.

5 It is important to point out that the marketing/managing of cultural hybridity is, of course, not limited to the English/British context. Leela Tanikella (2003), for one, reminds us that, "postcolonial Caribbean nation-states celebrate, and concurrently manage diversity... [with] ... national slogans such as Jamaica's 'Out of Many, One People,' Trinidad and Tobago's 'Together We Aspire, Together We Achieve,' and Guyana's 'One People, One Nation, One Destiny' suggesting a preoccupation with producing 'a people' unified through national symbols" (p. 155). However, in each case, the overt government-sanctioned marketing of unity through hybridity-speak "obscures the aporias of official multicultural policies, and through inaction, in effect, alibis the overpolicing and the continued maintenance of white privilege in education, the work place, and the public sphere (Huq, 2003, p. 120).

6 Rajinder Dudrah's (2002) definition of bhangra music/music scene is as good as any: British bhangra music is part and parcel of the urban soundscapes of British cities implicated in wider struggles for minority cultural expression that contribute to the meanings and definitions of one's sense of place and locality. It incorporates the pleasures, pains, and politics of urban British South Asian lives, especially in large metropoles, where, alongside black British groups, South Asians have produced musical and cultural expressions that illustrate the complex and hybrid interplay of the different music styles, lyrics, and cultural identities that constitute a dynamic experience for young South Asians in urban locales (p. 360-375).

7 Not to be outdone, popular literature such as Zadie Smith's (2001) debut novel *White Teeth* has been a rousing success while also asking the hard questions about the state of race relations in Britain ("The Book That Has Set London Alight," February 5, 2002). Additionally, Bali Rai's (2001) acclaimed teen novel, *(Un)arranged Marriage*, offers a male's perspective on growing up as a young, working-class Asian under the pressures to both conform to his family's strict traditionalism and lead his own life with his "gorah" (white) girlfriend and "kalah" (black) buddy. Alex Wheatle's (2001) *East of Acre Lane*, set against the backdrop of the 1981 riots in Brixton, is an evocative story that deals frankly and honestly with issues of race and class within youth culture.

References

Alibhai-Brown, Y. 2002. In the English arts, a merry racial blend. *The New York Times*, July 21, pp. S2–1.

Banerjea, K. 2000. Sounds of whose underground: The fine tuning of diaspora in an age of mechanical reproduction. *Theory, Culture, and Society* 17(3), 64–79.

Barker, C. 1997. Television and the reflexive project of the self: Soaps, teenage talk, and hybrid identities. *The British Journal of Sociology* 48(4), 611–628.

The book that has set London alight. *The Evening Standard* (London), February 5, 2001, pp. 24–25.

Bourdain, A. 2001. *Kitchen Confidential: Adventures in the Culinary Underbelly*. New York: HarperPerennial.

Burdsey, D. 2006. If I ever play football, dad, can I play for England or India? British Asians, sport, and diasporic national identities. *Sociology 40*(1), 11–28.

Burdsey, D. 2007. *British Asians and Football: Culture, Identity, Exclusion*. London: Routledge.

Caglar, A. 1997. Hyphenated identities and the limits of "culture." In *The Politics of Multiculturalism in the New Europe: Racism, Identity and Community*, ed. T. Modood and P. Werbner, 169–186. London: Zed Books.

Carrington, B. 2001. Postmodern blackness and the celebrity sports star: Ian Wright, "race," and English identity. In *Sports Stars: The Cultural Politics of Sporting Celebrity*, ed. D.L. Andrews and S.J. Jackson, 102–124. London: Routledge.

Denzin, N. 2002. *Reading Race: Hollywood and the Cinema of Racial Violence*. London: Sage Publications.

Dudrah, R. 2002. Drum'n'dhol: British bhangra music and diasporic South Asian identity formation. *European Journal of Cultural Studies 5*(3), 363–385.

Edmunds, J., and B. Turner. 2001. The re-invention of a national identity? Women and 'cosmopolitan' Englishness. *Ethnicities 1*(1), 83–108.

Gardner, K., and A. Shukur. 1994. 'I'm Bengali, I'm Asian, and I'm living here.' In *Desh Pardesh: The South Asian Presence in Britain*, ed. R. Ballard, 142–164. London: Hurst and Company.

Giardina, M. 2003. "Bending it like Beckham" in the global popular: Stylish hybridity, performativity, and the politics of representation. *Journal of Sport and Social Issues 27*(1), 65–82.

Giardina, M. 2005. *Sporting Pedagogies: Performing Culture and Identity in the Global Arena*. New York: Peter Lang.

Giardina, M., and J. Metz. 2001. Celebrating humanity: Olympic marketing and the homogenization of multiculturalism. *International Journal of Sports Marketing and Sponsorship 3*(2), 203–223.

Gillespie, M. 1995. *Television, Ethnicity, and Cultural Change*. London: Routledge.

Giroux, H. 1995. Innocence and pedagogy in Disney's world. In *From Mouse to Mermaid: The Politics of Film, Gender, and Culture*, ed. E. Bell, L. Haas, and L. Sells, 43–61. Bloomington, IN: Indiana University Press.

Gopinath, G. 1995. Bombay, U.K., Yuba City: Bhangra music and the engendering of diaspora. *Diaspora 4*(3), 303–321.

Hall, S. 2000. The multi-cultural question. In *Un/settled Multiculturalisms: Diasporas, Entanglements, Transruptions*, ed. B. Hesse, 209–241. London: Zed Books.

Harris, P. 2002. Riot city reaches boiling point. *The Guardian* (London), June 30, p. 10.

Hutnyk, J. 2000. Adorno at Womad: South Asian crossovers and the limits of hybridity-talk. In *Debating Cultural Hybridity: Multi-Cultural Identities and the Politics of Anti-Racism*, ed. P. Werbner and T. Modood, 106–138. London: Zed Books.

Huq, R. 2003. From the margins to the mainstream? Representations of British Asian youth musical cultural expression from bhangra to Asian underground music. *Young: Nordic Journal of Youth Research 11*(1), 29–48.

Johal, S. 2001. Playing their own game: A South Asian football experience. In *Race, Sport, and British Society*, ed. B. Carrington and I. McDonald, 153–169. London: Routledge.

Karenga, M. 1997. Black arts: Mute matter given force and function. In *The Norton Anthology of African American Literature*, ed. H.L. Gates, Jr. and N.Y. McKay, 1973–1977. New York: Norton.

Kellner, D. 1995. *Media Culture: Cultural Studies, Identity, and Politics between the Modern and the Postmodern*. New York: Routledge.

Kelly, J. 2004. *Borrowed Identities*. New York: Peter Lang.

Leonard, M. 1997. Britain*. London: Demos.

Marwah, G. 2002. Blend it like Chadha. *The Sunday Tribune* (India), July 21, 2002. Retrieved December 5, 2002 from http://www.tribuneindia.com/2002/ 20020721/ spectrum/main4.htm.

McCarthy, C. 2002. Understanding the work of aesthetics in modern life: Thinking about the cultural studies of education in a time of recession. Unpublished manuscript. Institute of Communications Research, University of Illinois.

McCarthy, C., M.D. Giardina, S. Harewood, and J. Park. 2003. Contesting culture: Identity and curriculum dilemmas in the age of globalization, postcolonialism, and multiplicity. *Harvard Educational Review* 73(3), 449–465.

Mirón, L.F., and J.X. Inda. 2000. Race as a kind of speech act. *Cultural Studies: A Research Annual* 5, 85–107.

Modood, T., R. Berthoud, J. Lakey, J. Nazroo, P. Smith, S. Virdee, and S. Beishon. 1997. *Ethnic Minorities in Britain: Diversity and Disadvantage*. London: Policy Studies Institute.

O'Herir, A. 2003. Dirty pretty things. Retrieved December 6, 2006 at http://dir.salon. com.

Ong, A. 1999. *Flexible Citizenship: The Cultural Politics of Transnationality*. Durham: Duke University Press.

Orwell, G. 1933/1972. *Down and Out in Paris and London*. New York: Harvest Books.

Qureshi, K. 2006. Trans-boundary spaces: Scottish Pakistanis and trans-local/national identities. *International Journal of Cultural Studies* 9(2), 207–226.

Rai, B. 2001. *(Un)arranged Marriage*. London: Corgi.

Runnymede Trust. 2000. *The Future of Multi-Ethnic Britain*. London: Profile Books.

Silk, M. 2001. Together we're one?: The "place" of the nation in media representations of the 1998 Kuala Lumpur Commonwealth Games. *Sociology of Sport Journal* 18(3), 277–301.

Silk, M., and D. Andrews. 2001. Beyond a boundary? Sport, transnational advertising, and the reimagining of national culture. *Journal of Sport and Social Issue* 25(2), 180–201.

Smith, Z. 2001. *White Teeth*. New York: Vintage International.

Stoddard, E., and G. Cornwall (1999). Cosmopolitan or mongrel? Creolite, hybridity, and 'douglarisation' in Trinidad. *European Journal of Cultural Studies* 2(3), 331–353.

Tanikella, L. 2003. The politics of hybridity: race, gender, and nationalism in Trinidad. *Cultural Dynamics* 15(2), 153–181.

Wazir, B. 2001. Identity crisis: Born in Manchester but loyal to Lahore. *The Observer* (London), July 24, p. 16.

Werbner, P. 1997. The dialectics of cultural hybridity. In *Debating Cultural Hybridity: Multi-Cultural Identities and the Politics of Anti-Racism*, ed. P. Werbner and T. Modood, 1–28. London: Zed Books.

Wheatle, A. 2001. *East of Acre Lane*. London: Fourth Estate.

Wilson, R. 2003. Globalization, spectral aesthetics and the global soul: Tracking some 'uncanny' paths to trans-Pacific globalization. *Comparative American Studies* 3(1), 35–51.

5

Diasporan Moves
African Canadian Youth and Identity Formation

JENNIFER KELLY

The ability of the United States to dissipate its cultural forms around the globe via digital pulses has an effect on the formation of African Canadian youth identity as well as the social construction of racialized understandings (via concepts, images, and symbols) and identities among all social groups. These shared racialized understandings are not individual responses but are constructed intersubjectively—shared to a degree by all members of a culture or subculture (Fiske, 1994, p.157). It is through this process of accessing outer national sources that media becomes one of the key mechanisms for centralizing cultural power (via cultural reception) through the articulation of ideology into social formation. Within these practices of consumption youth draw on media culture in order to represent and give meaning to everyday experiences and their identities. It is within this social space of symbolic activity that one can identify the ways in which youth receive and appropriate media culture within a capitalist economy.

This chapter will focus on the narratives of school youth whose heritage lies within the continent of Africa and its diaspora. Rather than using a traditional race relations model that reifies race (Rex, 1970/1983) I prefer to adopt a critical cultural studies framework, which allows for explication of issues related to meaning making and reception of media along with recognition of culture as ordinary (Williams, 1958/1993) and African diaspora as heterogeneous (Gilroy, 1993). As a central concept within my study

> ... diaspora points to difference not only internally (the ways transnational black groupings are fractured by nation, class, gender, sexuality, and language) but also externally: ... We are forced to think not in terms of some closed autonomous system of African dispersal but explicitly in terms of complex past of forced migrations and racialization—what Earl Lewis has called a history of overlapping diasporas (Edwards, 2004, p. 30).

I also draw on Canadian social critic and poet George Elliott Clarke's (1996) descriptor "African Canadian" which clearly exemplifies not just the actuality of the heterogeneity of African Canadian communities but also "overlapping diasporas" that encompass:

> ... persons and expressive cultures, located in or derived from Canada, possessing, to some degree, an ancestral connection to sub-Saharan Africa. The phrase encompasses, then, recent immigrants to Canada from the United States, the Caribbean, South America, and Africa itself, as well as indigenous, African-descended community (p. 118).

Methodology and Historical Context

John Thompson's (1990) "depth hermeneutic" framework is a useful methodological approach that allows one to understand the research participants' perspectives while at the same time being able to locate those perspectives within a wider political, socioeconomic and historical framework. Depth-hermeneutic consists of three phases: The first is related to the development of a social-historical understanding of "blackness" and black identification in Alberta and Canada; the second phase involves analysis of the students' discourse as narrative; whereas the third can be seen as interpretation/reinterpretation of previous social-historical and discourse analyses in relation to each other. Although youth culture is at the forefront of discussions of black identification, it is noted that within public representations of Canadian identity, blackness is subsumed. Historically, construction of dark bodies as "Other" has been prevalent in the Canadian discourses and understandings of nation, citizenship, and identity.

For example, if we examine the cultural and economic formation of Alberta as a province at the turn of the twentieth century we find that from 1907–1912, various strategies were employed by the immigration authorities in order to discourage the movement of blacks from Oklahoma to the Canadian west. Analysis of archival documents such as newspapers, government documents, magazines, and minutes of political meetings during this period of immigration reveals differing and competing racial discourses that intersect with regional, gendered, and political allegiances. The most consistent discourses drew on biological determinism and social Darwinism to construct Anglo-Celts as biologically different from and superior to blacks and other unassimilable groups. Through these racialized discourses, the dominant white group constructed blacks as its binary opposite. In this relation, whites were opposed to nature, while blacks, it was assumed, aligned with nature. Such a process naturalized and fixed differences between black and white by reducing the culture of black peoples to nature (Hall, 1997). Discourses of race constructed blacks as antithetical to the budding capitalist environs that dominant groups in Canada wanted to cultivate. Blacks were posited as opposite to the thriving, hardy, and self-reliant northern Europeans. They were perceived as "lacking" initiative, with a "sense of humour and predisposition to a life of ease [that] render[s] [their] presence undesirable" (Cooke, 1911, p. 11). For black women, stereotypes were gendered and racialized, as concern was expressed about the ability of such "unsuitable" bodies to produce future potential citizens who did not conform to conceptions of the "Ultimate Canadian" bred of the "best stock that could be found in the world" (Cooke, 1911, p. 11).

Such discursive practices played out through existing regionalized, classed, and gendered discourses. For example, women were no less tainted with racism, and the Anglophile women's organization, the Imperial Order Daughters of the Empire, protested black immigration to Alberta and black male immigration, in particular, by claiming that black men were a sexual threat to white women. This argument illustrates the ways in which subjectivities often operate at the intersections of social categories.

Those black immigrants who made it into Alberta between 1907 and 1911 formed the core of the early black settlers. Between 1901 and 1911, Alberta's population increased 5.5 times, from 73,000 in 1901 to 374,000 in 1911. The 1911 census placed the numbers of blacks residing in Edmonton and Calgary at 208 and 72, respectively. These pioneers settled primarily into four isolated rural communities: Junkins (now Wildwood), Keystone (now Breton), Campsie near Barrhead, and Amber Valley, 20 miles from Athabasca (Carter and Akili, 1981; Hooks, 1997). This group remained the dominant black group in the province until the second wave arrived.

With the relaxation and opening up of the immigration laws in 1962, and again in 1967, the Alberta black population increased with immigrants from Caribbean countries such as Jamaica, Trinidad, Guyana, and Barbados. These revisions of the Immigration Act that finally took place were prompted not by any major desire by government and immigration authorities to further develop a "racially" pluralist society but rather primarily by economic expediency. The federal government realized that Canada would not be able to rely on its traditional source for skilled immigrants, namely, Europe. In Alberta, this loosening of the immigration laws coincided with a demand not only for skilled oil field workers but also workers in construction and building trades, welding, pipe fitting and K-12 teachers. This shortage of labor and partial lifting of the racialized immigration barrier was the impetus for the second large-scale immigration of peoples of African descent to Alberta. This group of immigrants was diverse in terms of geographic origins and occupational skills, many being "technicians, tradesmen of all kinds, as well as clerical workers" (N. Darbasie, personal communication, September 2002). These workers from the Caribbean were later joined by students from the Caribbean and the continent of Africa who would graduate from the University of Alberta and go on to enter a wide spectrum of professions. In the 1980s and 1990s, these groups of diasporan blacks were joined by blacks from African countries, who were fleeing war or trying to make a better life for themselves and their children. According to 2001 census data, 31,395 blacks live in Alberta. Allowing for variations in the figures, this would translate to approximately two percent of the population in both Edmonton and Calgary being black. Of the black population in Edmonton, 4,280 were born in the Caribbean and Bermuda, whereas 6,620 were born in Africa (Statistics Canada, 1996; Torczyner, 1997).

Ironically, the influx of the newer immigrants from the Caribbean and various African countries served to subsume the presence of early African Canadian pioneers. Because of the numerical dominance of this new wave and the lack of knowledge of an earlier black presence in Alberta, there was initially little formal attempt to be inclusive and build a sense of community. Blacks from the Caribbean were often regarded as representing the universal in terms of black groups. This brief historical overview situates the ways in which blackness can be understood in relation to the development of Alberta in the past century; it is significant because the way students understand their place within the Canadian nation draws on this historical tradition. Furthermore, Canadian traditions are located within the colonial relations of British and American domination and dependency. In the 21st century this process of othering continues and is at times reinforced through liberal multicultural discourses that are dominant in Canada. Rinaldo Walcott (1997) provides a cogent argument for this positioning:

> The multicultural narrative is constituted through a positioning of white Anglophone and Francophone Canadians as the founding peoples of the nation, with "special" reference to Native Canadians. All others exist and constitute the Canadian ethnic mix or multicultural character. Thus, the colonizing English and French are textually left intact as "real" Canadians while legislation is needed to imagine other folks as Canadian (p. 79).

This discursive tension between "real" Canadians and "other" Canadians reinforces the sense of "black" and "Canadian" as binary opposites. A binary articulated through the idea of "just come"—it is an idea that is "crucial to the nation-state's construction both of black invisibility and hyper visibility" (Walcott, 1997, p. 42).

To adequately identify these understandings today means highlighting the pervasive influence of the American media on adolescent culture, both in the way in which blackness is perceived within Alberta and as it is positioned in relation to the global representations emanating from the United States via Madison Avenue and Hollywood.

The Students

This diverse population, a result of differing immigration patterns, was reflected in the student sample for the research. The percentage of black students in the high school from which the research sample is taken is difficult to ascertain because the school board does not identify its students on the basis of racialized identities or ethnicity. However, a safe estimate would be that the black student population is less than 2%. Of the 14 students interviewed in my broader study,[1] 8 are highlighted within this chapter. The study relied on students' self-identification as "black" in order to gather a subset of the African Canadian students willing to participate in the research. Purposive sampling was undertaken to ensure that those who participated in the project consisted of male and female students (15 to 18 years of age) of African descent, with family ancestry in the Caribbean, continental Africa, Canada, and the United States. They come from a variety of diasporan backgrounds: Etta is a female student who was born in Edmonton and has heritage in the Caribbean and in sub-Saharan Africa. Euda grew up in Edmonton in a deeply religious family. Her heritage is firmly within the Caribbean. Wayne came to Canada from Jamaica during his high school years and has no recent association with any country in Africa. He is a deeply committed Christian. Denzil has "mixed heritage" with one parent having emigrated from a country in Africa while the other was born and raised in Canada of European parents. Melvin was born in Edmonton but both his parents have strong association with different Caribbean islands. Doreen, born in the Caribbean, still has strong affiliation with the Caribbean through her parents. Gerald's parental heritage is mixed, with one parent coming from sub-Saharan African while his other parent has European heritage. Omar was born in Canada with both parents coming from a country in sub-Saharan Africa. The descriptor "origin" is, however, problematic because it implies a biological-racial self, thus reinforcing the historical understanding of race. As a partial answer to this problem of classification, I have chosen to identify such students as having "mixed parentage," whether that be in terms of "race," ethnicity, or continents. Although it would be useful to give a detailed description of the youth interviewed in the research, I am also cognizant that an in-depth description of the students could reveal their identities and therefore contravene my ethical responsibility with regard to confidentiality and anonymity.

My concern is to examine through symbolic forms (Thompson, 1990) what it means for school youth to identify as black in Alberta, Canada. Through individual interviews and focus groups, discursive tensions are evoked around who can identify themselves as black and who cannot. Contrary to the dominant "color-blind" discourse of many educators in the school system, these students' narratives also positioned them and others, at times, as racialized subjects. Although the school would like to perceive students synchronously as having an identical consciousness as "just students," the narratives indicate that they have racialized perceptions of themselves and others with whom they interact in school:

Doreen: They call them brown. I don't [know] why.

J : So you have brown, and you have black. What else do you have?

Doreen: Whites and, like, Orientals.
J　　: Oh, Orientals. And "Oriental" is ... ?
Doreen: That's everything from, like, Asia.

A few students—for example, Etta—alluded to demarcation of physical space into racialized/ethnicized social spaces:

> Well, like, people consider that [pause] ... I guess in the Hexagon they have little corners which, if you look, you can see them. Especially... they have a large East Indian group. And [pause] the Orientals are never really in the Hexagon. 'Cuz they actually have basically their own hallway on that side of the school. They have what you call [laugh] China-town ... the whole hallway is basically Oriental.

Although these school areas were marked and noted within the interviews, racialized boundaries were not perceived as being strictly policed, and several narratives allude to interaction taking place between different racialized groups. In positioning themselves as racialized subjects, the students identified themselves as "black" and were, to varying degrees, conscious of blackness as a political category that could be mobilized and used discursively to their advantage. In terms of the school site as a space of numerical dominance for students of African descent, several of the students indicated that there had been a decrease in the number of black students attending the school, and with that decrease the dynamic within the black group had changed. So it is that such changes and dynamics are also reflected in the types of data generated in this research at this specific historical conjuncture; as the dynamics change so, too, will the data generated.

Translated Blackness

In advancing the argument concerning the heterogeneity of these African diasporan youth, one theme that emerged from the generation of data relates to how identification as black is accomplished in various complex ways through understanding the self in relation to Canadian identity and other national identities encompassed within the diaspora and the African continent.

Although school youth construct a sense of what Stuart Hall (cited in Chen, 1996) identifies as translated blackness, this sense of blackness is one that is influenced by understandings of symbolic forms constructed primarily via youth culture in the United States. Such a placing of African-American cultural formation within the Canadian context means that African-American discourses of blackness dominate in an almost hegemonic sense, wherein Canadian identity is often interpreted in relation to its U.S. counterpart. This phenomenon is not new. Andre Alexis (1995) has alluded to the complex relationship and importance of the United States in the lives of African Canadians. For him, black American identity is portrayed as a universal identity for all blacks; a position he argues that some try to remedy, "trying to sing, dance, or write Canada for ourselves, to define our own terrain and situation" (p. 17). This tension in terms of the projection of U.S. experiences onto and into Canada is also evident in discussions of Canadian literary criticism. As George Elliott Clarke reveals, "African Canadians utilize African-American texts and historical cultural icons to define their own experiences (a fact which can seduce the unwary into believing that no uniquely African Canadian perspective exists)" (1996, p. 57).

This belief that there is no uniquely African Canadian experiences can be seen in the ways in which students orient themselves to an African-Canadian identity. For some school youth, the lack of recognition of a historical presence of blackness within the Canadian public sphere reinforces the sense of blackness as "Other," as outside the norm of what it means to be a Canadian. Even for those school youth whose ancestors have a long presence in Canada, it is difficult to identify or imagine any symbolic representation within Canadian society with which they can align themselves. Therefore, for some youth, Canadian identity is perceived as problematic, not readily available, and thus we can surmise that official citizenship does not automatically lead to recognition of self or acceptance by others as "Canadian."

It is not surprising, then, that overall, the students' narratives displayed differing and often-ambivalent orientations towards the adoption of African Canadian as a point of identification. For youth such as Etta (born and raised in Alberta), identification with a specific nationality is constructed through discourses on historical origins and "roots" rather than discourses that emphasize routes.

The following extracts highlight the ways in which the discourses of identity change according to the context and the raced subject positions of the participants. For this student, identification is managed and performed:

J : Do you see yourself as African or Canadian, or... West Indian or Caribbean?

Etta: What do I identify with the most? Yeah, well, first thing that pops into my head, I guess, must be I feel more like [Martinquane]. When I am here in Canada, I feel that I am [Martinquane] more than anything else. To me if I am Canadian I identify with [pause] ... like, white people. Right. But if I am in [Martinique] ... I am Canadian. That's how it is. 'Cuz they know that I am not from there. They know what family I'm from, whatever. But I am born in Canada, so I am Canadian. And for me, it is a little different, because technically I am half-African... But maybe I am biased with the whole thing. I do not see myself as an African.

For Etta the situation is not straightforward. It involves a process of self-reflection and, to some extent, "double-consciousness" as she reads the social situation to take account of the perceptions that the other person has:

J   : You wouldn't call yourself a Canadian?
Etta: Not here, I don't suppose. Well, I always go ... 'cuz I am born here so I
      don't want to lead anyone [on]. Usually, I say I am born here. But obvi-
      ously my mum's from [the Caribbean]. Cuz, usually ... that's what people
      are asking. I figured that out. Cuz they don't expect [pause] to hear that
      you are Canadian. They just know what they want to hear. Like, whether
      you are born here or not. I've learnt that. Cuz some people always ask
      you. If I say, "Oh, I am Canadian," they will say, "Oh, well, where are
      your parents from?" Or something like that. They ask you a further ques-
      tion. So I usually always put it in one sentence. Depending on who it is.
J   : Who it is?
Etta: It depends I guess, like [pause] ... I don't know. If a white person ask
      me, normally I'd say [pause] ... I am [Caribbean]. 'Cuz "Canadian" to
      them [pause] ... most of them don't understand what that means. But to
      a black person—especially if they are not from here—I usually tell them
      I am born here, but where my mum's from, 'cuz that's what they want to
      know.

Context and ethnicity of the audience can modify this complex process of identification and negotiating of a descriptor. Thus, the need for collective identity and fragmentation of identity varies according to social situation. Euda's narratives below indicate when fragmentation of collective might be necessary and when she would not necessarily call herself black:

Euda: If I was with a whole load of black people, I would then become a
      [Barbadian]

These narratives also reveal a problematic positioning resulting in specific discursive practices that result in a "disciplining of the self." This intertextual reading of identity and what it means to be Canadian supports, in some ways, a more open-ended pluralist definition of identity; one that changes accord-ing to context, a reflection of the intersubjective nature of interaction and identity formation. So context becomes important in determining whether the students construct black identity as an "outernational project" or not. At times they regard black identity as a singular construct contained by state boundaries. At other times they do not (Gilroy, 1995). As Henry Giroux (1996) argues such understandings are not innocent and often operate through pop-ular memory. It is an understanding that "neatly links nations, culture, and citizenship," leading to a position that "constructs the nation as an ethnically homogenous object" (1996). The ways that the students identify, or not, with a specific national identity are related to context as well as the availability of symbolic representations with which they can identify. Thus, taking on identification with Jamaica or Trinidad varies according to the racialized identity of the questioner as well as the geographic context of the social exchange. Although the latter fluidity in identification might subscribe to Hall's evocation that "identities are about becoming" (cited in Chen, 1996), such variability in identification does not imply a totally decentered sense of self. Instead, it can be argued that although "postmodern politics of temporary alliances, partial identities, is attractive as against the dyed-in-the-wool prejudice and exclusions of xenophobia, racism, and sexism, alliances and affinities mark some degree of ongoing identity and commitment, however provisional" (Andermahr, Lovell, and Wolkowitz, 1997, p. 125). These provisional alliances and affinities among the students, such as identification, were also dependent upon context, so that while, at times, their identification as black was paramount, at other times a national identity related to geographic region would emerge as a suffix and qualifier of their blackness.

A lack of strong identification with the descriptor "Canadian" becomes an important factor when placed in relation to the media definitions of African American to which the students were exposed. The narratives indicate that the proximity of the United States to Canada and the plethora of images of blackness that emanate from the United States come to play a part in the ability of the students to define themselves as Canadian. Thus, some students perceived African American as an identification that was as relevant to their sense of self as that of African Canadian.

Often, everyday meanings develop in relation to other cultural formations. As such, the narratives often drew on the United States in terms of defining the meanings and representations of blackness and black identity that exist in Canadian society. For Denzil, the proximity of the United States resulted in some leakage of U.S.-defined "black" culture into what could be defined as black Canadian. At times, this leakage comes to define other perceived black cultural formations as subordinate to that of the United States. Speaking about the influence of the African country from which his family emigrated, Denzil suggests that it offers little in terms of understanding the meanings associated with blackness in Canada,

J   : Are there things about your mum's culture that you bring to being black?

Denzil: There's nothing about the culture. 'Cuz being black, quote, unquote, is being black American.

J   : So, is there a black Canadian identity then?

Denzil: No, er [pause]. When you say African American, it encompasses, like, black people in North America.

However, in putting this latter perspective to Melvin, another student, a different response was garnered. For him, there is a clear distinction drawn between African American and African Canadian identity, with representations of Canadian blackness being identified as more syncretic. In addition, Melvin calls on liberal multicultural discourses dominant in Canada to both understand meanings surrounding "culture" and to differentiate Canadian culture from that of the United States. For him, it is the ability to mix with students from other racialized groups and the consequent construction of syncretic cultures that provides the "difference" from the United States:

J : What would you think if someone said to you, "Well, there isn't an African-Canadian culture"... and that what we have here in Canada is African-American culture?

Melvin: Oh, no, no. Well, it's just, like, there is, like [pause], Canadian and American, and it's all different. And people learn differently from different environments. And that's how you, like, mould and shape, like, the culture... in different places. Because you are going to react to different stuff different ways. 'Cuz I am sure that I wouldn't even be the same person if I lived down in the States.

J : You don't think so?

Melvin: No. My mentality would probably be different, especially if I was, like, meeting different people through the schools... like, being black [pause]... 'Cuz I know people from the States that just, like... used to just chill, like, with pure black people.... Well, I am not saying I didn't do that before [in school] but, like, I... still did chill with whoever. But then they used to, like, "cuss off" like other races, too, and they would always be, like, stuff going off against them. And, like, here I still, like... go through and do whatever with every race. And they kinda, like, single themselves out that way.

Although Gerald agrees that there is a slippage between the signifiers "African American" and "African Canadian," his narrative also goes on to specify that this slippage is primarily around youth culture,

Gerald:... I can't really explain it. It's just like there is no [pause], to me I've never seen anything that's, like, African Canadian. Like, everything that black kids identify with [pause] that I know about is, like, African American. Like, rap is African American, all the movies you watch are African-American movies, clothes you wear, [the] styles are African-American. Everything is, like, American.

Thus, Gerald's identification with blackness is primarily through youth culture, a youth culture that is linked to the United States. His recognition of youth culture as an important part of black identification is in line with recent theorization of black youth culture. Although the identification of students as black would appear to be a generic descriptor, the narratives indicate that the conception of black identity under discussion is specifically a youth identity. This point was also evident in the way that Gerald constructs blackness as related to dress and youth culture:

J   : So, give me an example of someone who you think dresses black? On the media or somebody that you know?
Gerald: All the black people except for people like old men. Like Denzel Washington. I always see him in suits and stuff, like, basically anyone else. See Snoop [pointing to The Source cover page on the table]— that's dressing black.

Or take, for example, the ways in which Melvin asks me to elaborate and differentiate in terms of whom I am referring to when I speak of black culture.

Melvin: It all depends. Like [pause] ... you mean black people as a whole? Or different age groups, or ... .
J   : You would make a distinction, then? Age groups, then ... ?
Melvin: Yeah, because ... still when you are, like, young you are not, like, down into nothing, like, deeper in life. So you just, like, go with, like, the things that everybody is into and stuff ... that make the things that black people are into. Like, we talk the same and, like, you know, listen to our music and what not and "do our thing." And, like, I am sure when you get like older, it, like, comes more visible that there is, like, different symbols and, like, different things that, like, represent [pause] your black culture. But, like, um, it's not really recognized to me at this moment. So I'm still digging deeper into life. Like, I've just begun.

Also evident within Melvin's narratives is that black identity is not an innate state of being but rather a social process of becoming that is heavily influenced by peers. He represents himself as "youth" on the way to becoming and adopting a differing "black adult" identity based on differing meanings and symbols. The construction of identity indicated by the narratives is one that draws primarily on U.S.-based youth culture and is open to change as one goes through adolescence to adulthood.

Of relevance in both Gerald and Melvin's narratives is the way that the discourses construct not just African-American identity as similar to African-Canadian but, specifically, African-American youth identity. These similarities are recognized and weighted as part of a yearning for African-American youth styles. In linking the two descriptors with regard to black identity, it becomes evident that similarities between the two are based on consumption of specific youth style. Media culture, music, and dress style, in particular, are identified as important markers of black identity. Frank's narratives clarify how he sees these two identities of black American and black Canadian as fluid in relation to each other:

Frank: They, like, try to do the same things. Everybody wants to do what other people do. Like, "rappers do this," then everybody wants to do this. It's, like [pause], want to listen to rap music and stuff like that.

Evident from the above presentation of student narratives is not only that African-American youth culture is aligned with African-Canadian youth culture but also that some use "black" interchangeably with African American and African Canadian. "Black" is used in a way that makes the term interchangeable between those whose heritages are in differing geographic areas and reinforces slippage between the signifiers African Canadian and African American. The point of constancy that links these differing geographic areas would seem to be a conception of black identity that is linked with phenotype and age and a trace of historical memory as much as anything else. Substantiation of this postulation can be found in the following extract that self-evidently defines hip-hop as a black cultural form—as Gerald said, "Cuz, basically, it's made up of black people!"

Perhaps not surprisingly, for those students born in Africa or whose heritage is more recently from countries in Africa, identification with the continent was more readily accepted. However, this identification was hybridized and as with other students of the diaspora strongly accented with hip-hop culture. This is to be expected in that such identification offers the possibility of an immediate sense of community and belonging for new students (Ibrahim, 2000; Forman, 2001). In contrast, students with close familial links to the continent seem not to use music or dress style as a source of identification with countries in Africa. Music described as black seems to be primarily from North America and the Caribbean, with few of the students being regular listeners of music from any countries in Africa:

J   : Do you ever listen to music from continental Africa?
Omar: Well, my parents do. I listen to it. In the car, my dad, he plays a lot. Um [pause], I used to go to, like [pause], potluck parties with my parents, things like that. That's what they used to play. I listened to that. I don't listen to it by myself, but when it's there I do.

Unlike rap, R&B, and reggae, music from the African continent is limited in its general availability. In comparison to the number of students who could access rap and R&B and reggae via *MuchMusic* or MTV on cable or satellite or via audiotapes sent by relatives in the Caribbean, few mentioned any comparable public spaces within which they could access or consume African music from the continent.

However, it also cannot be read that they were totally assimilated into Canadian society, as they may well draw on other sources and resources (churches and community groups), not evident through the narratives, to give meaning to identification with the continent.

In the themes discussed above, Hall's conception of black identity (discussed in Chen, 1996) as operating along vectors of sameness and difference coheres with the ways in which the youth constructed their identities. These intragroup differences were not evident at all times but tended to emerge during social situations that highlight a tension between individual identity and group identity. Although this identification of a black/national self through different music consumption patterns was primarily among the young women, I would urge caution in attributing this difference as due only to gender, since girls who were non-Jamaican but with Caribbean heritage were overrepresented in the sample.

To be sure, there was no real attempt among the students to represent themselves as distinctly Canadian through musical choices, even for those who were aware of the relations of power and dominance between the U.S. and Canada. The flow of dominance from the U.S. in music production, via rap and R&B, was interrupted only by reggae, a product of Jamaica, which is embedded with similar signs and codes as rap and has had more media exposure than other musical formations associated with the Caribbean region. Although the students from North America and the Caribbean are part of an African diaspora, there is little recognition, knowledge, or musical identification with the continent. In the long run, such a lack of connection may undermine the youths' ability to view music as constructed in a social formation.

Conclusion

In the context of my study, the students are the audience and the texts are the visual, aural, and print images produced in the U.S. that are received and consumed by African Canadian youth. Such images offer the audience of youth the opportunity to review and pursue a variety of differing subjectivities in general and black subjectivities more specifically. The study indicates the importance of youth culture and mediazation in terms of how youth identify with blackness and how they consequently come to understand their sense of self in Canadian society. This understanding of self is contoured by a specific historical conjuncture, where youth culture is heavily saturated with representations of blackness that have become a viable economic commodity. Thus, issues of black identification consistently collide with youth culture in order to produce various symbolic codes through which these students give meaning to their experiences. Through what can be identified as discourses—through language (verbal and nonverbal), a racialized regime of representation, and social interaction—the students make use of these space-distanced media to develop a cultural formation. Such a formation, although specific to the students' own social location, nonetheless reflects and reinforces a globalized capitalist economy in terms of its consumerist orientations. Youth culture is very much at the forefront of the intersection of the local and the global. Identities produced relate not just to Canada but also the Caribbean, the U.S., and the continent of Africa (i.e., African diasporan identities).

Notes

1 For a fuller discussion of the themes, arguments, and historical background highlighted in this chapter refer to Kelly, *Borrowed Identities* (2004) and Kelly, *Under the Gaze: Learning to Be Black in White Society* (1998).

References

Alexi, A. 1995. Borrowed blackness. *This Magazine* 28(8), 14–20.

Andermahr, S., T. Lovell, and C. Wolkowitz. 1997. Identity. In *A Glossary of Feminist Theory*, ed. S. Andermahr, T. Lovell, and C. Wolkowitz, 124–125. London: Arnold.

Carter, V., and W.L. Akili. 1981. *The Window of Our Memories*. B.C.R Society of Alberta.

Chen, K. 1996. Cultural studies and the politics of internationalization: An interview with Stuart Hall. In *Stuart Hall: Critical Dialogues in Cultural Studies*, ed. D. Morley and K. Chen, 392–408. New York: Routledge.

Clarke, G.E. 1996. Must all blackness be American?: Locating Canada in Borden's "tightrope time," or nationalizing Gilroy's Black Atlantic. *Canadian Ethnic Studies*, 28(3), 56–71.

Cooke, B. 1911. The black Canadian. *McLean's Magazine* 23(1), 3–11.

Edwards, B.H. 2004. The uses of diaspora. In *African Diaspora in the New World and Old Worlds: Consciousness and Imagination*, ed. G. Fabre and K. Benesch, 3–38. New York: Rodopi.

Fiske, J. 1994. Audience: Cultural practice and cultural studies. In *Handbook of Qualitative Research*, ed. N. Denzin and Y. Lincoln, 189–198. California: Sage.

Forman, M. 2001. "Straight outta Mogadishu" Prescribed identities and performative practices among Somali youth in North American high schools. *Topia: A Canadian Journal of Cultural Studies* 5, 1–19 [retrieved from http://www.utp-journals.com/topia/2forman.html 20/09/02].

Gilroy, P. 1993. *The Black Atlantic*. Cambridge, MA: Harvard University Press.

Gilroy, P. 1995. Roots and routes: Black identity as an outernational project. In *Racial and Ethnic Identity: Psychological Development and Creative Expressions*, ed. H. Harris, H. Blue, and E. Griffith, 15–30. New York: Routledge.

Giroux, H. 1996. *Fugitive Cultures: Race, Violence and Youth*. New York: Routledge.

Hall, S., ed. 1997. *Representation, Cultural Representation and Signifying Practices*. London: Sage.

Hooks, G. 1997. *The Keystone Legacy: The Recollections of a Black Settler*. Edmonton, AB: Brightest Pebble.

Ibrahim, A. 2000. "Hey ain't I black too?: The politics of becoming black. In *Rude, Contemporary Black Cultural Criticism,* ed. R. Walcott, 109–136. Toronto: Insomniac.

Kelly, J. 1998. *Under the Gaze: Learning to Be Black in White Society.* Halifax, NS: Fernwood Press.

Kelly, J. 2004. *Borrowed Identities.* New York: Peter Lang.

Rex, J. 1970/1983. *Race Relations in Sociological Theory.* London: Routledge and Kegan Paul.

Statistics Canada. 1996. *1996 Census: Ethnic Origin, Visible Minorities.* Ottawa, ON: The Daily Statistics Canada.

Thompson, J. 1990. *Ideology and Modern Culture.* Stanford, CA: Stanford University Press.

Torczyner, J. 1997. *Diversity, Mobility, and Change: The Dynamics of Black Communities in Canada.* Quebec: McGill University.

Walcott, R. 1997. *Black Like Who?* Toronto: Insomniac Press.

Williams, R. 1958/1993. Culture is ordinary. In *Border Country,* ed. J. McIlroy and S. Westwood, 89–102. Leicester, U.K.: National Institute of Continuing Adult Education.

6

Popular Culture and Recognition
Narratives of Youth and Latinidad[1]

ANGHARAD N. VALDIVIA

In the contemporary global situation, the movement of populations and cultural forms stands out as a major component of everyday life (Appadurai, 1996). Within this environment of forced and voluntary mobility, Latina/os[2] are one of the most dynamic segments of the U.S. population, with the youth component growing at a faster pace than other age cohorts. Simultaneously, as the symbolic register of our national imaginary, mainstream popular culture represents our values, fears, and desires within a matrix of power. That Latina/os are becoming more visible in mass media is a documented fact by many media scholars. However, and for the purposes of this book, my focus in this essay centers on Latina/o youth. How much do we know about Latina/o youth and popular culture scholarship? How much do we know about youth in Latina/o scholarship? Are Latina/o youth represented in mainstream popular culture and, if so, how? What are the implications of representation for Latina/o youth recognition? Do Latina/o youth engage with mainstream popular culture and, if so, how? This set of interrogations cannot be answered fully as the research has only begun to be conducted. Nonetheless, from what is available we can proceed to make some cautionary hypotheses as well as to pursue productive venues of further research. Narratives of youth and Latinidad are just beginning to be written, and this essay is an effort to make a democratically informed intervention into a budding discourse of ethnicity and difference.

Latina/o studies scholars trace mainstream popular culture visibility to either Selena's death in 1996 (Paredez, 2002, in press), to the late 1990s "Latin explosion" due to migration and demographic growth (Mayer, 2003), or to the U.S. Census announcement that Latina/os had officially become the most numerous minority in the U.S. (Valdivia, 2004). Historically, this is neither the first Latina/o explosion nor the first time that Latina/os achieved salience and prominence in mainstream popular culture. For example, Beltrán (2005, 2007) documents an earlier period in the 1920s when Latina/os (e.g., Dolores del Rio) were major Hollywood stars. Economic booms and busts fuel national sentiment towards migration in general and Latina/os in particular. Current

101

migration from Latin America, coupled with economic uncertainty, especially after 9/11, results in a climate where there is undeniable growth in the U.S. Latina/o population as well as border panics that have to be accounted for by both politicians and the popular press. As a result, this latest historical promi-nence is being documented in qualitative scholarship (see Molina Guzmán and Valdivia, 2004; Molina Guzmán, 2006; Báez, 2007; and Beltrán, 2002) that explores the representation of Latina/os in celebrity culture in general and Hollywood film in particular, as well as racialized and gendered narratives in the news (Molina Guzmán, 2005; Vargas, 2000). This literature finds promi-nent female celebrities whose bodies sign in for the national identity crisis that begins to acknowledge ethnic diversity as well as a gendered and devalued coverage of the Latina/o news subject. In quantitative research that measures the percentage of Latina/o characters in network television (Children NOW, 2004), research suggests that the "presence of Latino characters on prime time television has increased since 2001," including "for the first time, a show... [that] featured an opening credits cast comprised exclusively of Latino charac-ters" (p. 2). As of 2006 this trend of increased representation in entertainment media and news narratives continues unabated.

Studying Latina/o Youth

What is seldom mentioned in terms of the Latina/o population in mainstream representation in particular is that a large component of both long-standing and recent immigrant populations are composed of youth. Youth of color make up 40% of the population aged 19 and under in this country (Children NOW, 2004). The median age for native-born Hispanics is 17 (Pew Hispanic Center, 2005), with the broadest part of the nativity pyramid being in the under-4 age group (Pew Hispanic Center, 2005a). Yet despite this documented youth bubble, which is projected to grow as a percentage of the total Latina/o population, we are just beginning to conduct cultural research on Latina/o youth. Latina/o youth in school have surpassed the African-American public school population since 1996 (Marin, Lee, and Orfield, 2003; Horn, Flores, and Orfield, 2003); although visible in our communities, they are strangely missing from our mainstream popular culture. According to Children NOW (2004), "youth comprise the most racially diverse population in the country" (p. 9) but gains in general representation of Latina/os were not matched by those on youth roles. Certainly in the case of news, coverage of youth of color reinforces the criminality paradigm, despite decreasing rates of crime among youth of color (Youth Media Council, 2002).

The fact that youth of color compose nearly half of the population under 19 has not gone unnoticed by public policy and scholarly circles. Within media studies, scholars find that youth function as a proxy for the larger concerns of our culture. Thus, we often encounter youth as a problem, as deviants, and as the epitome of the latest moral panic. However, the deviant paradigm that often applies to minorities in general, Latina/os in particular (Casas and Dixon, 2003; Dixon and Linz, 2000; Vargas, 2000), and youth (see, for example, Mazzarella, 2003; Wyn, 2005) applies to youth of color with a vengeance (Tovares, 2000). For example, the Youth Media Council (2002) found that for every 11 stories about youth and crime there was one about youth and poverty. Even stories about education focused on crime. Furthermore, when solutions were offered, "83% focused on punishment, increased policing, or incarceration" (p. 9). Similarly, and sometimes linked in the academic literature, popular music as a signifying practice of youth can be and has been linked to deviant and abnormal behavior. As rock and roll, through heavy metal and more recently rap and hip-hop, youth music has been identified as a source of, at best, antisocial and, at worst, criminal and suicidal tendencies from which our youth need to be protected. Hip-hop and rap have been further linked to racial issues—namely, African-American urban ghetto tendencies, and thus have linked the moral panic of youth music with that of racial tensions and the underclass. In the news these come together, in the sense that minority youth who listen to these forms of popular music are also linked to criminality (e.g., Lipsitz, 1998).

Criminality is not the only "problem" paradigm or moral panic wherein Latina/o youth stand out. Another well-funded area of research involves medical and scientific literature, especially issues of smoking (e.g., Casas et. al., 1998; Dusenbury et. al., 1992), obesity (e.g., Cruz et. al., 2004; Davis et. al., 2005), and sexual activity, including condom use and HIV/AIDS (e.g., Ford and Norris, 1997; Sellers et. al., 1994). This medical scholarship singles out Latina/o youth as "at risk" for a broad range of behaviors that threaten their health as well as the health of the national body. This discursive construction of the Latina/o body as infectious and of the health implications of border-crossing microbes, bodies, and cultural ways of being has been well documented by Latina feminist scholars (Leger and Ruiz, 2007; Ruiz, 2003; Tapia, 2005). Tapia, in fact, has illustrated how teen antipregnancy campaigns symbolically construct the problem teen as a sexually active, socially irresponsible Latina.

In media studies scholarship, despite a veritable explosion in the scholarship of Latina/o celebrities, there is very little written about Latina/o youth. Perhaps part of the issue lies in their virtual lack of representation. ABC's 2006 fall lineup including the show *Ugly Betty*, with *Real Women Have Curves* protagonist America Ferrera in the lead role of the remake of the Latin American telenovela, *Betty La Fea* (literally Ugly Betty) (Rivero, 2003), alongside the *George Lopez Show*, might go part of the way in addressing that symbolic annihilation. Historically, U.S. network television has not been a model for ethnic representation. Scholars find that the children's networks such as Nickelodeon (Seiter and Mayer, 2004) and the Disney Channel (Valdivia, forthcoming) have been far more inclusive, partly because of the freedom that comes with

24-hour programming and not having to adhere to the rigid formulas of Saturday morning network fare. Hollywood film has foregrounded the already-mentioned celebrity Latinas such as Jennifer Lopez, Salma Hayek, and Rosie Perez but has not necessarily cast the spotlight on Latina/o youth, except within the outcast and criminal paradigm dating back to *West Side Story* (1961). In the new media of video and digital gaming, old tropes of the dark male subject as threatening and violent take up the criminal representation again as well. The exception would appear to be the children's networks, with the Disney Channel nurturing the career of current celebrities such as Jessica Alba and America Ferrera, both of whom were part of their children's troupe much like Britney Spears and Justin Timberlake.

Representation, however, is not the only way to study youth and the media. Media and cultural scholars also turn to issues of identity formation, reception, and consumption of media products. This type of research often includes a bit of representational analysis—for example, asking youth how or if they see themselves represented—but also extends beyond that into identity formation and notions of subjectivity and belonging. These are fruitful areas to pursue in the contemporary setting of globalization and mobility. Given that ethnic youth often straddle not only generations but cultures and nations, engaging them about their media choices and practices in relation to issues of ethnicity and nation promises to shed illumination on a previously understudied area. The well-documented characteristic of the Latina/o population to think of ourselves in multiplicitous terms as hyphenated beings further underscores the global currents that Latina/os embody and process. The particular location of Latina/o youth in this dynamic, considering that they often transact identity formation and media engagement across national divides, promises to shed light on issues of youth and globalization.

Although recent scholarship has sought to study the dynamic situation of migrant youth (see, for example, Mosselson, 2006) or of suburban Latina/os (Macias, 2006), there is often very little attention paid to media and popular culture. Mosselson's brilliant ethnography of Bosnian refugee girls in New York City, although an excellent study of migration, class, and hybrid ethnicity, has nearly nothing on media perceptions. Similarly, Macias' trenchant study of third-generation Southwest Latina/os makes little mention of youth and none about media. On the other hand, Finders (1997) ends up almost foregrounding media use in her study about junior high girls and their "hidden literacies." However, although this study explores some class differences, the composition of the participants is ethnically homogeneous—all white. In a study about a multicultural sample of children creating their own superheroes and their narratives, Dyson (1997) presages many of the issues that might be taken up with youth in a much younger age cohort. Foremost in her project, Dyson seeks to find the moments of agency that children carve out in a highly structured world.

Studies combining a focus on youth, media, and popular culture, and ethnicity and nation are few and far between. Foremost in this literature is the work of Vicky Mayer, *Producing Dreams, Consuming Youth: Mexican Americans and Mass Media* (2003). Mayer conducted ethnographic work in a community center in San Antonio, TX, where she was able to engage with Mexican-American[3] youth about media, identity, and cultural production. Similarly, in *¿Que Onda? Urban Youth Cultures and Border Identities*, Bejarano (2005) explores the dynamic situation of ethnic youth living on the Southwest border. Forthcoming research continues the investigation into these questions. Vargas (2007) chooses the term *transnational* to refer to the young Latina women she studies in relation to gender, popular culture, and family. She deploys the concept of "ambiguous loss" to explore the process of migration. She also encourages the girls to make their own media collages to represent their experiences with the process of migration. González Hernández (2007) studies border-crossing teens—that is, young people who literally and regularly criss-cross the Tijuana–San Diego border, much like 40% of that border population does. The hybrid identity of these teens, especially the middle-class ones, evokes the work of García Canclini (1995).

Given that there is little research on Latina/o youth outside of the deviant paradigm (whether in terms of criminality or of medical issues) and that there is more research on African-American youth, and, of course, tons of research on dominant culture youth, we can draw on that combined body of work, yet strike out into productive research paths that take into account the difference and specificity of Latina/o youth. As with general Latina/o studies, youth Latina/o studies inhabit that unstable location between the inclusivity of pan-Latinidad and the specificity in which individuals and groups may live out their lives and experience their media. Taking all of these issues into consideration, we can begin to map out some of the contours of a grounded approach to the study of Latina/o youth and popular culture.

Latina/o Youth and Popular Culture: A Grounded Approach to Research

First, Latina/o youth represent a different group not just in racial/ethnic terms but also because of the transnational situation that many Latina/os live in. The notion of *bi* or *tri* belonging, as in Mexican American or Chino-Latino, is unlike most African Americans who trace distant roots to the continent of Africa but not a recent or near recent root to a particular country that they may actually think of returning to or that they occasionally or frequently visit and/or stay in touch with through diasporic networks. This multiple subjectivity can be both enabling and restraining. It can be experienced as multiplicity and/or fragmentation. Popular culturewise, this multiple subjectivity means that many Latina/o youth engage with a range of popular cultures, not just a singular one, given that they may be rooted in more than one place. Opportunities for hybrid reception and creation extend beyond the mainstream and alternative media diet of singly rooted youth to a transnational and multi-national recipe of the popular that may, at times, be contradictory. Multiple roots can be enhancing and enabling but can also pull a person in many different ways. Compared to the easier belonging of native or distant ancestry youth, this recent and multiplicitous identity has to be addressed.

Second, youth, as a particular social and age category, have less agency than their parents in terms of deciding when and if to move. Additionally, they have fewer resources and less access to institutions that would help them to stay in touch with loved ones or significant others that they left behind, as well as limited assistance in reaching out for help in their new situation. In her effort to get teens to develop media collages of self in her quest to study their migration as "ambiguous loss," Vargas (forthcoming) gives an incredibly touching narrative of how certain teens, for example, leave their parents, siblings, and/or other loved ones behind. Some find the transition and loss so harrowing that they actually may lose their memories. One teen relates how she could not engage in popular culture consumption, such as collecting magazines, dolls, and other fan materials, because her parents, always planning for eventual migration, knew they would not be able to take much across the border. All of these tales of transition and migration reveal the loss and lack of agency reported by Latina/o youth as well as the importance of media and popular culture to their identity, whether in their homes or their new countries. The challenge to scholars is to figure out the spaces and occasions when Latina/o youth exercise agency despite intense structures. In this pursuit the work of Dyson (1997) proves to be particularly insightful.

Third, and related to the above, Latina/o migrant youth fall between the cracks of responsibility and attention and so may become even more dependent on popular culture and media both for entertainment and for cues as to their new place and role in society. Parents, if they are physically present, are often overwhelmed by issues of migration, prejudice, limited opportunities, etc. They are, in effect, "not there" for their youth. Younger children may receive more care, but youth are left to tough it out on their own. The ambiguous loss of what is left behind is coupled by the psychological absence of their caregivers (Vargas, 2007). In this case, media potentially can provide a form of escapism, engagement, and pedagogy for a new identity. Much like the Sears Roebuck catalog played an Americanizing role at the turn of the previous century, media and popular culture play that role, especially for that segment of the Latina/o youth population that finds itself falling between the cracks of parental and institutional attention.

Fourth, media and popular culture are taken-for-granted aspects of the contemporary modern world, including the United States. In the hyper-consumerist economy that we live in, many assume that this is a universal characteristic, indeed the most prominent signifier of youth culture. This may very well be the case for youth, regardless of ethnicity, in the middle class and above. However, this is a very different thing in the working and under-class. Nonetheless, we cannot assume that Latina/o youth are undifferenti-ated in terms of economic assets nor can we assume that all youth are equally empowered vis-à-vis consumerism. Issues of consumerism have to be studied in relation to class and socioeconomic standing. For instance, Mayer (2003) found that we cannot assume even that all youth have access to media. Both by virtue of their age—that is, their older siblings or parents or grandparents may have "dibs" on media use in their households or by class when they live in family situations where television and basic tape or CD technology are beyond the economic means of the family economy—working-class youth may actu-ally have very little access to the technology and cultural forms many of us take for granted. Some of the girls in the Mayer (2003) study could not watch television when they wanted to because their parents or older siblings dictated channel and program choice. Many could not afford to buy batteries to run their CD players.

The digital divide certainly applies to working-class populations, and Latina/o youth compose a disproportionate share of this population. Yet they undeniably want access to media and digital technologies. One such case study provides ample illustration about this desire. When engaging in an Internet action-research project that included the provision of computer and Internet access to disadvantaged San Diego area children for the purposes of creating their own community newspaper, Seiter (2004) found that the research team's preconceived pedagogical notions had to be balanced against the participants' choices in using the technology. Whereas the research team had predicted and hoped for community-building outcomes for the access to Internet techno-logy, many times the youth wanted to download popular celebrities and art-ists and print them out as a way to participate in popular culture fandom. Printed-out images of Jennifer Lopez could be taped to their bedroom walls. Seiter comments,

> From the moment students got on the Internet, their interest in researching and writing about local stories disappeared. Every proposed topic was a story about a national or global entertainment phenomenon: Pokemon, Britney Spears, Christina Aguilera, N'Sync, and the Back-street Boys. The first edition of the paper (pre-Internet) was composed entirely of local stories generated through the photography sessions... (pp. 93–94).

The near-majority of the participants, 49%, identified as Latina/o and yet from the listed items, we can see that they sampled a broad range of media and popu-lar culture. In previous research Seiter (1993, 1999) has documented the debates about popular and consumer culture and how this predisposes working-class children to think of their own cultural tendencies as inappropriate and less worthy, but after this project she found that it is indeed difficult to recuperate a progressive pedagogy from the hyper-commercial releases so widely available. This leads to yet another challenge for scholars of Latina/o youth and the media and popular culture: namely, that increasing access for the disadvantaged may improve their belonging, but in commodity and celebrity fan culture, rather than something deemed more progressive or pedagogically valuable.[4]

Fifth, the bulk of the studies mentioned focus on either recent migrants, transnational, and/or working-class youth. This certainly adds to the "deviancy" paradigm that so pervades much of the research. Although it is undeniable that a disproportionate share of Latina/o youth live under the poverty line, there is also a statistically significant, and sometimes long-standing, portion of the Latina/o population, whether recent immigrant or not, that is middle or upper-middle class. These youth are grossly understudied. One suspects that there may actually be quite a large amount of research conducted on this segment of the population by marketers and advertising agents, but this research is usually proprietary and not open for public review. The intensification of commodification and consumer culture means that this segment of the audience, affluent youth, is the most interesting to marketers and best lends itself to market-friendly representations such as the Disney Channel. If we are to take *Lizzie McGuire* and *Cheetah Girls*, both hit Disney shows, as any indication of Latina/o youth representation, it is the ambiguous Latina that plays best in commodity popular culture; it is this decidedly upscale target audience that is represented and sought. Both Miranda (from *Lizzie*) and Channel (from *Cheetah*) are sidekicks whose *Latinidad* is barely distinguishable—available to those with a highly honed Latina radar. Otherwise, they sign in as the assimilated, hyper-consumerist, beautiful youth that make up the bulk of Disney Channel original programming. Representation-wise, we are beginning to see more of these middle-class Latina/o youth, having had a surfeit of working-class youth as urban deviants, a previously mentioned tendency dating back to *West Side Story* (1961), in entertainment and news narratives.

In terms of Latina/o middle-class youth as audience, there is nearly a total gap in the research. An exception is the work of González Hernández (2007) who studies middle-class youth living in the Mexican border city of Tijuana—*Tijuanenses*—in relation to their preferences and identification as they are caught between and exposed to both U.S. and Mexican popular media. He finds that the double competence these youth develop includes not only a preference for U.S. media but also disdain toward Mexican migrants who flock to the border city in hopes of crossing over to San Diego. International popular culture, which in this border town is heavily influenced by the U.S., acquires a legitimacy among middle-class youth that cannot be rivaled by their national media; *Tijuanenses* deem it as more playful, educational, and of strategic and pragmatic use than that produced in Mexico.

This leads to a sixth item of potential research, and that is that media use is grossly understudied in terms of the conflicting pulls of family, culture, and the need to "fit in." These pulls exist both for recent immigrants as well as long-standing native populations. Given that youth are partly defined as members of a transitional subjectivity, fitting in becomes all the more important. Mayer (2003) and Bejarano (2005) interview a number of young Latinas who express frustration regarding these issues. Bejarano's chapter is appropriately subtitled "falling between the cracks." The multiply constructed category of Latinidad contributes the additional variable of age and generation to the mix of contradictory affiliations and belongings. Popular culture preferences may be rooted in one place for the grandparents, another for the parents, and yet another for youth. Thus, difference is experienced by youth both in relation to the mainstream culture and to their own family, not just across age but nation and culture.

Attesting to the heterogeneous effects and influence of popular culture is a seventh consideration of the linking and sustaining aspects of transnational popular culture. For recent immigrant Latina/o youth or for long-standing transnational youngsters, that is, the ones that regularly go back and forth as many Mexican Americans and Puerto Ricans do, media and popular culture are a central way to stay in touch with their relatives and home country communities. Mayer (2003) found that girls could stay in touch with their cousins and friends through discussions of telenovelas. Given that the Latinas living in the U.S. had access to these telenovelas on Univisión or Telemundo, they could discuss plot and character development with those in the home country. Telenovelas, in fact, become a way of maintaining a link, even as the girls mostly already knew that they are a derided form of popular culture. Although Internet culture, including some form of e-mail, might be the more "obvious" way of staying in touch, as previously mentioned, this would only be an option to that segment of the Latina/o youth who have steady access to computer technology and whose interlocutors in the home countries do as well.

An eighth issue is language. For youth this is an issue in terms of identity but not so much in terms of comprehension. Immigrant youth can learn a new language much faster and easier than their older generations. If bilingual, there are very few school systems that view that as an asset rather than yet one more predictor of low achievement and deviance. English-only movements further marginalize bi- or multilingual people. Language continues to play an important role as a signifier of Latinidad, even if youth have lost their Spanish proficiency. Within youth culture, language remains a way for youth subgroups to differentiate between themselves as well as for outside groups, such as educators or parents, to police youth, although for very different purposes. A Chicana girl in Bejarano's study (2005) complains of the many sources policing her language skills. Her Anglo peers police and deride her

English. Recent immigrants police and deride her Spanish—something that is accentuated if and when she travels back to the home country. Educators also want proficiency in English whereas parents do not want her to lose her Spanish. This girl articulates the many contradictory censors to her bilingualism. Rather than reinforcing this girl's ability to learn two languages and thus navigate two or more cultures, all seem to use this skill against her to position her as somehow incomplete, inauthentic, or deviant.

Moving on to greater tensions within ethnic formation, a ninth item to consider is the instability in struggles within Latinidad. That is, although from the outside, and certainly as constructed within mainstream popular culture, there is a tendency to paint Latinidad as an undifferentiated group of brown people, the *Bronze Race*, this intrinsic Latina/o solidarity is not quite borne out in everyday, lived experience. As this essay has already suggested, from within Latinidad there is a great deal of differentiation according to class, race, date of immigration, national origin, Spanish accent, education, accent, gender, sexuality, etc. Bejarano (2005) found that there is a great deal of conflict between Chicanos—that is, long-standing U.S. Mexican-American populations—and recent immigrants from Mexico, *Mejicanos*. Often, youths would not hang out together, and the popular culture, language, and style that they chose to perform their identity marked that difference and relationality. The fact that immigrants now come from all over the Americas generates a whole new range of tensions. Southern Cone immigrants from Argentina, Uruguay, Paraguay, and Chile tend to be lighter skinned and more educated than those from the indigenous countries such as Peru, Bolivia, and Guatemala. Racism is not absent from within Latinidad where lightness still has a valence. The gap between middle-class and working-class Latina/os does not seem to be an easy one to bridge. All of these divisions and tensions implicate youth as they are the ones thrown together in schools, for example. How do they negotiate these conflicts while carving out a space of survival and identity? There is nearly no research on Latina/o youth sexual minorities, other than in the previously mentioned medical literature of disease and infection. What is the role or potential of media and popular culture as a community building and coalition-forming tool? Can youth produce forms of popular culture that, in turn, can foster community growth and understanding?

Finally, all of these considerations lead us to consider the concept of hybridity. Both in terms of popular culture and of population, the resulting mix will be hybrid. Latina/o youth not only intermingle across Latinidades but with the other ethnicities in their communities. Suárez-Orozco and Páez (2002) document the tendency for lighter Latina/os to intermarry with non-Hispanic whites and the converse tendency for Afro Latina/os to marry with non-Hispanic blacks. Either way, Latina/o youth intermarry or reproduce across national, ethnic, and racial lines. Likewise, the popular culture that they engage in will come from a number of sources and will, indeed, be composed of hybrid cultural forms, such as *reggeaton,* a popular music whose Caribbean roots include Anglo and Hispanic traces. Of course, by the time this article goes to press, reggeaton will have already been touted as last year's cultural form, but that is the nature of contemporary popular youth culture; it is fast moving and changing. In terms of representation, Latina/o youth tend to appear unassimilatable in deviant discourses and as ambiguous ethnics in consumer-driven types of media. In the one, they remain outside of the hybrid space, whereas in the other they nearly disappear, noticeable mostly to those of us who can recognize the elements of Latinidad in their characters and/or surroundings.

Studying Latina/o youth and/in popular culture promises to become a growing area of research. Although we cannot exactly say that there is no research on Latina/o youth, we can certainly discern narrative patterns that accord with the standing of Latina/os in contemporary U.S. culture. Given that it was seldom acknowledged that Latina/os existed in a previous binary black–white national imaginary, it comes as no surprise that there is much more research on both white and black youth. The trope of deviance has been extended from black to Latina/o youth as has been the trope of eternal urban underclass. There is little work on middle-class Latina/o youth. In terms of popular culture, the representations can be mapped along the above patterns of exclusion and difference. Cinematically, entertainmentwise and news narrativewise, Latina/o youth tend to show up more as problems, gang members, outsiders, and deviants. Efforts to engage youth in cultural creation face formidable barriers of access to technology and other resources, especially for disadvantaged segments of the Latina/o population. Mayer's title, *Producing Dreams, Consuming Youth* (2003) is itself a telling document to the tendency to incorporate all that is youth culture into capitalist formations. Incorporating popular culture collages as a way to get Latina/os to talk about their identity (Vargas, 2007) has yielded valuable information. The fine line between youth agency and the myriad structures certainly impinge on their relationship with media and popular culture.

Notes

1 Thanks to Kortney Ziegler and Shivali Tukdeo for research assistance.

2 Throughout the essay, I will use the preferred term *Latina/o* to refer to that segment of the U.S. population that has recent or past Latin American roots. Admittedly, this is a porous demarcation. However, when quoting or referencing a study or scholar who uses *Hispanic* instead, I will use their terminology.

3 This essay uses the broader ethnic category of Latina/o while Mayer's work focuses on a particular and the most numerous segment of that category, Mexican Americans.

4 This dilemma certainly reminds cultural scholars of the high culture/low culture debates wherein elites want to use education to save the masses from their debased forms of culture. It also highlights the tensions between agency and structure. In this case, the agency of the youth who finally have access to both Internet and printing technology while the capitalist structure makes commodity and fan culture most easily accessible.

References

Appadurai, A. 1996. *Modernity at Large: Cultural Dimensions of Globalization.* Minneapolis, MN: University of Minnesota Press.

Báez, J. 2007. In press. Towards a Latinidad feminista: The multiplicities of Latinidad and feminism in contemporary cinema. *Popular Communication* 5(3).

Bejarano, C. 2005. ¿Que Onda? *Urban Youth Cultures and Border Identity.* Tucson, A2: University of Arizona Press.

Beltrán, M. 2002. The Hollywood Latina body as site of social struggle: Media constructions of stardom and Jennifer Lopez's "cross-over butt." *Quarterly Review of Film and Video* 19(1), 71–86.

Beltrán, M. 2005. Dolores Del Rio, the first "Latin invasion," and Hollywood's transition to sound. *Aztlán: The Journal of Chicano Studies* 30(1), 55–86.

Beltrán, M. 2007. When Dolores Del Rio became Latina: Latina/o stardom in Hollywood's transition to sound. In *Latina/o Communication Studies Today*, ed. A. Valdivia, New York: Peter Lang.

Casas, J., A. Bimbela, C. Corral, I. Yafiez, R. Swaim, J. Wayman, and S. Bates. 1998. Cigarette and smokeless tobacco use among migrant and nonmigrant Mexican American youth. *Hispanic Journal of Behavioral Sciences* 20(1), 102–121.

Casas, M., and T. Dixon. 2003. The impact of stereotypical and counter-stereotypical news on viewer perceptions of blacks and Latinos: An exploratory study. In *A Companion to Media Studies*, ed. A. Valdivia, Malden, MA: Blackwell.

Children NOW. 2004. Fall Colors 2003–2004 Prime Time Diversity Report. Oakland, CA: Children NOW.

Cruz, M., M. Weigensberg, T. Huang, G. Ball, G. Shaibi, and M. Goran. 2004. The metabolic syndrome in overweight Hispanic youth and the tole of insulin sensitivity. *The Journal of Clinical Endocrinology and Metabolism* 89(1), 108–113.

Davis, J., E. Ventura, M. Weigensberg, G. Ball, M. Cruz, G. Shaibi, and M. Goran, 2005. The relation of sugar intake to {beta} cell function in overweight Latino children. *American Journal of Clinical Nutrition* 82(5), 1004–1010.

Dixon, T., and D. Linz. 2000. Overrepresentation and underrepresentation of African-Americans and Latinos as lawbreakers on television news. *Journal of Communication* 50(2), 131–155.

Dusenbury, L., J. Kerner, D. Baker, G. Botvin, S. James-Ortiz, and A. Zauber. 1992. Predictors of smoking prevalence among New York Latino youth. *American Journal of Public Health* 82(1), 55–58.

Dyson, A. 1997. *Writing Superheroes: Contemporary Childhood, Popular Culture, and Classroom Literacy.* New York: Teachers College Press.

Finders, M. 1997. *Just Girls: Hidden Literacies and Life in Junior High.* New York: Teachers College Press.

Ford, K., and A. Norris. 1997. Sexual networks of African-American and Hispanic youth. *Sexually Transmitted Diseases* 24(6), 327–333.

Garcia Canclini, N. 1995. *Hybrid Cultures: Strategies for Entering and Leaving Modernity.* Minneapolis, MN: University of Minnesota Press.

González Hernández, D. 2007. Watching over the border: A case study of the Mexico United States television and youth audience. In *Latina/o Communication Studies Today*, ed. A. Valdivia, New York: Peter Lang.

Horn, C., S. Flores, and G. Orfield. 2003. Percent plans in college admissions: A comparative analysis of three states' experiences. A report by the Harvard University Civil Rights.

Project. Retrieved March 23, 2003 from http://www.civilrightsproject.harvard.edu/research/affirmativeaction/tristate.php.

Leger, M., and M. Ruiz. 2007. "Hot-Blooded": Latino bodies and politics of health and disease. In *Geographies of Latinidad,* ed. M. Garcia and A. Valdivia, Durham, NC: Duke University Press.

Lipsitz, G. 1998. The hip hop hearings: Censorship, social memory, and intergenerational tendencies among African Americans. In *Generations of Youth: Youth Cultures in Twentieth-Century America,* ed. J. Austin and M. Willard, New York: New York University Press.

Macias, T. 2006. *Mestizo in America: Generations of Mexican Ethnicity in the Suburban Southwest.* Tucson, AZ: University of Arizona Press.

Marin, P., E.K. Lee, and G. Orfield. 2003. Appearance and reality in the sunshine state: The talented 20 program in Florida. A report by the Harvard University Civil Rights Project. Available at http://www.civilrightsproject.harvard.edu/research/affirmativeaction/florida.php.

Mayer, V. 2003. *Producing Dreams, Consuming Youth: Mexican Americans and Mass Media.* Piscataway, NJ: Rutgers University Press.

Mazzarella, S. 2003. Constructing youth: Media, youth, and the politics of representation. In *A Companion to Media Studies,* ed. A. Valdivia, Malden, MA: Blackwell.

Molina Guzmán, I., and A. Valdivia. 2004. Brain, brow, and booty: Latina iconicity in U.S. popular culture. *The Communication Review* 7(2), 205–221.

Molina Guzmán, I. 2005. Gendering Latinidad through the Elian ciscourse about Cuban women. *Latino Studies* 3(2), 179–204.

Molina Guzmán, I. 2006. Mediating *Frida*: Negotiating discourses of Latina/o authenticity in global media representations of ethnic identity. *Critical Studies in Media Communication* 23(3), 232–251.

Mosselson, J. 2006. *Roots and Routes: Bosnian Adolescent Refugees in New York City.* New York: Peter Lang.

Paredez, D. 2002. Remembering Selena, re-membering *Latinidad*. *Theatre Journal* 54(1), 63–84.

Paredez, D. In press. Becoming Selena, becoming Latina. In *Women in the US-Mexico Borderlands: Structural Violence and Agency in Everyday Life,* ed. D. Seguar and P. Zavella, Durham, NC: Duke University Press.

Pew Hispanic Center. 2005. Hispanics at mid-decade. Table 6: Median age by sex, race, and ethnicity. Retrieved October 4, 2006 at http://pewhispanic.org/files/other/middecade/Table 6.pdf.

Pew Hispanic Center. 2005a. Hispanics at mid-decade. Table 7a: Population pyramids for ethnicity and nativity groups. Retrieved October 4, 2006 at http://pewhispanic.org/files/other/middecade/Table 7a.pdf.

Rivero, M. 2003. The performance and reception of televisual "ugliness" in *Yo soy Betty la fea. Feminist Media Studies* 3(1), 65–81.

Ruiz, M. 2003. Border narratives, HIV/AIDS, and Latina/o health in the United States: A cultural analysis. *Feminist Media Studies* 2(1), 37–62.

Seiter, E. 1993. *Sold Separately: Children and Parents in Consumer Culture.* New Brunswick, NJ: Rutgers University Press.

Seiter, E. 1999. *Television and New Media Audiences.* New York: Oxford University Press.

Seiter, E. 2004. Children reporting online: The cultural politics of the computer lab. *Television and New Media* 5(2), 87–107.

Seiter, E., and V. Mayer. 2004. Diversifying representation in children's TV. In *Nickelodeon Nation: The History, Politics, and Economics of America's Only TV Channel for Kids*, ed. H. Hendershot, New York: New York University Press.

Sellers, D., S. McGraw, and J. McKinlay. 1994. Does the promotion and distribution of condoms increase teen sexual activity? Evidence from an HIV prevention program for Latino youth. *American Journal of Public Health* 84(12), 1952–1959.

Suárez-Orozco, M., and M.M. Páez. 2002. The research agenda. In *Latinos Remaking America*, ed. M. Suárez-Orozco and M.M. Páez, Berkeley, CA: University of California Press.

Tapia, R. 2005. Impregnating images: Visions of race, sex, and citizenship in California's teen pregnancy prevention campaigns. *Feminist Media Studies* 5(1), 7–22.

Tovares, R. 2000. Influences on the Mexican American youth gang discourse on local television news. *Howard Journal of Communications* 11(4), 229–246.

Valdivia, A. Forthcoming. Mixed race on Disney channel: From *Johnnie Tsunami* through *Lizzie McGuire* and ending with the *Cheetah Girls*. In *Mixed Race in Hollywood Film and Television*, ed. M. Beltrán and C. Fojas, New York: New York University Press.

Valdivia, A. 2004. Latina/o communication and media studies today. *Communication Review* 7(2), 107–112.

Vargas, L. 2000. Genderizing Latino news: An analysis of a local newspaper's coverage of Latino current affairs. *CSMC: Critical Studies in Mass Communication* 17(3), 261.

Vargas, L. 2007. Media practices and gendered identity among transnational Latina teens. In *Latina/o Communication Studies Today*, ed. A. Valdivia, New York: Peter Lang.

Youth Media Council. 2002. Speaking for Ourselves: A Youth Assessment of Local News Coverage. San Francisco: We Interrupt This Message.

Wyn, J. 2005. Youth in the media: Adult stereotypes of young people. In *Talking Adolescence: Perspectives on Communication in the Teenage Years*, ed. A. Williams and C. Thurlow, 23–34. New York: Peter Lang.

7

Mobile Students in Liquid Modernity
Negotiating the Politics of Transnational Identities

PARLO SINGH AND CATHERINE DOHERTY

On a day-to-day basis, educators design learning environments based on images of learners and imaginings of their worlds. Such imagining constructs a tacit model of the learner. It also informs the selection of curricular content, the design of pedagogy, and modes of evaluation (Bernstein, 1990; Singh, 2002). In Australian higher education settings, approximately 23% of the total student population is now full-fee-paying international students, typically of Chinese heritage from Southeast Asia (Department of Education Science and Training, 2003, 2005; Nesdale et al. 1995). Thus, the international student is widely imagined and known under an "institutional abstraction" (Apple, 2004, p.126) or category of "the Asian learner." This category invokes essentialized attributes (rote learning style, passive learner) understood to require pedagogic intervention and amelioration. Michael Apple (2004) argues that such ingrained "commonsense categories" need to be interrogated in terms of their effect on the ultimate distribution of knowledge, the historical and social circumstances that initially produced the categories, and the conditions that sustain and reify the category in educational practices over time. He also highlights how any label works to essentialize the individuals it is applied to and reduces how they can be known, even by themselves:

> The label and all that goes with it is likely to be used by the individual's peers and his or her custodians (e.g., teachers and administrators) to define him or her. It governs nearly all of the conduct toward the person, and, more importantly, the definition ultimately governs the student's conduct toward these others, thereby acting to support a self-fulfilling prophecy (p. 129).

Thus, when it comes to "knowing" internationally mobile students, it is not necessarily any intrinsic identity that will impact on pedagogic design; rather, it will more likely be a matter of who they are imagined to be in these temporal-spatial locations and thus what pedagogic identities (Bernstein, 2000) are made available to these students with which to "suture" their identity projects (Hall, 1996). This is not to suggest that knowledge about international students is simply imagined into being and does not refer to something "real"—such as different language proficiency, cultural traits, religious customs, and educational dispositions. Rather, we suggest that when one discourse such as cultural difference takes on a particularly powerful explanatory significance, other discourses of the learner may be marginalized.

We suggest that much of the literature on international students does not account for the ways in which Asian student identities may be constructed in relation to Asian modernities, labor markets, and Asian diaspora spaces (Brah, 1996). The few studies that have attempted to analyze the interview discourses of Asian students in Australian settings (Kenway and Bullen, 2003; Kettle, 2005; Rizvi, 2000) present a counter-discourse to the institutional abstraction of the "Asian learner" as passive, tradition-bound, and a rule follower. For example, Fazal Rizvi (2000) argued that Asian international students talk of a "global imagination in which the notions of mobility, transculturalism, and diaspora are especially significant" (p. 222). Jane Kenway and Elizabeth Bullen (2003) described the tactics of pragmatism, resistance, ambivalence, reinvention, affirmation, and solidarity reported by their sample of international women postgraduate students. In Margaret Kettle's (2005) study an international student expresses a strong sense of personal agency as he negotiates a trajectory from "nobody" to "somebody" during his educational journey. These studies construct very different narratives of who the Asian or international learner might be, and how they might be known.

Where does this leave institutionalized pedagogy that builds its common-sense categories solely from concepts of "culture," "cultural difference," and fixed cultural identities? In short, social change may well have outstripped the capacity of such established conceptual tools. Thus, although the concept of culture is alive, well, and thinkable in the dominant discourse of internationalized higher education, its relevance could be dead or fast fading in understanding how individuals plot their careers within global flows of finance, ideology, migration, and opportunity. Following Zygmunt Bauman (2000, p.8), culture could now be interpreted as a zombie concept—"simultaneously dead and alive." Arjun Appadurai (1996) suggests that "culture," the concept, remains alive as a discursive ploy: "a pervasive dimension of human discourse that exploits difference to generate diverse conceptions of group identity" but warns that it should no longer be unproblematically used to refer to "a property of individuals and groups" (p. 13). To invoke nostalgic, determinist versions of culture and cultural difference in order to understand the mobile student at the expense of any alternative frame is to make a fetish of such difference and to elide the proactive agency and global imagination of these students, and their biographical solutions to living in more uncertain, liquid times.

In this paper, we purposefully shift the focus more to the students' mobility and explore how the strategy and motives behind their transnational mobility might be a more productive way of understanding this group and their flow through higher education institutions. We are thus interested in investigating international student identities as a "process of becoming" (Hall, 1996) by means of investing in diverse cultural and linguistic capitals. We are also interested in how such identity projects fit with and negotiate the discursive frames of the Australian teachers they encounter and the identity politics produced in such negotiations. In the next section, we build a theoretical framework better suited to explore such life politics in current globalizing times.

Liquid Modernity and Biographical Solutions

It is now commonplace for social researchers to suggest that the old logic of stable identities is no longer tenable (Appadurai, 2000; Bauman, 2000; Castells, 1996; Giddens, 1990, 1999). In contrast to the relative stability of the old "solid" containers (Bauman, 2000) of nation, class, and ethnicity and the inherited "givens" of life from these allocated positions, these theorists argue that the new affordances of instantaneous communication, global travel, electronic finance, and mobile capital have produced a new, more flexible or fluid social condition. Bauman (2000) terms this condition "liquid modernity," extending the "liquid" metaphor to characterize the melting of previously solid bonds of collective identity into the less determined, more vicarious forms of "individually conducted life policies" (p. 6). As Anthony Giddens (1999, p. 65) puts it, "[Self]-identity has to be created and recreated on a more active basis than before." Ulrich Beck (1992) similarly highlights the increasing "individualization" of "life situations and biographical patterns" (p. 128), as the individual engages with institutional offerings, such as employment and educational opportunities, to assemble a life through strategic decisions and risk taking:

> Decisions on education, profession, job, place of residence, spouse, number of children and so forth, with all the secondary decisions implied, no longer can *be*, they must be made …. This means that through institutional and biographical prescriptions, *construction kits of biographical combination possibilities* [original emphasis] come into being (p. 135).

Beck (1992) suggests that there are contradictions across "institutional biographical patterns" and that "how one lives becomes the *biographical solution of systemic contradictions*" (p.137, original emphasis). In this frame, the international student's route through "global" or "internationalized" educational institutions can be understood as a biographical solution to the systemic contradictions emerging between a globalizing economy, the dominance of English as a global language, the transnational networks forged via Asian diasporas, and local educational opportunities.

In a parallel problematization of established sociological precepts, John Urry (2003, p. 1) calls for a sociology beyond societies "that examines the diverse mobilities of peoples, objects, images, information, and wastes; and of the complex interdependencies between, and social consequences of, these diverse mobilities." He argues that the foundational concept of a geographically located "society" is unraveling and is now better conceptualized as a nexus, a point of intersection in the networks of flows and routes of people, images, and objects. His 13-point manifesto for the new method of such a sociology includes two points pertinent to our purpose here:

- To develop ... a sociology which focuses upon movement, mobility and contingent ordering, rather than upon stasis, structure and social order ....
- To examine how class, gender, ethnicity, and nationhood are constituted through powerful and intersecting temporal regimes and modes of dwelling and traveling (Urry, 2000, p. 18).

Such a theoretical gaze allows a more nuanced analysis of the "stratified and tangled networks" (Urry, 2000, p. 19) of global routes and flows that these young people inhabit. His idea of "contingent ordering" captures how any established patterns in the routes and channels that these mobile students follow are susceptible to change in economic orders, global politics, and the like. Very little remains locked in under these liquid conditions.

Transnational or Diasporic Identities

The concept of transnational identities forged in the opportunities of "flexible accumulation" in global markets and the mobility of globalized times (Nonini, 1997; Nonini and Ong, 1997; Ong, 1997; Ong and Nonini, 1997) offers an alternative vocabulary to fixed cultural identities reliant on national boundaries or ethnic histories. Transnational identities have outgrown national boundaries but can skillfully negotiate the respective "zones of graduated sovereignty" (Ong, 1997). In their body of work, Aihwa Ong and Donald Nonini build on James Clifford's (1997) notion of cultural routes and culture in travel to account for the Chinese diaspora's strategic engagement both within and beyond various capitalist, family, and national regimes to pursue "transnational imaginaries" (Ong, 1997, p. 172). Identity in these conditions is not a static, inherited quality, but "formed out of the strategies for the accumulation of economic, social, cultural, and educational capital as diasporic Chinese travel, settle down, invest in local spaces, and evade state disciplining in multiple sites" (Ong and Nonini, 1997, p. 326).

Similarly, Avtar Brah (1996) defines diasporic identities as being simultaneously local and global. Diasporic identities are "networks of transnational identifications encompassing imagined and encountered communities" (p. 196). Brah continues,

...diasporas emerge out of migrations of collectivities, whether or not members of the collectivity travel as individuals, as households, or in various other combinations. Diasporas are places of long-term, if not permanent, community formations, even if some households or members move on elsewhere. The word *diaspora* often invokes the imagery of traumas of separation and dislocation .... But diasporas are also potentially the sites of hope and new beginnings. They are contested cultural and political terrains where individual and collective memories collide, reassemble, and reconfigure (p. 193).

Thus, both diasporic identities and transnational identities carry connotations of being "contingent orders" (Urry, 2000), ways of being and dwelling sutured from what is possible in the circumstances and what one aspires to.

Education in Middle-Class Strategy

Middle-class strategy is receiving more attention in the sociology of education in order to understand how educational opportunities become stratified through the proactive work of the middle classes' interests and their tactics to protect their relative advantage through strategies of closure or exclusion. Stephen Ball's (2003) work in the U.K. highlights how educational markets have become crucial sites for class struggles in more liquid times. The young person's progress is now being carefully and "prudentially" engineered through strategies of choice and the investment of capital by "anxious" middle-class parents intent on reproducing their class advantages in the face of risky global markets that make such status less secure. Here, we extend these understandings of class strategies to derive "profits of distinction" (Bourdieu, 1986, p. 245) in global educational markets and transnational investments made by fractions of the Asian middle class to understand the mobility of international students. In the next section, we draw on work exploring the role contingent identities, educational choice, and geographic mobility play in the middle-class strategies of Asian communities.

Asian Middle-Class Strategies: Strategic Essentialism and Western Consumption

In cognate work, Michael Pinches (1999) reviews the cultural politics surrounding members of the newly emergent Asian capitalist class, "as they are variously constructed by themselves and by others, through ethnic stereotyping, lifestyle and consumption patterns, interpersonal conduct, moral judgments, and nationalist or class ideologies" (p. xi). Against a backdrop of rapid economic and cultural change, Pinches (1999) explores the rhetorical tension between different accounts of the middle classes' economic success—on one hand attributed to "traditional Oriental values," whereas, on the other, equally attributed to the rampant spread of Western consumerism. He argues that this irreconcilable binary overlooks their relational nexus,

> Each of these representations of the new rich in Asia needs to be understood in reference to both the global and the local, and, most significantly, the interplay between them .... Indeed, it is this interplay,

mediated through the unprecedented movement across state borders of people, capital, consumer goods, fashion and lifestyle images, and contending politico-religious ideologies, that underpins the heightening of both cosmopolitanism, and ethnic or nationalist differentiation in Asia (Pinches, 1999, p. 10).

Pinches (1999) also highlights the importance of educational credentials as status markers, and the pursuit of such as a significant strategy to achieve the less tangible cultural capital associated with social refinement. Thus, fractions of the Asian middle class attempt to reproduce their class advantages via "profits of distinction" (Bourdieu, 1986, p. 245) in global education markets.

These studies of transnationalism, diasporas, middle-class strategy, and representational politics argue for a more multifaceted concept of identity that fractures any overriding ascription of cultural identity with considerations of class positioning and family/gender regimes, and their interplay—all notable silences in the institutional abstraction of the "international student" in Australian higher education. Thus, from a variety of fronts, we arrive at the realization that identities (or cultures) are not fixed or ascribed by membership in collectivities, but are rather works-in-progress, meshing the positions and resources on offer in dialogue with the biographical solutions of the individual. This frame also allows us to account for both "horizontal" (Urry, 2000, p. 3) geographical mobilities and vertical social mobilities, and how they intermesh in educational choices as biographical solutions, that is, as active choices to invest time, money, and effort in the hope of realizing imagined futures and new identities.

The Empirical Study

To empirically investigate how these *more liquid and mobile life politics* are played out through a strategy of engaging with international educational markets, we conducted 24 semi-structured interviews with groups of two to three students studying in English for academic purposes (EAP) or academic preparation courses at an Australian university, and the nine teachers who were at the time involved in teaching these students. These interviews constituted one part of a larger study[1] into the curriculum and pedagogy designed for international students, which also involved video taping sequences of classes and another layer of teacher interviews with stimulated recall accounts of episodes in their teaching.

Academic preparation programs offer a point of reception and pathways into undergraduate and postgraduate university studies in Australia for international students who are deemed to not yet have the prerequisite English language proficiency, academic study skills, or cultural orientation. Where indicated, EAP programs pitched at a variety of levels precede the "foundation" program which articulates with mainstream undergraduate programs, or similar bridging programs for entry into postgraduate offerings. The duration of such courses varies between 12 weeks and 1 year, depending on the English language proficiency and academic entry level of the students. Progress to the next level or mainstream offerings is typically determined by in-house assessments mapped against IELTS (International English Language Testing System) score levels.

Most of the teachers in these programs are employed on a casual or contractual basis, work from prescribed curriculum programs, and have high teaching contact hours with minimal time for curriculum modification or reinvention. In addition, many of these teachers have to navigate between their professional ethic of respecting cultural difference, and the "acculturating" imperative of preparing students for the Western higher education system (Singh and Doherty, 2004). Such pedagogic work is unique in the higher education sector in that it is explicitly designed to act as a transition or contact zone between diverse language and cultural orientations.

For this paper, interviews involving 36 students attending a foundation course and 9 teachers involved in this and similar programs have been analyzed.[2] Of the 36 students, 4 were not from Asian nations (2 South America, 1 Europe, 1 from Africa). The remainder, whose comments will form the focus of this study of Asian identities, were from Taiwan (8), Hong Kong (6), Singapore (4), Indonesia (4), Japan (2), and individuals from East Timor, India, Korea, Malaysia, Philippines, Papua New Guinea, Thailand, and one whose nationality was not stated. The nine teachers were all Australian citizens with English as their first language and 7 to 28 years of experience. Six of the teachers had experience across different educational sectors; five had international teaching experience. Six of the nine had postgraduate qualifications in TESOL, and another was studying for such a qualification at the time.

In analyzing the interview scripts, we are interested in, firstly, how students construct their identities-in-the-making; secondly, how they negotiate their positioning by the subjectivities offered in their particular educational setting; and, finally, how the teachers' discursive frames appraise the students' motives. For the former, we are interested in identifying the investments each individual has made in order to accrue the linguistic and/or cultural capital on offer (for example, English-language competence and Western educational qualifications), and what it means to them and their life chances. Secondly, we are interested in how the students take up, display or disrupt the cultured identities constructed for them as "international students," understanding "culture" here as a discursive ploy (Appadurai, 1996). Finally, we contrast these accounts with the teachers' accounts and appraisals of their students' identity projects. We cannot erase the possibility that the interview setting and the framing of the questions contributed to the discursive positioning of the students or teachers, and impinged on the accounts given. Our purpose here, however, is to show how a complex politics of identity emerges around such accounts of motivations and strategy, which will shape the subject positions that the student can legitimately take up in such educational spaces.

We interpret the interview accounts as auto-ethnography. To this end, we are interested in articulating the contributions by a number of theorists such as Mary-Louise Pratt, Aihwa Ong, and Gayatri Chakravorty Spivak. For example, Pratt (1992, 1998) highlights the strategy of auto-ethnography in the contact zone. By contact zone, she is referring to spaces where disparate cultures meet and through their contact play out various strategies of power and resistance. The internationalized university could be considered a current example of such a site of intercultural interface (Kenway and Bullen, 2003; Singh and Doherty, 2004). By auto-ethnography, Pratt (1998, p.175) is refer-ring to

> ... a text in which people undertake to describe themselves in ways that engage with representations others have made of them.... Autoethno-graphic texts are representations that the so-defined others construct *in response to* or in dialogue with those (ethnographic) texts.... They involve a selective collaboration with and appropriation of idioms of the metrop-olis or the conqueror. These are merged or infiltrated to varying degrees with indigenous idioms to create self-representations intended to inter-vene in metropolitan modes of understanding (emphasis in original).

Auto-ethnographies thus construct accounts with the resources for representation at hand, that is, from the "contingent order" forged in the politics of cultural contact. This resonates with Stuart Hall's (1991, 1996) concept of rearticulation as the identity process of reassembling elements of discursive representations to negotiate new positions.

As one such strategy of auto-ethnography, the term "self-orientalization" has been coined by Aihwa Ong (1997) to highlight the opportunistic take-up of triumphal Orientalism by Chinese diaspora capitalists and Asian leaders to produce transnational solidarity. Ong argues that such self-orientalizing is a strategic discursive response to certain settings, deployed by the transnational capitalist to further their ends opportunistically, rather than a claim to some intrinsic cultural truth. Similarly, Gayatri Spivak (1990) uses the term "strate-gic use of essentialism" to signal two ways of representation—representation as delegation in the political sense and representation as portrait or depic-tion. Crucially, Spivak suggests that it is "not possible to be non-essentialist" (p. 109). Rather, she suggests that we should think about the ways in which individuals represent themselves (depict, portray), and in the process repre-sent members of particular social groups (delegation). In other words, it is important to engage in the cultural politics of representation—who is being represented, where, how, when, and to what tactical or strategic ends?

Analyzing Students' Self-Reports

The analysis of the student interviews is treated in more detail elsewhere (Doherty and Singh, forthcoming). The summary of students' self-representations is provided here to allow a contrast with the teachers' representations of the same cohort of students.

1. Investing in Western cultural capital and English-language competence: All of the students reported spending many years acquiring English-language skills in both the home country and in Australia. For many students, Australian universities were worthy of further capital outlay—time, money—in order to acquire English-language skills and Western credentials, and the profits from these investments were understood in accrue terms in their home countries' local yet globalized settings. Their choice of international study, however, was often described as a second option, given the limited and highly competitive opportunities available in their home countries. Australian universities were not only considered less expensive than U.S. and U.K. universities, but geographically closer to home, and part of the growing Asian diaspora. Other family members had often studied or were presently studying in Australian universities and the choice of an Australian university was at times made by the patriarch of the family to extend the network of transnational familial alliances. Students' goals to acquire English competence and Western credentials demonstrate not only their own but their family's transnational imaginary driving investments in Asian diasporic spaces—spaces that cross national boundaries. By their accounts, the students' common biographical solution of investment in international higher education attempts to manage the contradictions among limited local opportunities in the field of higher education, professional aspirations, recognition of English as the global lingua franca, knowledge of the way local economies are connected to global economic flows, and alliances in a global Asian diaspora often mediated by familial and patriarchal ties.

2. Fulfilling the orthodox script—the self-Orientalizing account: This second step in the analysis sought to identify how students took up and located themselves within the orthodox institutional discourse of the "culturally different Asian learner," and duly constructed an "East vs. West" binary in their self-accounts. Many of the students drew contrasts between the East and the West in regard to classroom practices and the wider social sphere, including family relations, censorship, fashion, recreation, religion, and work ethic. However, most students limited their claims to "in my country," and carefully resisted making

broader claims regarding pan-Asian attributes. Where some students expressed an inherited sense of "Western" practices being superior, other students merely saw it as a matter of having to "adapt" to, and fit in with, the local practices. These students had chosen to invest in the Australian higher education system because of limited opportunities elsewhere—they had to make good of this investment— even if this entailed strategic take-up of oriental discourses.

3. Intervening in the orthodoxy—auto-ethnographic interventions in the institutional abstraction: The third step in the analysis of student interviews identified how the students disrupted the orthodox orientalist discourse. The students' accounts displayed four tactics to disrupt the orthodox discourse of "cultural difference." Firstly, some students highlighted similarities between their home and host country rather than differences. These similarities, they argued, were based on a historical legacy of British colonialism which left behind for example, a "Western" system of education or arose from the common experience of global consumer culture. Secondly, students often dismantled the broad parameters of the East/West binary by talking about differences within the West—for example, differences between U.K. and U.S. educational discourses that were appropriated selectively by their home nations. Thirdly, students provided different explanations for the "cultural traits" attributed to the "Asian learner." For example, the attribute of passivity was not associated with static cultural traditions but rather with English-language proficiency. Finally, students engaged with the notion of cultural difference between the so-called East and West but did not ascribe any superior value to the West. Rather, they spoke of moving fluidly between their home and host nations in order to acquire the educational and other resources during their international sojourns.

Analyzing Teacher Accounts of Students' Reports

The analysis above summarizes student accounts of their routes, motives, and strategies and shows how they suture personal accounts from a variety of discursive resources and strategies available in the "contingent ordering" (Urry, 2000, p. 18) of relations. In this section, we turn to the accounts given by the nine teachers of their students' motives, routes, and strategies, and how the teachers reflect on and relate to such motivations and identity projects. To this end, our analytical questions were "How do the teachers account for the students' motivations and purposes?" and "What judgment of such motivations and purposes do their accounts carry?" In general, the teaching staff was well qualified with extensive experience across sector and teaching areas. Teaching experience within the group ranged from 7 to 28 years. Four of the nine teachers had some international experience, and this varied but largely involved some work in Papua New Guinea (a former Australian colony) and various Pacific Island countries. In addition, one teacher had experience teaching in Saudi Arabia and Bangladesh, another had experience teaching in European countries. Only two of the teachers spoke a non-European language; one teacher spoke PNG Pidgin, another spoke some Indonesian. Generally, however, most of the teachers were monolingual, speaking only English. All of the teachers were white Anglo Australian, except for one who described herself as Asian Australian. It is important to note, however, that the discursive strategies employed by this teacher did not differ markedly from the others.

Despite the orthodox institutional abstraction of the international student as a cultured identity, the teachers' accounts consistently constructed the student identity projects foremost with reference to their economic status and aspirations. This was not so much in terms of specific career paths but, rather, in terms of class position, vertical mobility, and relative advantage. This was reported sometimes dispassionately: "They're looking for success and advancement in their chosen career... " (Interview Teacher One); "They will get a degree to go back to their country and make a lot of money" (Interview Teacher Three); "... and thereby have an edge... to move upwards fairly rapidly" (Interview Teacher Five). At other times, this account carried explicit disapproval:

> I actually think I can be quite cynical about this. Many of the students with the money who come to Australia, they come to Australia to get a university degree to keep them in their upper echelons of their societies.... They want to keep being leaders and... they're quite open and honest about it (Interview Teacher Two).

In this data slice, the teacher thus expresses not only her disappointment with the students' motives but also a sense of disapproval of their failure to disguise this goal as something more palatable or tactful. Another teacher rationalizes and accommodates such candor as a cultural attribute in contrast to notional Australian sensibilities: "Hey, that's okay. That's their culture... I suppose we've got this real thing about being money, against being money-grubbers, haven't we?... Well, these guys are just really up front about that" (Interview Teacher Three). Goals of monetary gain thus may not be misplaced, but rather could benefit from more appropriate expression. Teacher Four judged those students who reported coming for the cultural experience as well as the credential as "the more mature students" in contrast to the "less mature students" who "more blatantly" were concerned with "getting into university" (Interview Teacher Four).

By these accounts, the students were considered to be overly intent on pursuing lucrative careers. Their focus on occupational aspirations, in these accounts, often rendered the required generic preparatory programs as a necessary and irksome phase, if not hindrance, between them and their goals,

> Basically it's a stepping stone to them. In a lot of cases many of them wouldn't do it if the university didn't put the requirement on them. They want it to get them into university. That's all they want (Interview Teacher 2).

This teacher continued to imagine that "It would be very nice if the students wanted the skills necessary to cope at university out of the course, but the reality is not" (Interview Teacher 2). Another teacher (Interview Teacher Three) told of successful students who only in hindsight valued the preparatory programs.

Similarly, Teacher Two mourned the lack of interest in more general classroom texts: "Doing some history reading topics ... they can be interesting in their own right but it's not where they [the students] want to be." In the same account, the teacher told of her experience in more specialized programs where "English for M.B.A. and English for health science ... worked really, really well because ... you've used all the authentic text from the courses that they're actually going to go do. ... So there is an intrinsic value." Although this insight offers a workable solution, she then pointed out the difficulty for teachers to work outside their "own safety zone." She thus communicated a sense of regret about the students' sharp, purposeful focus and identified inevitable tensions, resistances, and cross-purposes built into this preparatory limbo.

Teacher three also reported being "surprised" by the number of students who stated that their parents had made the choice of a higher education program without reference to the student's interests. "And listen, that was a generalization but it tends to be the predominant ... yeah, you know what, may be the majority." Another teacher read this family regime as a pressure on students, which in turn produces their characteristically pragmatic focus: "They're aware that a huge amount of their family resources are invested in them." The students' wealth itself was judged a problem and a growing one at that by one teacher, which, by this account, ironically made the cultural tourism agenda more possible and more detrimental to the classroom program:

> The others are here because some of them are here because they've got lots and lots of money, and they want to spend some time in Australia ... they're the ones who hardly ever come to class and hardly ever complete any work.... We seem to have quite a few more of them this semester. (Interview Teacher Six).

Such hedonism was not judged to be the kind of cultural experience these teachers imagined and wished for the students. Teacher Nine considered it "a shame" that the students did not seem to want "the Australian experience ... It saddens me greatly that they don't seem to get a sense of Australia being a good place to be in. They don't tend to love it." By her account, her response is to build such appreciation into the curriculum, "If I can anywhere I will try and bring in the Australian experience for them." She thus was determined to be the cultural ambassador even if the students did not want it.

Discussion of Teacher and Student Interview Data

These analyses draw threads of congruence across and between teacher and student accounts of the mobile students' identity projects and motives. In many ways, the teacher accounts align with the students' versions with reference to furthering career prospects in globalized labor markets. However, what distinguishes the teachers' accounts from the students' is the moral evaluations made of the students' motives. The majority of the teachers' accounts expressed degrees of disappointment, regret, helplessness, and cynicism, with veiled criticism of such "pragmatic" agendas.

So what is happening here? Teachers motivated by "intrinsic" interest in cultural exploration are being offended by the students' "extrinsic," "instrumental" motivations in using education as a resource for upward mobility. Such projects are seen to diminish the teacher's relational identity as ethnographic informant, and their professional interest in celebrating cultural diversity. Students' "pragmatism" reduces the teachers' role to mere service worker delivering more conversational opportunities and writing skills. One teacher, by her report, resorts to insinuating her desired "Australiana" content into the curriculum, as a corrective measure to the purported educational instrumentalism displayed by the students. The teachers express a sense of being robbed by students' desire for short cut pedagogy, yet most fail to account for the substantial time and capital investments these students are making. The teachers and programs are reportedly not resourced to provide the focused, occupationally driven English for Specific Purposes programs (ESP) that would "intrinsically" motivate the students. As a result, the students' reluctance to engage with the generic material for its own sake suggests that these programs will continue to be locked into an institutional contradiction, and students and teachers are thus set up to be disappointed with each other.

It is crucial to point out that the work of many of these teachers is fast becoming de-skilled and casualized; many talked of the high demands of intensive teaching work on short-term contracts across a number of institutions and employing authorities. In many cases, the teachers felt that their own socioeconomic standing was lower than that of the full-fee-paying international students whose needs they were servicing. It is difficult to judge whether such "moral judgments" would similarly be made of "Australian students" as these teachers are only employed to work with "international students." But given the increasingly market-driven approach to higher education, such moral judgments may become more evident across the sector.

Additionally, there is a sense of nostalgia expressed in the teachers' shades of regret—a nostalgia for previous days of less business-like pedagogy, for mythic philosophies of "learning for its own sake." Roland Robertson (1992) identifies the nostalgic attitude as a predictable reaction to the more fluid life politics under conditions of globalization, "The very fluidity of global change has invited ... nostalgia for secure forms of 'world order,' as well as a kind of projective nostalgia for the world as a home" (p.162). We would suggest that the moral judgments carried in the teachers' accounts are also the expression of a form of nostalgia for more stable cultural spaces and identities.

Conclusion

This chapter explored the identity politics of a specific category of youth, namely Asian international students enrolled in Australian higher education institutions. We argued the relevance of a politics of identity to education given that programs and pedagogies are designed around, between, and in spite of, such understandings. Specifically, we compared and contrasted the students' own accounts of their identity project work—their youth moves—with those of the Australian teachers who work in the contact zones of intensive English-language instruction programs in the higher education sector. The analysis drew out some of the tensions and interplay between classed and cultured identity work of these students and explicated teachers' judgments of the students' biographical solutions to uncertain times.

We framed this study of identity and representation politics in the broader social changes underway, and what this means for how educational journeys are strategically navigated and negotiated across and beyond national boundaries. We focused particularly on discursive strategies for inhabiting both classed and cultured identities and for negotiating the "contingent orders" encountered in life routes. Identity construction within essentialized categories is still pursued, but different settings will precipitate different responses and constructions of self.

We argued that discourses of cultural difference (with traces of orientalism) may be produced by Australian TESOL teachers to legitimate their knowledge position in the international higher education sector. Such discourses may also be strategically deployed by Asian international students as cultural markers of a distinctive modernity, that is, Asian vs. Western modernity. At the same time, however, students may disrupt and contest these discourses through the strategic deployment of auto-ethnographic narratives.

Notes

1 This study was funded by the Australian Research Council.
2 Student interview schedule: (1) Why did you choose to study English in Australia? (2) How long have you been learning English? What do you think that you are best at in English and what do you find most difficult? (3) Is the teaching here the same as the teaching in your home country? How is it the same? How is it different? (4) Is the English you're using here different from the English you were using at home? (5) Can you tell me about something in the course that you really liked? Was there something you didn't like?

How could it be made better? (6) Do you think we can talk about such a thing as "Asian values" and "Western values"? Can you tell me about this? (7) What did you want to get from this program? Do you think that you got it?

References

Appadurai, A. 1996. *Modernity at Large: Cultural Dimensions of Globalization.* Minneapolis, MN: University of Minnesota Press.

Appadurai, A. 2000. Grassroots globalization and the research imagination. *Public Culture; Society for Transnational Cultural Studies* 12(1), 1–19.

Apple, M. 2004. *Ideology and Curriculum.* New York: RoutledgeFalmer.

Ball, S.J. 2003. *Class Strategies and the Education Market: The Middle Classes and Social Advantage.* London: RoutledgeFalmer.

Bauman, Z. 2000. *Liquid Modernity.* Cambridge, U.K.: Polity Press.

Beck, U. 1992. *Risk Society: Towards a New Modernity.* London: Sage Publications.

Bernstein, B. 1990. *The Structuring of Pedagogic Discourse.* London: Routledge.

Bernstein, B. 2000. *Pedagogy, Symbolic Control and Identity* (rev. ed.). New York: Rowman and Littlefield Publishers.

Bourdieu, P. 1986. The forms of capital. In *Handbook of Theory and Research for the Sociology of Education,* ed. J. Richardson, 241–258. New York: Greenwood Press.

Brah, A. 1996. *Cartographies of Diaspora: Contesting Identities.* London: Routledge.

Castells, M. 1996. *The Rise of the Network Society,* Vol. 1. Oxford, U.K.: Blackwell.

Clifford, J. 1997 *Routes: Travel and Translation in the Late Twentieth Century.* Cambridge, MA: Harvard University Press.

Department of Education Science and Training. 2003. Students 2002: Selected Higher Education Statistics. Canberra, Australia: Commonwealth of Australia.

Department of Education Science and Training. 2005. Students 2004 (Full Year): Selected Higher Education Statistics. Canberra, Australia: Commonwealth of Australia. Retrieved October 18, 2005, from http://www.dest.gov.au/sectors/ higher_education/publications_resources/profiles/students_2004_selected_ higher_education_statistics.htm.

Doherty, C., and P. Singh. Forthcoming. Mobile students, flexible identities and liquid modernity: Disrupting Western teachers' assumptions of "the Asian learner." In *Learning and Teaching across Cultures in Higher Education,* ed. D. Palfreyman and D. McBride, Palgrave Macmillan.

Giddens, A. 1990. *The Consequences of Modernity.* Cambridge, U.K.: Polity Press.

Giddens, A. 1999. *Runaway World: How Globalization Is Reshaping Our Lives.* New York: Routledge.

Hall, S. 1991. The local and the global: Globalization and ethnicity. In *Culture, Globalization and the World System,* ed. A. King, 19–39. London: Macmillan Press.

Hall, S. 1996. Introduction: Who needs "identity"? In *Questions of Cultural Identity,* ed. S. Hall and P. Du Gay, 1–17. London: Sage.

Kenway, J., and E. Bullen 2003. Self-representations of international women postgraduate students in the global university 'contact zone.' *Gender and Education,* 15(1), 5–20.

Kettle, M. 2005. Agency as discursive practice: From "nobody" to "somebody" as an international student in Australia. *Asia-Pacific Journal of Education,* 25(1), 47–62.

Nesdale, D., K. Simkin, D. Sang, B. Burke, and S. Frager. 1995. *International Students and Immigration.* Canberra, Australia: AGPS.

Nonini, D. 1997. Shifting identities, positioned imaginaries: Transnational traversals and reversals by Malaysian Chinese. In *Ungrounded Empires: The Cultural Politics of Modern Chinese Transnationalism,* ed. A. Ong and D. Nonini, 203–227. New York: Routledge.

Nonini, D., and A. Ong. 1997. Chinese transnationalism as an alternative modernity. In *Ungrounded Empires: The Cultural Politics of Modern Chinese Transnationalism,* ed. A. Ong and D. Nonini, 3–33. New York: Routledge.

Ong, A. 1997. Chinese modernities: narratives of nation and of capitalism. In *Ungrounded Empires: The Cultural Politics of Modern Chinese Transnationalism,* ed. A. Ong and D. Nonini, 171–201. New York: Routledge.

Ong, A., and D. Nonini. 1997. Toward a cultural politics of diaspora and transnationalism. In *Ungrounded Empires: The Cultural Politics of Modern Chinese Transnationalism,* A. Ong and D. Nonini, 323–332. New York: Routledge.

Pinches, M. 1999. Cultural relations, class and the new rich of Asia. In *Culture and Privilege in Capitalist Asia,* ed. M. Pinches, 1–55. London: Routledge.

Pratt. M.-L. 1992. *Imperial Eyes: Travel Writing and Transculturation.* London: Routledge.

Pratt, M.-L. 1998. Arts of the contact zone. In *Negotiating Academic Literacies,* ed. V. Zamel and R. Spack, 171–185. Mahwah, NJ: Lawrence Erlbaum.

Rizvi, F. 2000. International education and the production of global imagination. In *Globalization and Education: Critical Perspectives,* ed. N. Burbules and C. Torres, 205–225. New York: Routledge.

Robertson, R. 1992. *Globalization: Social Theory and Global Culture.* London: Sage.

Singh, P. 2002. Pedagogising knowledge: Bernstein's theory of the pedagogic device. *British Journal of Sociology of Education,* 23(4), 571–582.

Singh, P., and C. Doherty. 2004. Global cultural flows and pedagogic dilemmas: Teaching in the global university 'contact zone.' *TESOL Quarterly,* 38(1), 9–42.

Spivak, G.C. 1990. *The Post-Colonial Critic: Interviews, Strategies, Dialogues.* New York: Routledge.

Urry, J. 2000. *Sociology beyond Societies: Mobilities for the Twenty-First Century.* London, Routledge.

Urry, J. 2003. *Global Complexity.* Cambridge, U.K.: Polity Press.

III
Youth and the Global Context
Transforming Us Where We Live

8

The Children of Liberalization
Youth Agency and Globalization in India

RITTY LUKOSE

Introduction

Since the early 1990s, popular and state discourses proclaim India to be
a powerful and emerging global power. This is "India Rising" as a recent
magazine puts it (Zakaria, 2006). The liberalization of the Indian economy has significantly transformed the political, economic, and cultural
landscape of a country in which images of third-world poverty, a backward, uneducated, rural, and traditional society, and an inefficient and
corrupt bureaucratic state and economy jostle with images of a world-class
information technology industry, a robust and growing economy, and a
media-saturated, highly educated, urban, affluent, and globally oriented
consumer middle class.[1] The political assertiveness of India as a nuclear
power, its economic strength and power, and a new-found cultural assertiveness globally in the areas of film, literature, music, art, and fashion
have created a sense that India is fast approaching its moment of arrival on
the global stage, no longer struggling at the bottom of the modernization
ladder.

The promise and potential of India as a new global power significantly rests
on its youthful population. Media discussions of liberalization often point to
demographic statistics that indicate 54% of Indians are now below the age of
25, making India one of the "youngest" nations in the world ("The World's
Youngest Nation," 2004). Within the southwestern state of Kerala, where the
research for this article is based, people between the ages of 15 and 25 are said
to make up 45% of the total population of the state ("The World's Youngest
Nation," 2004, p. 52).[2] Emblematic of a popular discourse, journalistic
coverage has labeled this age category "zippies"; they have also been called
"Liberalization's Children," a play on and contrast to the so-called generation of "Midnight's Children," those born at independence in 1947, the first
generation to grow upj in independent India under the Nehruvian socialist
understanding of national development.[3] The definition of the "zippie"

combines marketing clichés that exhibit an almost giddy sense of entitlement and possibility, as this mock dictionary definition illustrates:

> ... A young city or suburban resident, between 15 and 25 years of age, with a zip in the stride. Belongs to Generation Z. Can be male or female, studying or working. Oozes attitude, ambition, and aspiration. Cool, confident, and creative. Seeks challenges, loves risks, and shuns fear. Succeeds Generation X and Generation Y, but carries the social, political, economic, cultural, or ideological baggage of neither personal and professional life marked by vim, vigor, and vitality (origin: Indian) ("The World's Youngest Nation," 2004, p. 41).

This construction of generation, emblematic of a wider discourse, links a particular image of youth to a larger sense that India is transforming in the face of liberalization. Although "Midnight's Children" might have lacked ambition, been risk-averse, felt "uncool" or been fearful, "Liberalization's Children" are urban, hip, cool, full of ambition, and confident. This construction of the social category of youth directly links the values and attitudes of this new generation to the economic liberalization of the economy and the cultural impact of globalization.

This celebratory discourse of globalization, however, is a highly contested one. Drawing on a variety of discourses of anti-imperialism, grassroots development, critiques of corporatization and environmentalism, antiglobalization movements, campaigns, and discourses have challenged the triumphalism of corporate globalization. Examples are numerous and varied: the attacks on the fast-food chain Kentucky Fried Chicken by a peasant-based movement protesting against large multinationals and their control of high-yield seeds in the South Indian state of Karnataka, the investigation of a Coca-Cola bottling plant in the state of Kerala accused of disrupting the water supply in a nearby village, the lawsuits and banning of the sale and distribution of Coke and Pepsi in some states because of allegations of high levels of pesticides in these drinks, the struggle against the introduction of genetically modified seeds by large multinationals, the fight against the "theft" by multinationals of the intellectual property rights of indigenous knowledge systems—the list could go on. Not always falling neatly into distinctions between the left and the right of the political spectrum, antiglobalization protests and mobilizations draw on anticolonial rhetoric and economic and cultural nationalist positions in different and overlapping ways (Menon, 2005).

One group of protests stands out for its focus on the links between corporate globalization, the rise of a global consumer culture, and its impact on youth. One of the most fractious and intense protests surrounded the staging of the Miss World pageant in Bangalore in 1996.[4] Although I focus here on the pageant in order to explore the contours of antiglobalization discourse in India, this pageant is indicative of several such protests and mobilizations that target youth. Other forms of youth cultural practice, such as the increasingly popular celebration of St. Valentine's Day, are often met with protests from mainly Hindu rights activists. More recently, the state government of Kerala has sought to ban fashion shows, cell phones, and text messaging at college events, all seen to be part of an invasive global consumer culture ("Kerala Bans...," 2005).

The mobilization over a 2-month period of 12,500 police and paramilitary personnel from city, state, and central security forces to ensure the pageant would take place was the largest use of state power to help what was essentially a multinational, private, commercial venture fend off widespread protests from a diverse array of political organizations. The protests came essentially from two sides. Women's groups on the Hindu right opposed the pageant on the grounds that it would import a decadent Western culture which undermines "Indian culture." The left-affiliated and independent women's groups distinguished themselves from the more conservative critics whom they felt focused on a unitary and conservative notion of "Indian tradition," "a euphemism for the subordination of women." Rather, they focused on the liberalization of the economy and the growing influence of multinational corporations which, they argued, had created a climate in which events like beauty contests thrive, events that demean and commodify young women.

The pageant reveals the ways in which consumption is a discursive site for contesting and imagining the Indian nation, in which the bodies of young, middle-class females are crucial for a consumer-driven middle class oriented towards the global economy. The contested cultural politics of globalization involves the demonization of consumption, a consumption crucially linked to the commodification of young women's bodies. The Hindu right and left feminist perspectives are obviously different in important respects. The conservative position rests on a deployment of "tradition" that masks gender oppression and patriarchy within as well as outside "India." Similar to the cultural nationalists of the later nineteenth century that Partha Chatterjee has discussed, these nationalists of the Hindu right place women under the sign of a privatized tradition that must be defended against the corruption of Western materialism (Chatterjee, 1990). The left-feminist perspective rejects "Indian culture" as patriarchal. Yet, it also rejects simplistic identifications of "modernity" with the space of women's freedom. This "modernity," rooted in the structures of patriarchy and capitalism, collaborates with the patriarchy of continuously reinvented "tradition" to produce new forms of gender oppression. Both positions, however, are operating in tandem in their rejections of the commodification of women. For the Hindu right, this commodification is associated with an invasive, alien, foreign culture. For the feminists, it is associated with an imperialist form of capitalist oppression. This is an oppression that targets the "modern miss," as one prominent women's activist argued, while having little to say to those who cannot consume beauty products—those who are too poor and too busy struggling to survive.

At one level, the contestations over beauty pageants, celebrations of St. Valentine's Day, and fashion shows point to articulations of agency and resistance among young people in the context of increasing globalization. Specifically, it gestures towards the resistance of young women who, in the face of community and family pressure, nevertheless choose to wear "provocative dress," participate in beauty pageants, and engage in romance in public, articulating a kind of consumer agency that challenges norms of gender and sexuality. In some sense, globalization appears as an enabling space for the articulation of young women's agency.

However, as the politics of globalization reveals, both as an object of political discourse and as a set of political, economic, and cultural restructurings, globalization is a much more complex terrain of politics and possibility. Throughout the 1990s, students I worked with engaged in strikes, challenging the government's attempts to privatize higher education, part of a larger mobilization on the part of young people to challenge the government's new economic liberalization policies intended to privatize the Indian economy and open it to foreign markets (Lukose, 2005). At the same time, "globalization," although seen as a large, unilateral economic program by the students, took on highly fractious and local meanings in their lives. Globalization was, simultaneously, an objective set of government policies to be challenged and the wider context in which politics mixed with other youthful practices: fashion, movie-going, and music-listening. Challenging these government policies did not prevent these students from articulating the need and the necessity to leave Kerala—perhaps for the U.S., Canada, or the Persian Gulf—in search of jobs, given the nearly 30% unemployment rate of educated workers in the region. The structured scripts of these students' lives— barely functioning schools, no job prospects at home—reveal the workings of a hierarchical and unequal national and international division of labor and opportunity that these students astutely and painfully apprehend. Yet, this over-determined script does not prevent them from challenging the retrenchment of the state in educational matters or protesting what they see to be the intensification of unequal geopolitical relations through globalization. At the same time, it is precisely these new geopolitical realities that allow these students to claim "modernity" as youthful, modern consumers, a claim that is key to their self-fashioning within the age, gender, class, and caste hierarchies of the region.

"Globalization," then, is a complex terrain of discourse and politics, as well as a shifting terrain of spaces and structures of opportunity and hierarchy. Given that youth cultural practices have become a key site for a contested politics of globalization in India, how are we to understand the "agency" of youth in the context of globalization? Within a broader discourse, those who celebrate and denounce the impact of globalization use youth practices, in particular youth consumer practices, as an index of the power, reach, and impact of globalization.

Either young people are painted as vanguards of a new, global dispensation or victims of a global consumer culture. Within the polarities of this discourse, how can the cultural studies of youth shed light on youth, agency, and globalization in a way that pays attention to the intersection between the broader cultural politics of globalization and its everyday lived realities?

Tracking Agency and Resistance in Youth Cultural Studies

Arguably, the central organizing framework for youth cultural studies is the identification and tracking of agency and resistance among young people. As with cultural studies more generally and other related intellectual formations, identifying agency and resistance have gone hand-in-hand with the very identification of the subject itself—whether it be a youth, woman, queer, black, or the subaltern. Given the progressive political commitments of these varieties of cultural studies across and within disciplines, the identification of the subject of critical analysis is folded into the project of identifying and articulating the forms of agency and resistance that this subject articulates.

The problematization of the category of agency/resistance has come from several quarters. One strand, from a feminist viewpoint, challenges the ways in which conceptions of agency exclude women and questions of gender. So, within youth cultural studies, the early feminist critique of youth resistance and agency pointed to the ways in which this literature relied on an unproblematized understanding of public performance and style that seemed to exclude girls from its purview and that could not grasp the more private agentive worlds of girls' social and cultural lives (McRobbie, 1991; Nava, 1992; Bhavnani et al., 1998). On the other hand, both within and outside feminist studies, there has been a concern with what Lila Abu-Lughod calls the "romance of resistance" (1990, p. 41). In an important article, Abu-Lughod traces the ways in which a single-minded search for resistance obscures the ways in which such seemingly resistant practices are actually evidence of becoming more enmeshed in overlapping and more complex networks of power. She urges that we use expressions of resistance as a "diagnostic of power," providing a window into the complex webs of power and culture that structure people's lives rather than as an index of their resistance to simple understandings of structure (1990, p. 42).

A concern with the limits of agency has also been reflected upon by Lawrence Grossberg as he considers the internationalization of cultural studies (1993). He urges that we disabuse ourselves of the idea that agency is some "ontological principle" that all humans share, across all contexts (1993, p. 15). He urges that we de-link subjectivity and agency and understand agency to be articulated in highly specific historical, cultural, and social contexts. Although he holds on to the idea that agency is about "empowerment" and the "making of history," he urges a much more contextual understanding of the production of agentive fields and possibilities, something he feels is necessary as cultural studies itself globalizes.

In the context of trying to understand the cultural politics of youth and globalization in Kerala, the above problematization of agency is helpful but, as I will demonstrate, obscures some questions that are necessary for a critical apprehension of agency, youth, and globalization in postcolonial contexts. For both Abu-Lughod and Grossberg, although they call for a more contextually sophisticated understanding of agency and resistance, what constitutes agency and resistance is left relatively unexamined. For example, Abu-Lughod refers to the desire and practice of young Bedouin women wearing sexy lingerie as an example of resistant behavior against gender and age norms, which could and should be contextualized within a critique of capitalist modernity. But what are the structures and categories through which the desire for and wearing of sexy lingerie become resistant? In other words, what are the conditions of possibility that produce certain practices and young women as resistant? In a sense, an interrogation of youth, globalization, and agency requires not only an attention to the complex fields of power and culture that surround acts of resistance but an attention to the conditions of possibility that produce these acts as resistant in the first place.

One way to more fully contextualize the resistant practices of young women in the face of globalization, this chapter 5 will suggest, is to draw a distinction between agency and resistance. Grossberg helpfully suggests that we de-link subjectivity and agency, recognizing that the identification of the subjectivity of the protagonists of our critical analysis does not necessarily and inherently point to their agency in the face of structure and power. However, an important dimension of globalization that this article will focus on, both as discourse and structure, is the circulation of consumer agency. As will be argued further on, globalization conflates subjectivity with consumer agency. In this context, it becomes necessary to critically apprehend subjectivity as agency in such a way that agency is not simply conflated with resistance. For example, to return to the Abu-Lughod example, the desire for and the wearing of sexy lingerie on the part of younger women as a form of resistant behavior is part of the encroachment of capitalist modernity, not simply because these are new commodities that come from elsewhere, but because they are rooted in ideas about consumer agency that construct these consumer practices as resistant. Critically understanding the structuring of subjectivity as a form of consumer agency is crucial to contextualizing "resistant" youth cultural practices in the context of globalization.

Consumption and Globalization in the Postcolony

Within cultural studies, and youth cultural studies in particular, the link between consuming practices and agency is usually made through a focus on processes of identity formation. Consumption, fashion, and style afford new ways of understanding identity formation and agency, one that often uses "fashion" less as a specific type of practice and more as a metaphor for the workings of culture, gender, and power. Performative theories of identity, particularly the work of Judith Butler (1990), have usefully reconceived gender less as a set of fixed roles and identities and more as highly stylized performances that are continuously produced and reproduced. In this way, gendered subjectivities and different ways of being masculine and feminine emerge not as expressions of essential gender roles and identities but as fluid, power-laden performative practices that have possibilities for subversion, play, and expressions of agency and resistance.

The analysis to follow draws much from this reconceptualization of identity as enacted, embodied, and performed. However, one dimension of the literature on fashion, style, and consumption bears some scrutiny. In its desire to argue for the importance of consumption as a site for a newly reconceived understanding of identity, cultural studies renders consumption as an already existing, readily available set of social practices that need to be examined and deciphered. Secondarily, questions are posed about the presence or absence of agency, the mediation of identities, and the relationship of this already existing domain to other domains (e.g., production). Much of the focus of performative theories of identity is on the micro-level practices that constitute the processes of identity formation within the context of self-fashioning. As others have noted, the larger sociohistorical and political-economic contexts of such processes are not always elaborated in such analyses (Ferguson 1999; Weston, 1993). Drawing on such critiques, the problem might productively be rendered slightly differently. The issue is not simply an inattention to the larger social contexts and political economy of identity processes, but a naturalization of the very context of identity production itself, namely the space of consumption. Paying attention to the historical and cultural-ideological contexts of discourses of consumption as they intersect with consuming subjects and objects enables both an attention to the larger contexts of identity formation as well as a denaturalization of the context of identity production itself in such a way as to make visible constructions of consumer agency.

While there is no doubt that consumption as a structured field of practice "exists," it is also itself an object—something to be produced through discourse, practice, and imagination. In other words, consumption itself becomes a fetishized object, a terrain of social and cultural practice that cannot be simply assumed. This fetishistic quality of consumption rests crucially on highly mediated constructions of the subject of consumer agency. This subject then becomes a condensed, congealed, and highly objectified (fetishized) signifier of consumption itself. As Arjun Appadurai states, under new regimes of globalization, "… the consumer has been transformed through commodity flow into a sign" (1996, p. 42). This transformation, crucially affected by global advertising, produces "creative and culturally well-chosen ideas of consumer agency" (1996, p. 42). This production of images and ideas about consumer agency constitutes consumption as a highly contested terrain that must itself be produced, rather than simply assumed as one half of a capitalist system. Importantly, this circulation of signifiers of consumption affects the ways in which subjects of consumption negotiate the how, why, when, and what of consumption as practice. In this way, rather than oscillate between the fact of the commodification of young women's bodies by global consumer culture on the one hand or the agency of young women within consumer culture on the other, this chapter draws our attention to the ways that new globallinflected consumer spaces are structured by discourses of consumer agency that make these spaces both enabling and constraining for young women. This focus on constructions of consumer agency enables an attention to the tension between being both subject and object of consumption—a commodity and a consumer.

Further, as Beng-Huat Chua states, for East Asia much theorization and research on consumption that focuses on identity politics comes out of an argument about the importance of consumption vis-à-vis high/low debates about culture within the Euro-American context (2000, p. 19). The field of consumer practices is often taken for granted. Although the identity politics of consumer practices is certainly crucial, especially for the politics of youth and generation, the ideological context within which that politics is played out is quite different. The location of consumption as a structured field of practice and the meanings ascribed to that field have different histories in distinct places (Appadurai, 1996; Breckenridge, 1995; Burke, 1996; Comaroff and Comaroff, 1991; Deshpande, 1993; Hendrickson, 1996; Pinney and Dwyer, 2001; Tarlo, 1996). The specific genealogies and dynamics of this space of consumption must be attended to if we are to pay attention to the ways in which globalization engenders new forms of consumption that must intersect with postcolonial structures of meaning and power.

Within the debates analyzed below, discourses of consumption insert themselves into the cultural-ideological terrain of poscolonial states and societies that are struggling with the legacy of colonialism and anticolonial nationalism as they intersect with a new global order. This terrain is marked by debates about Westernization, tradition, and modernity that emerge out of colonial modernity and are newly reconfigured under the latest conditions of globalization. The cultural history and anthropology of South Asia also demonstrates that the terrain of preoccupation with Westernization, tradition, and modernity is a profoundly gendered one, in which the place of women along the public/private and tradition/modernity binaries becomes key to understanding the dynamics of this cultural–ideological terrain (Arunima, 2003; Chatterjee, 1990; Mankekar, 1999; Sarkar, 2001; Vaid and Sangari, 1989). Consumption, as "social practice" or "everyday life" operates in and through these political fields.

Understanding youth, agency, and globalization, then, requires a critical understanding of how the cultural politics of modernity in postcolonial locations shape the ways in which consumption is understood—a tradition of debate and contestation that profoundly influences the manner in which young people engage globalization. The ways in which articulations and expressions of agency are tied to the contested cultural production of postcolonial modernities is an important lens through which to critically apprehend youthful agency in globalizing times.

Fashioning Youth

Let me illustrate what such an analysis entails by examining the construction of consumer agency in the context of globalized modernity among young women in Kerala.

As the following demonstrates, expressions and practices of consumer agency are underwritten by spatiotemporal constructions of binaries between public and private, tradition and modernity. As Partha Chatterjee and others have delineated, a modern nationalist patriarchy developed in India under colonialism in which that which was public was ceded to the West (modern) and that which was private (the home, women, etc.) congealed around the idea of tradition (Banerjee, 1995; Chatterjee, 1990; Hancock, 1999). "Youth" as a category of modernity is also, in some crucial sense, "public."

Dominant representations, in everyday discourse, films, and magazines, drape women's bodies with the tropes of the traditional and the modes of the modern in ways that make the traversal of that public fraught with contradiction for young women. Always at stake is what I call the "burden of locality"—carrying the weight of a tradition into a public that could jeopardize it (cf. Appadurai, 1996). In Kerala, this has often manifested in the cultural politics of women's clothing styles, a long skirt (*pawada*) and blouse combination indexing a local "traditional" culture (*nadu*), and shorter skirts and jeans signaling modernity and "the West." However, despite the stubborn ideological salience of the public/private, tradition/modernity dichotomy, young women do occupy the public. Increasingly, in the public spaces of contemporary Kerala—streets, shops, schools, offices, etc.—young women, whether they be students, professionals, clerical workers, or "shop girls," neither wear the pawada/blouse combination, nor do they commonly wear skirts or jeans. The dress of choice is the so-called *churidar* or Punjabi "suit" (what might otherwise, in another looser-pant version, be called the *salwar kameez*). The wearing of the churidar among young unmarried women has increased dramatically in the last ten years. The notions of femininity associated with the churidar interrupt the more simple binarism of the "traditional" and "modern" women's fashions. For young women today, wearing the churidar, as opposed to the pawada, is adorning themselves in the clothing of an "Indian" public—one that takes them out of a pawada-clad tradition and yet protects them from the rampant sexualization of a "Western"-identified, skirt-clad modernity. The contemporary wearing of the churidar, I would argue, is an

embodiment of notions of modesty in the fashioning of a modern femininity—one that enables and yet circumscribes women's participation in the
public. I link the churidar to what I call a "demure modern," a gloss on the
Malayalam term *oudhuke* which most literally means "contained" or "closed."
I gloss the term here as "demure." The term is used in any number of ways
with respect to women: to walk in an "oudhuke way," self-contained, not looking about, moving quickly, or as an "*oudhuke pennu*" or "demure girl," one
who walks and talks properly, in a self-contained, quiet way.

Any discussion of these terms (*naden/oudhuke*/modern) must also reveal
the space–time dynamics that instructively demonstrate the stark inscription
of the contestations of modernity on the female body. *Naden*—the pervasive
term for "traditional"—comes from the word *nadu* which in Malayalam usually refers to "native place" or "home." A profoundly locational concept, it can
only be used or applied to someone who is understood to be where they do not
belong. To ask somebody where their nadu is implies being from someplace
else. In the spatial configurations of Kerala's geography, it can also refer to
the "interior" or the "countryside" (*naden purethu*). Insofar as the term refers
both to "place of origin" and the "traditional" (naden *rithi*—the traditional
way), the adjective *naden,* therefore, can only make sense along a space–time
grid that maps "native places" onto "traditional" time. And in the logic of
nostalgic memory, nadu points to another place and another time. *Modern* is
a very similar term. Conventionally understood as the marker of a temporal
break, the mutual imbrications of the projects of modernity and colonialism have produced a space–time dynamic where the relations between the
West and the non-West are mapped onto a distinction between the past and
a present–future. So, "modern" simultaneously refers to that present–future
and the "West." Thus, an anxiously modern male subject expels a pawada-
clad female body from a place in the present to which it cannot with certainty
belong into a "traditional" past constituted by, and also constitutive of, its
location in Kerala's nadu; simultaneously, a female body that is marked as
incorrigibly "modern" is propelled into a dangerous "West" somewhere "out
there."

The term oudhuke does not have the same space–time dimensions. It refers
most directly to a different space–time grid—that of bodily *habitus* and comportment. It refers to the "closed," "contained" body of one who walks with
her head down, arms close to the body, eyes averted. It refers to no place "out
there" but rather contains the female subject within the body itself. In some
sense, the resolution of the tension between an indigenous tradition and a
predatory modernity is literally the demure comportment of the female body.
The production of locality, in this instance, hinges on the female body.

This point might be better made if we compare the terrain of femininity to
the terrain of masculinity. I will not enter into a full discussion of the latter
here, but I will briefly address questions of masculinity in order to illustrate

my larger point about femininity. In Malayalam, one would rarely refer to a young man as either naden or modern. And one would never refer to a respectably clad bourgeois-type male as oudhuke. Therefore, the absence of a readily available concept for marking a respectably "modern" male, points, I think, to the specifically gendered nature of the term *oudhuke,* which I am trying to explore, and to its constitutive construction of the female body.

The "Modern" Girl in Global Space–Time

What implications does all of this have for thinking through the agency of youth in the context of globalization? As I stated earlier, a primary articulation of youthful agency in this context coheres around the consumer agency of young women in the face of family and community opposition. The practices and experiences that constitute this consumer agency are structured in and through the relationship between the performance of body and self in highly public consumer spaces.

The analysis of a local beauty pageant reveals the ways in which the gendered terrain I have layed out (naden/demure/traditional) underwrites spaces understood as indicative of global consumer culture. The contest was but one of several Miss Kerala pageants held in various parts of the world. Held under the aegis of the World Malayalee Federation, along with Miss Keralas from such far-flung places as Abu Dhabi, London, Chicago, and Houston, the Thiruvananthapuram Miss Kerala would travel to New York for the final level of competition, thereby mapping Kerala's own diaspora. The contest was held in a large hall in a palace of the former Maharajah of Travancore, a Nayar royal family. Consistent with its location, the beauty contest went on to define a hegemonic Kerala femininity in line with its upper-caste Nayar trappings. The contest had some very precise specifications. There were to be three rounds, each with a different style of dress. In the first round, the contestants wore the pawada/blouse combination. In the second round, they wore the sari, most wearing a Kerala sari distinguished by white cotton cloth and gold-thread borders. For the third round, the young women wore the *mundum/neerthu,* a two-piece garment resembling a sari. It is the traditional attire of mature, upper-caste Nayar women.

In each round, they were asked questions by a local television celebrity. The questions were quite specific, focusing on Kerala dance, drama, poetry, history, and literature. In round three, the round in which they wore the mundum/neerthu, they came out one by one, carrying a large *villaku* (lamp), in the Kerala style, which they carefully carried to the front of the stage and lit. (As one contestant put it, "It was really heavy.") This mirrors the lighting of the lamp by brides during Nayar marriage ceremonies. This nostalgic production of a specifically Nayar femininity is in line with a broader movement of cultural remembering defined in upper-caste, Nayar terms. Globalization affords the circulation of what Arjun Appadurai has called "the production of locality." Within the rubric of the global Miss Kerala competition, the Miss Kerala from Kerala is but one of many the world over. She has an equivalent position with respect to other Miss Keralas. Her Kerala-ness is not privileged with respect to the diaspora; in fact, her equivalence with them is required by a certain cultural politics of globalization. The structure of a globalized middle class makes it possible for there to be an equivalence between the likes of a Miss Kerala from Kerala and a Miss Kerala from New York. The contest reveals starkly the production of locality on a global stage. Miss Kerala must be a traditional girl (naden pennu) in her dress, comportment, and knowledge. Written onto the female bodies of a proliferation of Miss Keralas, the nadu, locality itself, becomes transportable and transposable.

So far, I have presented an analysis that would trace the body of the woman as object, tradition commodified—a body inscribed and consumed by a patriarchal middle-class masculine gaze. But, in many ways, the Miss Kerala pageant was seen as a failure. In order to examine why this is so, we must move from the structure of the event to its performative aspects. The beauty contest can be conceptualized as a literal and figurative stage for the enactment of gendered identities. Judith Butler points to the possibility of a breakdown of replicability—a "failure to repeat"—as a way of understanding gender identity as a real but tenuous construction (Butler, 1990, p. 141). It then becomes possible to view a woman's body as not simply inscribed and commodified, but also performed and enacted.

During the public performance of gender identity that took place during Thiruvananthapuram's Miss Kerala contest, certain dissonances emerged. The main problem emerged during the questioning. In short, all ten contestants had trouble answering questions about Kerala history, poetry, literature, dance, and drama, mainly because they simply did not know the answers and sometimes because they did not know the highly Sanskritized Malayalam necessary to answer. The problem became particularly acute during the third round. After walking slowly across the stage with the traditional lamp, laying it down, lighting it, and then walking over to the questioner, all that many of the women could say, when asked who had won the Kerala Sahitya Akademi (a government-sponsored literary organization) award for poetry two years prior was "Sorry, I don't know." At which point the audience, laughing and heckling, would shout back, "Then why did you come?" or "Go home girl!" It became comically clear that there was a mismatch.

The source of the mismatch is a contradiction between form and content. The form of the pageant is part of a whole repertoire of practices—acting, modeling, fashion shows—which constitute new, globally inflected "modern" feminine consumer spaces. A form of publicity that only "certain girls" engage in, the "modern middle-class miss" highlighted by the activist who protested the Miss World pageant discussed earlier. The content required a performance of the "traditional" comportment and habitus in a public space, which collided with other ("modern") bodily demeanors—walking as in a fashion show, but somehow doing so while wearing a pawada. In this instance, the beauty pageant is framed as a space of globalized consumer modernity, one that has little room for the demure modernity of the churidar-clad young woman who, in everyday contexts, navigates the tension between tradition and modernity, public and private, through her closed and contained body. Rather, the very public and highly globalized stage of the beauty pageant becomes a site for the staging of the tensions between such binaries.

Here we have the imbrication between two structures of patriarchy. One is rooted in the patriarchal family formed through India's colonial and then postcolonial, nationalist modernity into a binarism between tradition and modernity. This intersects with the patriarchal structures of emergent, globally inflected spaces of public consumption which commodify women at the same time that they target them as consumers. This young woman, a participant in the beauty pageant, struggles to articulate a sense of agency, albeit a consumerist sense of agency within this mutual imbrication. Reflecting afterwards on the audience reaction, she states,

> They say fashion is bad. So they have the girls wear the pawada, the sari, and all that. But what's wrong with fashion? I'm not saying fashion is a big deal. I don't say like other girls, you know. In the magazines the girls say "Fashion is a really important part of my life." I don't say that. It's just a little fun. That's all it is, just fun.

It is difficult to formulate precisely how one can rescue the "fun" of fashion from its simultaneous demonization by the protectors of "tradition" and by critics of capitalism who locate "fun" as a mere diversion, a market-driven, consumer, middle-class subterfuge. In this beauty pageant, the failure of the replicability of gender identities is founded on a collision between highly spatialized notions of tradition/modernity, India/West as they intersect when young women's bodies wrapped in clothing commodities move across the stage of beauty. The idea of "fun," marking experiences of pleasure, desire, and leisure, then, becomes one lens through which to understand the fraught relationship that young women have to new, globally inflected consumer spaces. The "modern miss," interested in fashion shows, modeling, beauty pageants, is a middle-class object of desire that must ultimately be tamed and disciplined. Burdened by tradition, preyed upon by modernity, she must learn to navigate these new spaces of consumption respectably and modestly. Her notions of "fun" are situated in and through notions of tradition and modernity, public and private, that make her claim on these new consumer spaces tenuous.

My analysis of the cultural politics of this beauty pageant reveals the spaces of global consumer culture to be shaped by a gendered terrain of femininities in which the meanings of tradition and modernity, what ought to be private and public, are highly charged. Here, the "resistance" of the modern girl is not self-evidently understood. More than just contextualizing her participation within the networks of power that an increasingly global capitalist modernity engenders, this analysis foregrounds the contested and complex cultural politics of Indian modernity in and through which her consumer agency is rendered as "modern" and "resistant." The discourses and contested cultural politics of globalization work through binaries and oppositions created in and through India's long engagements with colonial and nationalist rework-ings of the legacies of Western modernities as it seeks to globalize itself in the contemporary era. This involves highly spatialized understandings of India and the West, mapped onto distinctions such as public/private and tradition/ modernity. The figure of the young, Westernized female has been central to this project, and young women who navigate new spaces of globalized moder-nity bear the "burden of locality" within this cultural politics. In this context, it is worth noting a representational absence in the cultural economy of con-sumer agency that I have been tracking. In other work, I discuss the impor-tance of the upper caste/class male figure and the lower caste/class male figure within the new terrain of commodified masculinities and femininities that constitute contemporary youth consumer culture (Lukose, 2005a). What is strikingly absent is the lower caste/class female, so thoroughly privatized and traditionalized that, within this new global moment, she appears as little other than a figure in need of saving, the one who cannot afford beauty products, the one who is forever struggling to make ends meet.

Conclusion

Highlighting youth consumer practices, from their inception cultural studies of youth have tracked agency and resistance in a variety of ways (Bucholtz, 2002; Hall and Jefferson, 1976; Hebdige, 1979). These studies have focused on the ways young people deploy music and clothing styles as forms of "signifying practice," in order to form subcultural youth identities that are seen as acts of resistance against a dominant culture. This body of research has opened up the possibility that consumption does not simply produce victims of capi-talist hegemony but is a site for a complicated mediation of youth identities. More recently, this focus on youth cultural practices has extended beyond the Euro-American context to link a concern with globalization, youth cultural studies, and spatiality in non-Western contexts (Amit-Talai and Wulff, 1995; Bhavnani et al., 1998; Cole, 2005; Dolby, 2001; Durham, 2000; Liechty, 2003; Lukose, 2005, 2005a; Maira and Soep, 2005; Skelton and Valentine, 1998). Feminist cultural analysis, too, has renewed its interest in consumer culture. Rather than see consumption as singularly a site of patriarchal domination and the commodification of women's bodies, feminist writers and cultural historians have investigated the ways in which consumer culture is a complex site of female participation and constraint, enjoyment and objectification (Bhavnani et al., 1998; Felski, 1995; McRobbie, 1991; Nava, 1992; Peiss, 1986).

These cultural analyses focus on what women and girls do with consumer goods and how commodities give rise to meaning-making processes that are frequently at odds with the intended meanings and usages. It is this that opens up the possibility for the ascription of "resistance" and "agency" to the female consumer.

This chapter has explored the ways this framework, initially formed in and through Euro-American debates within cultural studies about the boundaries of culture and class resistance, travels to the globalizing worlds of young people in postcolonial contexts. Focusing on the critical apprehension of constructions of consumer agency as a key dimension of globalization, I have sought to explore the framework of agency/resistance in illuminating the ways in which young people's worlds are shaping the contours of globalization while being attentive to the contested and complex terrain of cultural politics that globalization has engendered. It is argued here that a critical understanding of youth, agency, and globalization in postcolonial contexts requires attention to the ways that globalization structures subjectivity through articulations of consumer agency, articulations that are embedded in a long-standing tradition of debate and struggle about the meanings of Indian modernity. Young women, their bodies, and what they wear have been central to those debates, providing a fertile terrain for the reworking of youth identities in the context of globalization.

Notes

1 Though started in the mid-1980s, the liberalization of the Indian economy accelerated with comprehensive economic reforms in 1991, during the Rajiv Gandhi government, in which India signed on to World Bank and IMF loans, reduced tariffs and duties on foreign goods, liberalized the private sector, and opened up the public sector to market forces.
2 The fieldwork that this chapter is based on has been ongoing since 1994. It has involved intensive research with college students in the southern state of Kerala, as well as following them longitudinally past their college years. The research has also involved media and documentary research. This research, during various phases, has been supported by the Fulbright-Hays Program, the American Institute of Indian Studies, the University of Pennsylvania, the National Academy of Education, and the Spencer Foundation.
3 Deshpande (1993) discusses the contours of Nehruvian developmentalism while discussing the ways that contemporary forms of globalization transform conceptions of citizenship and nationalism in India.
4 The details of the Miss World pageant that follow are taken from Menon (1996). For critical discussions of the pageant and its protests see John (1998), Menon (2005), and Niranjana (1999).

References

Abu-Lughod, L. 1990. The romance of resistance. *American Ethnologist* 17, 41–55.
Amit-Talai, V., and H. Wulff, eds. 1995. *Youth Cultures: A Cross-Cultural Perspective.* London: Routledge.
Appadurai, A. 1996. *Modernity at Large: The Cultural Dimensions of Globalization.* Minneapolis, MN: University of Minnesota Press.

Arunima, G. 2003. *There Comes Papa: Colonialism and the Transformations of Matriliny in Kerala, Malabar c. 1850–1940.* New Delhi, India: Orient Longman.

Banerjee, H. 1995. Attired in virtue: The discourse of shame (*lajja*) and clothing of the *Bhadramahila* in colonial Bengal. In *From the Seams of History: Essays on Indian Women,* ed. B. Ray, 67–106. New Delhi, India: Oxford University Press.

Bhavnani, K., K. Kent, and F.W. Twine, eds. 1998. *Signs, Special Issue on Feminisms and Youth Cultures,* 23.

Breckenridge, C., ed. 1995. *Consuming Modernity: Public Culture in a South Asian World.* Minneapolis, MN: University of Minnesota Press.

Bucholtz, M. 2002. Youth and cultural practice. *Annual Review of Anthropology.*

Burke, T. 1996. *Lifebouy Men, Lux Women: Commodification, Consumption and Cleanliness in Modern Zimbabwe.* Durham: Duke University Press.

Butler, J. 1990. *Gender Trouble.* London: Routledge.

Chatterjee, P. 1990. Colonialism, nationalism, and colonized women: The contest in India. *American Ethnologist* 16, 622–633.

Chua, B., ed. 2000. *Consumption in Asia: Lifestyles and Identities.* London: Routledge.

Cole, J. 2005. The Jaombilo of Tamatave, 1992–2004: Reflections on youth and globalization. *Journal of Social History* 38(4), 891–914.

Comaroff, J., and J. Comaroff. 1991. *Of Revelation and Revolution: Christianity, Colonialism and Consciousness in South Africa.* Chicago: University of Chicago Press.

Deshpande, S. 1993. Imagined economies: Styles of nation-building in twentieth century India. *Journal of Arts and Ideas* 25–26, 5–35.

Dolby, N. 2001. *Constructing Race: Youth, Identity, and Popular Culture in South Africa.* Albany, NY: State University of New York Press.

Durham, D. 2000. Youth and the social imagination in Africa: Introduction to parts 1 and 2. *Anthropological Quarterly* 73(3), 113–120.

Felski, R. 1995. *The Gender of Modernity.* Cambridge: Harvard University Press.

Ferguson, J. 1999. *Expectations of Modernity: Myths and Meanings of Urban Life on the Zambian Copperbelt.* Berkeley, CA: University of California Press.

Grossberg, L. 1993. Cultural studies and/in new worlds. *Critical Studies in Mass Communication* 10(1), 1–22.

Hall, S., and T. Jefferson. 1976. *Resistance through Rituals: Youth Subcultures in Post-War Britain.* London: Hutchinson Press.

Hancock, M. 1999. *Womanhood in the Making: Domestic Ritual and Public Culture in Urban South India.* Boulder, CO: Westview Press.

Hebdige, D. 1979. *Subculture: The Meaning of Style.* London: Methuen.

Hendrickson, H. 1996. *Clothing and Difference: Embodying Colonial and Postcolonial Identities.* Durham: Duke University Press.

John, M. 1998. Globalisation, sexuality and the visual field: Issues and non-issues for cultural critique. In *A Question of Silence? The Sexual Economies of Modern India,* ed. M. John and J. Nair, 368–396. New Delhi, India: Kali for Women.

Kerala bans camera cellphones in educational institutions. *The Hindu.* June 25, 2005. Retrieved October 14, 2006 from http://www.hindu.com/2005/06/26/stories/2005062607570100.htm.

Liechty, M. 2003. *Suitably Modern: Making Middle-Class Culture in a New Consumer Society.* Princeton, NJ: Princeton University Press.

Lukose, R. 2005. Consuming globalization: Youth and gender in Kerala, India. *Journal of Social History* 38(4), 915–935.

Lukose, R. 2005a. Empty citizenship: Reconfiguring politics in the era of globalization. *Cultural Anthropology* 20, 506–533.

Maira, S., and E. Soep. 2005. *Youthscapes: The Popular, the National, the Global.* Philadelphia, PA: University of Pennsylvania Press.

Mankekar, P. 1999. *Screening Culture, Viewing Politics: An Ethnography of Television, Womanhood, and Nation in Postcolonial India.* Durham, NC: Duke University Press.

McRobbie, M. 1991. *Feminism and Youth Culture: From Jackie to Just Seventeen.* Boston: Unwin Hyman.

Menon, N. 2005. Between the burqa and the beauty parlor?: Globalization, cultural nationalism, and feminist politics. In *Postcolonial Studies and Beyond,* ed. A. Loomba, S. Kaul, M. Bunzl, A. Burton, and J. Esty, 206–229. Durham, NC: Duke University Press.

Menon, P. 1996. Pageant and protests: A Miss World show under state protection. *Frontline,* December 13, 1996, 4–16.

Nava, M. 1992. *Changing Cultures: Feminism, Youth and Consumerism.* London: Sage.

Niranjana, T. 1999. Introduction. *Journal of Arts and Ideas* 32–33, 3–8.

Peiss, K. 1986. *Cheap Amusements: Working Women and Leisure in Turn-of-the-Century New York.* Philadelphia, PA: Temple University Press.

Pinney, C., and R. Dwyer, eds. 2001. *Pleasure and the Nation: The History, Politics, and Consumption of Public Culture in India.* New Delhi, India: Oxford University Press.

Sarkar, T. 2001. *Hindu Wife, Hindu Nation: Community, Religion, and Cultural Nationalism.* New Delhi, India: Permanent Black.

Skelton, T., and G. Valentine, eds. 1998. *Cool Places: Geographies of Youth Culture.* London: Routledge.

Tarlo, E. 1996. *Clothing Matters: Dress and Identity in India.* Chicago: University of Chicago Press.

The world's youngest nation. *Outlook.* January 12, 2004. Retrieved October 14, 2006 from http://www.outlookindia.com/archivecontents.asp?fnt=20040112.

Vaid, S., and K. Sangari, eds. 1989. *Recasting Women: Essays in Indian Colonial History.* New Delhi, India: Kali for Women.

Weston, K. 1993. Do clothes make the woman?: Gender, performance theory and lesbian eroticism. *Genders* 17, 1–21.

Zakaria, F. 2006. India rising. *Newsweek.* March 6. Retrieved October 14, 2006 from http://www.msnbc.msn.com/id/11571348/site/newsweek/.

9
Youth Cultures of Consumption in Johannesburg

SARAH NUTTALL

This chapter explores the rise of a youth cultural form widely known as "Y Culture." Y Culture, also known as *Loxion Kulcha* for reasons I explain below, is an emergent youth culture in Johannesburg which moves across various media forms. It articulates the clear remaking of the black body, its repositioning by the first postapartheid generation. More specifically, it signals the supercession of an earlier era's resistance politics by an alternative politics of style and accessorization, while simultaneously gesturing, in various ways, toward the past. It is a culture of the hip bucolic which works across a series of surfaces, requiring what Paul Gilroy (2000) calls "technological analogies," in order to produce enigmatic and divergent styles of self-making. While drawing on black American style formations, it is an explicitly local reworking of the American sign—a reworking that simultaneously results in and underscores significant fractures in Gilroy's paradigm of the Black Atlantic.[1] The conception of the body as a work of art, an investment in the body's special presence and powers, a foregrounding of the capacity for sensation, marks Y Culture. Selfhood and subjectivity are presented less as inscriptions of broader institutional and political forces than as an increased self-consciousness about the fashioning of human identity as a manipulable artful process.

The chapter draws on a notion of self-styling, or self-stylization, a concept invoked by Michel Foucault (2001) to describe those practices in which individuals "create a certain number of operations on their own bodies and souls, thoughts, conduct, and ways of being so as to transform themselves" (p. 225). Foucault wanted to explore how such "technologies of the self" negotiated the transition between the moment of political liberation and "practices of freedom" as such. His notion of self-styling bears on the forms of emerging selfhood and bodily life I discuss below, though in ways that certainly Foucault himself did not have in mind. The chapter shows, too, that in attempting to understand Y cultural forms, cultural analysis which relies on ideas of translation or translatability are useful only up to a point, and that what is required is an understanding of how cultural forms *move*. While "translation" relies on an idea of a gap—a gap between one meaning or text and another—what is needed in order to properly understand this cultural form is something closer to an interface in which meaning morphs into something else, rather than "losing" its initial sense. Although the idea of the gap in meaning inhabits our theorizing about culture generally, I argue that it deserves elaboration and adjustment when it comes to reading the innovations of contemporary urban cultural forms.

In the second part of the chapter, I consider a recent set of advertisements that have appeared on billboards and in magazines in the wake of Y Culture. I show how they simultaneously engage with and push in unexpected directions one of the most striking aspects of Y/Loxion Culture, an attempt at rereading race in the city. In analyzing the ads, I consider ways in which commodity images, and the market itself, come to produce some of the most powerful reimaginings of race South Africa has known in some time. At the same time, the idea of the gap (here, between what you have and what you want) is continually reconstituted at the heart of the commodity in order to propel new desires.

The discussion below intersects with but is not directly constitutive of emergent work in South Africa by scholars in education. The latter focus on the school as a key site for social reproduction. More specifically, such scholars have been focusing on (1) the destabilization of racial categorization through language practices, (2) the emergent fault lines between suburban and township-schooled youth, and (3) the complexity of multilingualism in urban South Africa (Makubalo, 2006; McKinney 2005, 2006; Soudien, 1998, 2003, 2004). Although some—in particular, Crain Soudien (2004)—have argued that the dominant model of integration in desegregated schools has been overwhelmingly assimilationist, others, while not overturning this in its entirety, have wanted to draw out more fully the transformation of cultural resources and the construction of new identities in such schools—that is, to focus on "the gaps and moments that might be available for remaking culture and identities" (McKinney, 2005, p. 1).[2] Wally Morrow (1998) has emphasized the limits of a politics of difference as a structuring educational device: "At this time in South Africa, the politics of difference is likely to reinforce traditional divisions, rather than to enable us to discover the social cohesion of which we were deprived during colonialism and apartheid" (p. 242). Nadine Dolby (2000) has theorized race in a South African school as simultaneously "full" and "empty" of meaning. She shows how racial identities have been shaped in a discourse of taste which relies on the racialization of global popular culture. Her notion of the "global popular" (1999) is understood as simultaneously a "ground for racial conflict, moments, and spaces of racial connection and the shifting of racial alliances" (p. 291). The global popular, she writes, serves as a critical site of youth's affective investments, and she argues, with Frith (1996), that the popular does not reflect racialized selves as much as it produces them.

The focus of my chapter is on a cultural form developed by young people initially in a postschool context but one which is now widely subscribed to within schools, particularly in Johannesburg, as its influence widens. The focus of the chapter on the stylization of self can be taken as a productive way of thinking about how learners present themselves and how their identities are constituted. Moreover, Loxion Kulcha, as we will see, emphasizes, in its self-description and in its conscious manipulation of taste, schooling background (see McKinney, 2005, p. 4). Furthermore, an analysis of Loxion Kulcha offers a sense of what constitutes insider knowledge, the social capital that young people wield in determining what is cool and what is privileged among peers (McKinney, p. 12). The chapter also aims to open up aspects of the focus of this book as a whole: ways, that is, in which youth identities are increasingly tied to "the new structures and conditions of modernity: the processes of an accelerating economic globalization, the intensification of commodification and consumer culture, the shifting nature of the public sphere, the changing role of nation and national identity … and new relations and dynamics made possible by technology."[3]

Johannesburg, the locus of this chapter, is a city of approximately 4 million people in a country of 46 million. It is Africa's financial capital, and it is characterized, as are many metropolises, by extremes of poverty and wealth, and by multiple locations of citiness—an inner city, a financial district, suburbs, edge cities, and townships.[4] It derives its distinctively modern aura, as Michael Watts (2005) has written, from its zine culture and its metropolitan imaginings, as well as from its memorializations, its urban theaters of late capitalism, and its psychic wounds and fugitive underground worlds. Central to this aura are, increasingly, consumer cultures and media technologies. To be in Johannesburg today is to feel the immense coincidence of the end of apartheid and the rise of globalization, new media cultures and cultures of consumption. In Johannesburg, the power of this concatenation of forces (political, cultural, and economic) and the velocity with which it has engendered change on a national level, is patently clear. South Africa's recent past was marked by the relative singularity of purpose and vision of massive local resistance to, and international solidarity against, apartheid, which led to the white regime's demise in 1994. The present, by contrast, can be characterized by heterogeneity, by a fracturing of the contemporary moment in South Africa, now a place that is moving in multiple and unforeseen directions, splintering into manifold forms of desegregation and resegregation, shaped, increasingly, by media cultures and cultures of consumption. As Johannesburg's black middle class rapidly outgrows its white counterpart, urban teenagers now represent a consumer base that spends R6.4 billion a year.

Y/Loxion Culture has been characterized by its capacity to generate ideas, images, and ways of being in the city quite different from before. Arguably, it has retained a political edge because, as we will see, it has involved acts of rereading, a citing of the apartheid past while drawing increasingly on its stylistics, which speak to the future. It intersects with a rising commodity culture but could also be thought of as a youth movement, a concerted attempt at creating a subculture in the city that defines the youth, trading on their powerful political role in the apartheid era. Subsequently, as we will see, brand managers began to capitalize on its stylistics as a means of reading the youth market.

The challenge that the chapter aims to take up is to be able to account for, by attending closely to, the rapid pace of change among contemporary urban youth cultural forms. Too often, academic critiques of commodity culture and the inequities bred by globalization miss the cultural shifts that commodity-based formations signify, their growing intraclass dimensions, and their manipulation of surfaces, long disfavored by a scholarly establishment accustomed to reading for depth. I attempt to do that here. Its aim, finally, is to begin to generate the analytical tools needed to read contemporary youth cultural forms which increasingly rely on terms and dimensions not available to an earlier generation.

Y Culture, Johannesburg Circa 2006

Y Culture was first launched by a radio station called YFM, today South Africa's largest regional station, beamed over the airwaves from Johannesburg to nearly two million listeners. The station was set up in 1996. Its primary audience was young, mostly black people, who tuned in to hear a mix of popular, mostly local, music. When democracy came to South Africa in 1994, there was nowhere, on the AM or the FM dial, for the majority of the country's young people to gather, no airspace dedicated to them. The South African Broadcasting Corporation (SABC) had a spare frequency it handed over to the team that would eventually found YFM. Stringent conditions were attached: The station would only be granted a license if eighty percent of its capital was black-owned, fifty percent of its staff was female and, within three years, at least half its playlist was made up of South African music. The station was to be a multilingual, urban entity that informed, educated, and entertained a young audience. All of this was well in line with the founding team's goals. YFM, says general manager Greg Maloka, was to be a "phenomenon ... for us and by us. We saw [its creation] as another June 16, 1976," he adds, alluding to the spontaneous uprising of tens of thousands of children and adolescents in Soweto, a massive call-to-action against the apartheid state which marked the beginning of the end of the white regime. Twenty-two years had gone by. Apartheid was officially dead. Suddenly, the youth market was all the rage (see McGregor, 2005).

YFM launched *kwaito*, South Africa's first globally recognized local music form, a potent blend of city and township sound that emerged after the democratic transition in 1994, mixing the protest dancing and chanting known as *toyi-toyi* with slow-motion house, local pop (known as "bubblegum"), and a dash of hip-hop. In 1998, the station spawned a print spin-off, *Y Magazine* (or *YMag*). Making use of state-of-the-art branding techniques, the magazine associated itself closely with both YFM and *kwaito*. Its tagline, prominently displayed on the spine of each issue, is an anthem to the art of being in the know—hip, cool, plugged in: "Y—Because You Want to Know." The same is true of the name chosen by the company that owns the publication, YIRED, a play on notions of being young and "wired"—up-to-date and connected in all the right places. In 2002, the YFM stable launched a fashion label called "Loxion Kulcha."[5] "Loxion" is an SMS-type contraction of the word "location," a synonym of "township"; "Kulcha" is an ironic deformation of the word "culture." The brand name invokes a remixing: an infusion of black township culture, long kept at a violent remove from the urban center, into the heart of the (once-white) city itself. In *YMag*, Loxion Kulcha is described as a "pride-driven line," a "brand born of the YFM era," one that remixes African-American styles to its own purposes and in ways that speak to its own, particular cultural precursors (Mtsali et al., 2000). Its designers, Wandi Nzimande and Sechaba "Chabi" Mogale, are "typical generation Yers, children of the 1980s who are old enough to understand what the political fuss [of the apartheid era] was about, yet young enough to keep an open mind [to the present and future]" (p. 62).

Y Culture is located most visibly in an area called the Zone in Rosebank, a residential neighborhood and business district that has been attracting a young hip workforce since the 1980s, thanks to a concentration of information technology, travel, and tourism enterprises, retail and fashion outlets, cinemas and restaurants. Increasingly, to serve this young workforce, a process of infill has occurred, in which shopping complexes expand by incorporating spaces and structures that predate them. The Zone—home to the YFM studios and to shops showcasing Loxion Kulcha and related fashion labels such as the popular Stoned Cherrie brand[6]—is one of these infills. Here, enclosed shopping venues and open areas are linked by indoor and outdoor "roads" in an approach to architecture that, as one critic observes, turns the notion of public space inside out (Farber, 2002, p. 73).

In the Zone, yellow and blue neon tubes, glitter tiles, columns clad in reflective aluminum, and exposed steel trusses give it an industrial look that combines elements of the factory and the club. As one makes one's way through its spaces, one is struck by their fluidity. Distinctions—thresholds—between public and private, pavement and mall, inside and out, seem to fall away. The Zone's indoor roads sometimes feel like catwalks—and at other times like a state-of-the-art gym (television screens hang over the walkways). Throughout, surfaces (shiny, mirror-like) and colors (an energetic metallic gray flecked with primary colors) differentiate the space from the neutral beige found in the city's other shopping centers.[7] Wherever possible, the Zone's architecture maximizes the intersection of gazes: people on the escalators produce a spectacle for diners seated at strategically located restaurants; the main indoor roads function simultaneously as means of access and vantage points; signifiers one would usually rely on to orient oneself outside (street signs, for instance) are reappropriated to define interior spaces (2002). As a locus of social interaction, The Zone is complex. On the one hand, as a privatized public space, it speaks of exclusion: Though it is possible for poorer citizens to come to the Zone, they are not welcome there.[8] At the same time, it is one of Johannesburg's relatively few up-market open spaces where some manner of the unexpected is possible: theater, mime, and dance groups perform here, parades are organized, and people come from all over the continent to trade in a large African craft market located near its entrance. The Zone is by no means a place of extensive social mixing. Heavily regulated and subjected to close scrutiny by expedient mall governors, the craft market at its door underscores this. Still, as a result of its presence, there is a sense here of broader horizons: a young person (or anyone else) walking around the Zone circulates within an imagined Africa much larger than Johannesburg alone.

Thus, despite the influence on it of American models of mall design and commerce, the Zone does not yet display the nihilism that characterizes consumer culture in the United States—an approach to selling "style" and "individuality" in which each customer is pegged to a specifically managed and increasingly reified identity. This, in part, is due to the still recent emergence of the black body from its history of "invisibility" under apartheid—an "erasure" from the city which Y Culture, in certain respects, seeks to recall, but that it is largely bent on transforming—and to the relative fluidity with which black middle-class culture locates itself in the urban matrix after a long period of exclusion. Elaborating on this point, we could perhaps also argue that under apartheid, black people faced the oppressive binaries of either being made entirely invisible—or being made hypervisible. It is this hypervisibility which Y Culture, but especially the advertisements I discuss in the second part of this chapter, works with and parodies.[9]

The Zone, as well as housing smaller fashion outlets like the Stoned Cherrie brand store and Young Designers Emporium, is home to the ubiquitous mall chain stores. Among these are Exclusive Books and CD Warehouse. Both are found at shopping arcades throughout the city and in urban centers across the country. At this particular branch of Exclusive Books, the bestsellers are not what they are elsewhere. The books that sell the best in most Exclusive Books locations are by pulp U.S. authors like John Grisham and Dan Brown. In the Zone, they take second billing. The top sellers are Niq Mhlongo's *Dog Eat Dog* (2004) and Phaswanes Mpe's *Welcome to Our Hillbrow* (2000). The first is the story of a young Sowetan trying to hustle his way through Wits University, long a bastion of white education; the second is a tale of xenophobia and AIDS in inner city Johannesburg. The Zone branch of CD Warehouse also differs from its sister stores elsewhere in the city. It carries a prominent and exhaustive range of kwaito CDs as well as some of the best sounds from the continent and black America. Next to CD Warehouse is the YFM Internet café and the Y-Shoppe, where local designers showcase their work and whose designs generally invoke the city by name or image, draw on puns or pastiches of the past, and play with the "Y" logo.[10] The shop leads to the heart of the radio station, the Y Studios, a slick, black-lined maze of soundproof booths. Through large windows, one can see DJs at work creating the Y sound at banks of sophisticated equipment. The DJs themselves are young, glamorous, mostly black-skinned and black-clad (see McGregor, 2005).

Remix

Y is a hybrid phenomenon that appeals to young people across borders of class, education, and taste. Key to its success in this regard is a dual remixing it effects—of the township and the city and the township *in* the city. The young designers who launched the Loxion Kulcha label are incarnations of this intraculture. Wandi styles himself a *kasi*, or "township boy," Chabi a *Bana ba di Model C* (a "Model C kid"). As such, they represent the remix at work in the making of Y. A *kasi* is typically someone who grew up in a black township, a world often associated with poverty, crime, overcrowding, and lack of resources. At the same time, whereas this is indeed the environment in which Wandi was raised and which he references in speaking of himself as a *kasi*, the word today has acquired so many connotations that it can now stand alone, quite apart from location, to imply a certain way of life (see Mbembe, Dlamini, and Khunou, 2004). Chabi's take on himself tells of a different world. When the South African education system was first integrated post-1994, privileged schools in formerly white, bourgeois neighborhoods opened their doors to black students. These schools were classified as "Model C" establishments. Though the term is no longer used as a formal education category, over time it has acquired a meaning of its own. It refers to black high-school students who have taken on a cross-racial style and social set.

Loxion Kulcha's intracultural success is less a matter of appearance than a matter of branding. The point may be to bring the township into the city, and cultural knowledge of where "township culture" is heading is certainly at the heart of what makes Wandi and Chabi hip, but Loxion Kulcha is not about spreading a "township look." The label—the brand, explicitly set forth and marketed with brio—is the thing here, as Mpolokeng Bogatsu (2003) quite accurately points out. This privileging of brand over look simultaneously reflects and shapes structures of class and race within the city's emergent youth culture.

Although Loxion Kulcha's market is intraclass (to the extent that it encompasses both city youth and those living in generally lower-middle-class township homes), sartorial markings are often seen to reveal sharp distinctions between Zone kids (well-to-do young people who make a habit of coming to Rosebank) and township kids, who do frequent the Zone, but do so to a far lesser extent and are not particularly welcome there. Rocking the brand is good, essential even, but it doesn't occult where you come from. Young people interviewed in the Zone make this quite clear: "Township girls," says one, "wear Rocabarroco [brand] shoes that are square-shaped with laces. . . . They will wear bright [colored] jeans with a collar-type shirt. A Zone kid will wear [blue] jeans and a nice [read hip, collarless] top." Another glosses this as: "They dress similarly, but you can tell them apart. Model C girls have an air of sophistication, whereas township girls could snap anytime." Some interviewees focus less on sartorial differences than on skin color. This they do, however, in ways that stand at a distinct remove from earlier, pre-1994 discourses of race and, by extension, class. Notes one young Zoner: "In our generation, we all kind of dress the same. Some blacks dress outrageously wrong and some whites do, too, but we all wear the same things. If you check around, you can't notice a difference between whites and blacks here, apart from the color of their skin" (Farber, pp. 11–16). Difference is still located on the skin, as color, even as skin color becomes less determined within this sartorially inflected set of practices and signs.

The foregoing underscores the fact that racial identities emerging from Y/Loxion Culture are new in relation to the apartheid-era legal classification of people as "White," "Black," "Indian," or "Coloured." These categories operated on an everyday basis through processes of urbanization, policing, and the manipulation of cultural difference to political ends. Since 1994, when this system was officially abolished, young people have occupied these categories in changing ways, using them to elaborate shifting identities for themselves in the new, "postracist" dispensation. Dolby (2000) argues that "taste" at times comes to displace orthodox constructs of race and culture as the carrier of social distinctions amongst urban school-going youths; this as popular culture comes to increasingly contest the church, family, and neighborhood as the primary site where racial identities are forged. The criteria that define bodies, clothing, and culture as "White," "Coloured," or "Black" are not stable, as fashion and music tastes undergo one metamorphosis after another.[11] Class dynamics work into the constitution of racialized taste patterns, at times taking on charged connotations despite constant style fluctuations. What is clear is that new youth cultures are superseding the resistance politics of an earlier generation, while still jamming, remixing, and remaking cultural codes and signifiers from the apartheid past.

How these codes are reappropriated and transformed makes for fascinating cultural (and business) practice. Stoned Cherrie, one of the most popular fashion labels at the Zone, puts signs of the past to striking use. Notably, it recycles images of boxing champions, beauty queens, and musicians from *Drum*, a politically engaged magazine for black readers popular during the 1950s, integrating them into contemporary fashion styles. *Drum* was associated with places like Sophiatown, the heart of Johannesburg's counterculture in the 1950s. It courted and actively constructed an expressly cosmopolitan target audience, "the new African cut adrift from the tribal reserve—urbanized, eager, fast-talking, and brash" (Nkosi, 1983). Stoned Cherrie's designs speak in several registers. In part, they play on the taste for "retro" (a current global trend in styling), by drawing on 1950s imagery—imagery for which *Drum*, a showcase for some of the best urban photography in South Africa, is a particularly fruitful source. At the same time, they make extensive use of parody, as they brand unquestionably dated, *vieux jeu* images onto mass-produced T-shirts. Retro and parody, in turn, combine to invoke nostalgia for "the location." Emblematic figures of Johannesburg's mid-20th century past—*pantsulas*, the "bad boys" of the 1950s; migrant and blue-collar workers; black cover girls whose very existence and whose sophistication stood on its head white culture's claim to superiority[12]—are recreated, brought to life anew, and remixed, in Loxion Kulcha. This past, recalled and reworked, is, in turn, cross-pollinated with references to African-American culture(s) and styles. In an analysis of how Loxion Kulcha remakes township culture and, more specifically, blends *pantsula* and African-American street culture styles, Nthabiseng Motsemme (2002) shows how *isishoeshoe* and *iduku* (shoes and headcloths worn by black married township and rural migrant women employed as domestic workers in the city during the apartheid era) have been recaptured, reinterpreted, and transformed into iconic fashion items on display in Rosebank. The point, here, is not a political one—not, in any event, in the sense that resistance movements to apartheid understood the term. There is no real (or intended) engagement here with the horrors of the pre-1994 past. This is underscored by another Loxion Kulcha product: a recent line of low-cut, tight-fitting T-shirts on which liberation theorist and apartheid martyr Steve Biko's image and name appear in a brilliant, stylized red.[13] It is not so much the Black Consciousness message spread by Biko that is being commemorated here, although "BC" still has a broad resonance for young people only vaguely aware of its message. Rather, something different is being introduced: a sartorial style is being marked as an in-your-face contemporary phenomenon through the remixing and recoding of an icon.

While township culture and identity have existed as long as the townships themselves, it is the *performance* of township culture that has emerged with new vigor in the contemporary context. "Like kwaito music," writes Bogatsu, "Loxion Kulcha claims the streets of South Africa's townships as its cultural womb but occupies the centre of the city with its new forms" (p. 14). Township culture is translated from a socioeconomically stagnant into a high-urban experience. The latter gives rise to what is increasingly known as "Afro-chic." A case in point: in the 2000–2002 Loxion Kulcha collections, overalls were big. Mostly, they were single-color outfits, inspired by the work clothes of migrant laborers and miners. Their design was similar to that of *mdantsane*, two-piece coveralls consisting of pants and a zip-up jacket generally worn by workers on a factory assembly line or by miners in a shaft. Unlike the protective garments on which they were modeled, however, the LK pieces emphasized bright, eye-catching primary colors. The utility-oriented, mass-produced overall was made chic, appropriated with great success to new cultural ends.

Here, too, class and race, rethought Y-style, emerge as key concerns. In LK's designs, the township is referenced—gestured to explicitly—yet, in the same breath, cast aside. To sport LK gear is to say one wants out of (or to brag that one has definitely left behind) the location. An insistence on staying in the township, Bogatsu notes, is increasingly marked within Y Culture as a self-defeating show of "negritude" (p. 21) wearing LK's flash-in-your-face overalls makes it clear: This is emphatically not how you plan to live your life. You have no intention of toiling the way your parents did. The economic violence done them is not forgotten, but neither is it openly critiqued. Instead a largely uncritical celebratory focus is placed on the city's burgeoning service economy. LK's overall becomes the signifier, worn with pleasure and pride, of a young workforce whose members labor as waiters and shop attendants in the Zone, becoming both providers for wide family networks and, when off duty, consumers who buy clothes and music in the area and hang out in Rosebank's many clubs.

A Stylistics of Sensation

Turning to a series of images from *YMag*, we can see how Y Culture signals to, but increasingly breaks with, the past in its adoption of an elaborated stylistics of sensation and singularization. A cover image accompanied by the words "Kwaito-Nation" reveals a striking example of the foregrounding of the capacity for sensation, of the new investment in the body's special presence and powers, and of the ascendancy of the sign of blackness. Here, selfhood and subjectivity can no longer be interpreted as merely inscriptions of broader institutional and political forces; instead, the images project an increased self-consciousness of the fashioning of human identity as a manipulatable, artful process.

Representations of the self as an expressive subject have for some time been seen by scholars to signal a subject that is fractured, multiple, shifting, and produced through performativity (see Butler, 1993, 1999). What Loxion Kulcha's image-texts emphasize, by contrast, are practices based on specific aesthetic values and stylistic criteria and enabled by various emerging techniques of the self (Foucault, 2001). The *YMag* "Kwaito-Nation" cover image bears this out, as do others published of late by the magazine. It shows sixteen *kwaito* artists. All are black men, and all are dressed in black, with one or two white shirts showing underneath. The emphasis is on the glamour and style of blackness, reflected metonymically in the color of the clothes themselves. In a fashion sequence six months later called "Angel Delight" the theme is the color white, and the shoot is dominated this time by women but also by a cross-racial group: white and Coloured women are foregrounded, and cross-racial and cross-gendered sexual desire is clearly being played with in the image (*YMag*, October–November 2002). Here, then, is a quite different version of *Y Magazine*'s projected reader, and this difference is part of a broader remixing of identity, including racial identity, in a shifting signifying chain.

The identities and forms of selfhood projected here are compositional. The self in this instance is above all a work of art. So, too, are the stylizations of the self projected in the magazine's images based on a delicate balance between actual emerging lifestyles of middle-class black youth and the politics of aspiration. An exchange in the letters-to-the-editor column in the June–July 2002 issue underscores this: "After reading *YMag* for a while now I've concluded that it would appeal more to the 'miss-thangs' and 'brother mans' living or trying to live the so-called hip life in Jozi. Some of us live in different areas in the country and you only portray a certain kind of youth. The rest of us then feel like the odd ones out, making us feel like aliens or something. Please broaden your scope so that most people can find it appealing, not just those who live in Jozi."[14] The editors' reply follows: "We are all aliens if you think about it, depending where you come from. But seriously, though, *YMag* is for you. *YMag doesn't necessarily portray reality as each of us would see it, that is, we're aspiring as well* [my emphasis]. We obviously can't reflect every kind of person under the good sun but every young person can and will find at least one thing they like inside *YMag*" (p. 12).

In acknowledging that their product is made for those who aspire to (but cannot necessarily claim) hip, cutting-edge, largely middle-class lifestyles in the city, the editors signal a potential "gap"—a gap of potential—between what is and what could be. The present and the possible interlace to form a stylistics of the future. We could also draw out this idea of a gap from the words of one young South African whom Tanya Farber interviewed in the Zone, "We understand where we come from, but I am not interested in politics and about what happened in the '1980s because I wasn't there. And even if I was, I live for the future" (Farber, p. 28). Since this interviewee is in his early 20s, he was in fact "there" in the 1980s, during the worst of the apartheid struggle and the height of the resistance to it. Indirectly acknowledging this by his phrase "and even if I was," he nevertheless insists on the fact that his project and investment lie in a search for the future. His words, we could say, mark him as a public representative of "the now" in South Africa, as he signals the remainders of the past but also speaks the future-oriented language of Y-Gen aspiration.

Y Magazine, in naming a subject who aspires, also draws consumers into a competitive system in which not everyone can have what he or she aspires to. In *Lifebuoy Men, Lux Women* (1996), Tim Burke, one of the few theorists of African consumer culture, points to pitfalls inherent in such processes. As the pleasures of consumption in the 20th (and 21st) century have become increasingly and explicitly tied to satisfaction of the flesh and its needs, he asks, have we not perhaps made too much of the body as a unique site for the elaboration of forms of self-stylization? And in so doing do we not "risk separating individuals from their bodies, seeing, for example, the bodies of women as separate from the selves of women"? This, of course, is not a specifically African phenomenon. Chakrabarty is similarly concerned with the gap between body and self that a culture of commodification would seem to imply: the commodification of culture as lifestyle, he argues, can never completely encompass the life-worlds upon which it draws. On the one hand, it requires a suppression of embodied idiosyncrasies and local conjunctures, but on the other it needs the tangibility of objects and people, a "corporeal index," as Beth Povinelli (2001) puts it, to lend credibility and desirability to its abstract claims. Thus, Chakbrabarty (n.d., in Mazzerella, 2003) draws attention to the gap at the heart of the commodity form, caught as it is between embodiment and abstraction.

Yet the making of the contemporary self is not so easily readable in the self-representations and subjective practices, the powerful parodic languages, the processes of self-styling in which the body plays such an important part— in the seductive "surface forms" of youth culture. Critics generally disavow the "surfaces" of youth culture as an insufficient analytic space (see Jean and John Comaroff, 2001). Yet, arguably it is here, on the surfaces of youth culture, that we come most powerfully to encounter the enigmatic and divergent ways of knowing and self-making that mark its forms. Pursuing the surfaces of cultural form implies a reading, however, that positions itself at the limit of the by-now ubiquitous cultural analytic notion of translatability[15]: It demands that we push beyond the dual notions of "reading" and "translating" to "understand."

Mind the Gap

A conventional reading of Y Culture would rely on tropes of translatability—and indeed the latter can take us quite far into the analysis of this cultural form. The cover stories of YMag signal a transnational, multilingual hybridity, which a focus on translation goes a long way toward explicating. The title "Skwatta Kamp: Hard to the Core Hip-Hop," for example, suggests the influence of American hip-hop on the local scene (Skwatta Kamp is a local rap group), even as it invokes the local topography of the squatter camp—the ubiquitous sign of homelessness and poverty in urban South Africa (August–September, 2002). "Vat en Sit: Shacking Up in Y2K" explores how young black South African couples flout older orthodoxies of sex and marriage; it draws simultaneously on the Afrikaans expression *vat en sit* ("take and live with," a colloquialism used by black migrant workers who would meet and live with women in the city despite having a wife in the rural area or town they came from—a practice of which both women were often aware) and on the English word *shack*, used to denote the makeshift quarters of the poorest in South Africa's townships and squatter camps, (June–July, 2002). "The

Colour of Music: Whiteys and Kwaito" signals an interest in and a projection of crossover cultural and racial cultural codes in postapartheid South Africa, as does "Darkies and Ecstasy: Is it the New Zol?"(YMag, February 2000).[16]

Translatability and multilingualism are built into the text of Y *Magazine*. This is less visible in the body of the text, as the main articles are written in English, than in the interstices. It is in the in-between spaces—the soundbites, the gossip pages, the reviews—that language emerges most forcefully as a locus for practices of translation. Acronyms, wordplay, colloquialisms, and "deep" meanings are some of the devices drawn on within the culture of translatability at work here. A review of a new CD release by local kwaito act Bongo Maffin reads, in Zulu, *Aahyh, Ngi yai bon'indlela en'ibalwe BM* ("Ah, I see the road and it says BM [Bongo Maffin]") (Nappy Head, 1998, p. 9). The phrasing plays on the widely admired style and road performance of BMWs and also recalls a classic of South African music, Dorothy Masuka's classic "Imphi indlela" ("Where's the road / the way").[17] The same review then shifts from Zulu to Tswana: *Kego tsaela 99, Bongo Maffin ifhlile* ("I'm telling you straight up, Bongo Maffin has arrived").

These shifts in language and frame of reference question standard notions of location and publics. They show us that the "world" appears increasingly as a set of fragments, bits and pieces with which young people grapple. Sutured onto these bits and pieces are the histories of isolation from, and connection to, the world that South Africans carry.[18] These fragments come to be refracted in ways that produce resemblances across different signs and languages between signs—what Achille Mbembe (2002) has referred to as "the powers of the false" (p. 14)—revealing the ability of Africans to inhabit several worlds simultaneously. As these fragments and their multiple meanings travel they also encounter resistant edges, and in Y Culture one of these edges is the sign of black America. As Y youth come to inhabit a culture of selfhood shaped in part by African-American hip-hop culture, they also rebel against it, resulting in a form of pastiche. A cut-and-paste appropriation of American music, language, and cultural practices is simultaneously deployed and refuted. An example of this can be found in the self-styling of Trompies, a kwaito group that epitomizes the contemporary version of *mapantsula*. The group is now sponsored by FUBU (For Us By Us), an African-American clothing label often worn by U.S. rap artists. In the June–July 2000 issue of *YMag*, Trompies members are accused of making a "fashion faux pas," as they call themselves *pantsulas* yet adopt a hip-hop style (Mstali et al., 2000, p. 19). At the same time, it is also acknowledged that the 1950s *pantsula* culture emanated from America. Although the black American is embraced as a "brother," the Y reader does not want to be assimilated into his culture (Masemola, 2000, p. 47).[19]

Tropes of translatabilty can reveal much, then, about the workings of Y Culture—but they can only take us so far. The idea of (cultural) translation relies, like the theorizations of Burke and Chakrabarty discussed above, on an idea of "the gap." Increasingly, however, scholarly work on the technologies of public forms, including popular cultural forms, has tended to move toward a focus on circulation and transfiguration replacing, or at least complicating, earlier preoccupations with meaning and translation. As analytic vectors of the social, the latter rely on methods of reading derived from the tradition of the book, a tradition that stipulates that a cultural text be meaningful—"that it be a text and confront us as a text whose primary function is to produce meaning and difference and to captivate us in the dialectic play between these two poles" (Gaonkar and Povinelli, 2003). Such a tradition, moreover, implies a theory of translation grounded in the question of how to translate *well* from one language to another, as meaning is borne across the chasm of two language codes. Once we set foot in a "terrain of chasms and gaps," as Gaonkar and Povinelli note, "we are swept up in the maelstrom of debates about incommensurability, indeterminacy, and undecidability in translation": translation is seen as a productive failure (p. 388). Rather than, or in addition to, asking what happens to meaning as it is borne across languages, genres, or semiotic modes (to "read for meaning"), we might ask what movements of cultural form and techniques for mapping them appear in worlds structured increasingly by cultures of circulation. In other words, as Gaonkar and Povinelli so usefully put it, we need "to foreground the social life *of* the form in question rather than reading social life *off* it" (p. 394, emphasis in original). Such an approach proves particularly productive in understanding Y/Loxion culture. The latter is a cultural form which cuts across sound, sartorial, visual, and textual cultures to reveal a process of "compositional remixing." In this setting, processes of circulation, parallels and slippages between genres play a fundamental role. In the reviews pages of *YMag*, crossover styles are elaborated so that a sound might be used to describe an image, or an image a word, or a clothing line a taste. "His writing is reminiscent of Tracy Chapman's singing," writes one book reviewer (Davis, 2000, p. 130). Another describes a book by way of allusion to a TV chat show (Gule, 2000 p. 89). A review of a CD by Thievery Corporation in *Y*'s sister magazine, *SL*, references fashion to describe sound: "Picture some cool geezer in a black Armani shirt, grey slacks, and DKNY sandals, smoking a doobie like a zeppelin. That pretty accurately describes the sound of Thievery Corporation" (Campbell, 1999, p. 105).[20] Thus, the processes of self-stylization that emerge from *YMag* further accessorize a range of cultural texts that, reframed within crossover media forms, become elements in the aestheticization of the self.[21] Race, especially blackness, as it plays out across these surfaces of form, itself becomes more of a mutating formation than before, less a finished and stable identity than something open to transformation, even proliferation—a phenomenon that actively resists attempts at reading or translation.

Revisiting the Analytics of the Gap

I turn, now, to a second set of cultural texts, a series of advertisements that have appeared since 2005 both in *YMag* and on billboards around Johannesburg. The ads elaborate on the cultural opening that Y Culture has provided, particularly in relation to the prominence given to "style" in the making of contemporary identity in the city. They take up notions of self-making and stylization in order to deconstruct South Africa's racial past—and they do so through an attempt at beginning to define notions of the "post-racial."[22] Drawing on the enormous popularity of Y Culture itself among young South Africans, they use irony and parody to work even more specifically and provocatively than *YMag* and its related brands have in the past with questions of race. A mix of image and text (a point I return to later), the ads emerge as important sites for reading the South African "now" for they just begin to make explicit ideas and passions that are "out there" in society, and therefore have an articulatory function—a function that palpably affects lifeworlds. Each of the advertisements can be thought of in terms of the commodity image. The latter, as William Mazarella (2003) reminds us, can be theorized as a compelling point of mediation between culture and capital and as an index of wider transformations within the field of public culture. The commodity image is at once a flash point for the key ideological issues of the day, a rendering of national community as aesthetic community, and, conventionally at least, a vector of cultural difference offered up for consumption.

The first two advertisements are for a brand of sports shoes called K-Swiss, an American make recently introduced in the South African market. The first is filmed against the backdrop of what was formerly a lower middle-class section of Johannesburg and is now a mixed-income neighborhood (see Figure 9.1). Though the neighborhood is not identified, it is in all likelihood Brixton, a part of the city popular among a certain set for its "retro" look. The ad shows a person in the process of being arrested by the fashion police while others look on. The people on the street stand beneath a sign that says "Whites Only." The scene is an explicit allusion to a widely known genre of image: an urban scene typical of 1970s South Africa, depicting a black man being arrested on grounds that he is not carrying a "pass" to legitimize his presence in the city. The image relies on both irony and parody to achieve its effect: It is not quite what it seems. The crime that the man being arrested has committed, it turns out, is not a "pass" but a "style crime": he is not dressed properly. Specifically, he is not dressed in the color white; most egregiously, he is not wearing the white sports shoes that are being advertised. The image works on many levels: it suggests that the greatest crime is now a "style crime"; that whiteness (and therefore blackness) is a matter less of race than of style, and that style is itself a crossover phenomenon, working across race. It also comments on the

Figure 9.1 Fashion police.

style pecking order in contemporary urban South Africa in the style stakes marked out on the street: The average guy white guy languishes at the back; next comes the black woman; coolest of all is the black man, shown here sporting a 1970s (now retro-cool) Afro hairdo and a body language that suggests cultural confidence and hipness as well as street credibility. In general, the ad plays with the notion that the way you look—the way you dress—defines you as "in" or "out," legal or illegal, official or unofficial; it insists on self-styling as a critical mode of self-making.

The second ad in this series works on the same principle: the past is acknowledged but ironically recast in the postapartheid present (see Figure 9.2). Here, the scene is a men's urinal. One man is cleaning the floor while others make use of the urinal. We might recall that under apartheid the spaces of segregation included macro-spaces such as schools, churches, and cemeteries but also, importantly, micro-spaces, which functioned as key loci for the staging

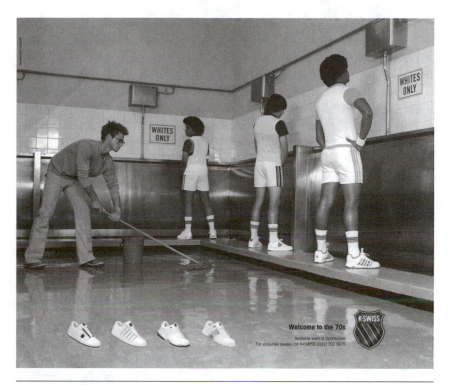

Figure 9.2 Urinal.

of humiliation. One such locus was the "whites only" urinal, which a black man could enter under one condition only: to clean it. The image with which we are concerned gestures to that past and its legacy in South Africa's collective memory, but with a twist. The men using the urinal are both black and white. What differentiates the users from the man cleaning the floor is not skin color but the color of their respective clothes. The users are dressed in the "sign" of whiteness, white clothes, and more specifically white shoes; the man cleaning the floor is *not* wearing the right shoes—he is badly dressed, the ad suggests, out of style, unwilling or incapable of playing the market to project a particular (life)style.[23]

The adverts were launched in 2004. South Africa was celebrating its first ten years of democracy and the company wanted to run a campaign that spoke to this particular context. The target market K-Swiss was aiming at was 14- to 26-year-olds: young people whom market research showed were increasingly thinking and acting in a cross-racial manner. The ads had been a success with this group; surveys showed that young people found the ads clever and "funny" (the only group who were not amused, he added, were 50- to 65-year-old white Afrikaans men).[24] They were based on market research showing that whereas South Africa was once the ultimate signifier of race difference, the situation is now much more striated and complex. A recent survey released by the Human Sciences Research Council shows that, in 1997, 47% of respondents described themselves in terms of racial categories. By 2000, the figure had fallen to only 12% (in the same period, references to gender- and class-related identities declined, whereas allusions to religious identity increased). What had been a fairly limited and predictable set of self-descriptions had given way to what the authors of the survey termed "a whole range of individual, personalized descriptions" (Klandermans et al., 2001). Another survey, Trend Youth (2005), which focused on black and white youth from emerging and affluent households in major metropolitan areas (and which included 2400 face-to-face interviews and 30 focus groups), shows clothing brands to be the main ingredients in the development of a "new and clearer South African identity" and notes that the country's 7- to 24-year-olds "are the most racially integrated [group] in the country, with friendships now based more on shared interests like music and fashion than on skin color."

The K-Swiss ads underscore, on the one hand, that the cross-racial lifestyles of urban youth today, although strikingly different from those one might have encountered 20 years ago, still cite (or quote) a racially segregated past that remains in the collective memory; on the other hand, they reveal that, increasingly, "desegregation" takes place under the sign of a reinscribed "whiteness," this time elaborated around social class rather than race. Formerly, the ads state in no uncertain terms that you had to be white to adopt a particular lifestyle; now you have to know how to be stylish—stylish, that is, by K-Swiss's standards. What they don't say but, of course, imply is that you no longer have to be white, but you do have to be middle class, or at least you must find the money to buy products such as those celebrated in the ads. Increasingly, in fact, young people who are not middle class are buying *fong kong*: fake products available especially in the inner city which are cheaper versions of Y or Loxion cultural style, thus enabling them to circumvent some of the restrictions of class and economic status.

Two further images, forming a paired advertisement, play on similar notions. Both are close-ups of men's faces, one black and one white. Together, they suggest a message that is at once subjective and "in your face." The visuals in the ads depend for their effect on the verbal text that accompanies each image, making the meaning of the paired images explicit and, again, distinctly in your face. The text in the first ad (see Figure 9.3) reads:

I HATE BEING BLACK. If it means some people think that they know my criminal record. My rhythm. My level of education. Or the role affirmative action has played in my career. I'm not someone else's black. I'm my own. And I LOVE BEING BLACK.

Figure 9.3 Hate being black.

The second text (see Figure 9.4) reads:

> I HATE BEING WHITE. If it means some people think that I'm not a real South African. That I'm racist. Privileged. Paranoid. Or Baas. I'm not someone else's white. I'm my own. And I LOVE BEING WHITE.

Taken together, these ads suggest an imperative that is both antiracist ("I hate being black"; "I hate being white") and pro-race ("I love being black"; "I

Figure 9.4 Hate being white.

love being black"). The message they project is that the fact of being white or black becomes banal, that older meanings can be erased or evacuated in order to be able to inscribe onto the words "black" and "white" whatever meanings one wishes. Yet in the ads themselves, the racial habitus remains—at the same time as, socially, culturally and politically speaking, there are now more possibilities for entering new racial spaces. Although these ads appear to rely on the texts for their impact (as I first suggested above)—to domesticate the visual, as it were—one could also note that a visual medium itself is being used here to critique conventional notions of the image, to show the extent to which we rely on the verbal to narrate and explicate the visual.[25] Thus, the ads stage a fascinating engagement with the nature of contemporary visuality.

As I remarked above, all of the ads aim to work towards what one could tentatively term "post-racial" configurations, while also revealing the complexity of this task. The difficulty of it all is underscored by a striking feature of the ads: They can simultaneously be seen to move beyond and to reconfirm the power of race in the contemporary public sphere of the city. A fine line is involved. The ads attempt to "soften" race and class differences by invoking the powerful notion of style and in particular self-stylization. Working with the idea that "everyone" wants to be stylish—to wear good shoes, for example—the ads undercut a more "antagonistic" reading of race and class difference. As we have seen, they rely for their effect on citation or quotation of historical, political context. Simultaneously, they tap into deeper issues at stake relating to the psychic life of things. That is, they tap into the place things occupy in a given historical moment, what desires they organize, what fantasies they provoke, via what epistemologies they are assigned meaning—or, as Bill Brown (2003) puts it, how they represent us, comfort us, help us, change us (p. 12). The psychic life of things activates deep impulses of desire which are commonly shared beyond race: it is these that the ads seek to draw out, rather than relying on less sophisticated technologies of race and class. The shift is made from a form of crude governmentality so characteristic of the apartheid period to a different sort of social potency, which displaces the terms of recognition. Earlier in this essay I considered some of the limits of a theory of "the gap." What these ads return us to is not only the gap of the social, which middle-class commodity cultures rely on in the very moment of aiming to bridge the gap of race, but also how the gap (of desire) is continuously reconstituted at the heart of the commodity. For, although the commodity seems to eliminate the gap, it must constantly reopen it in order to propel new desires to sell itself.

Finally, it is worth considering the ads I have discussed above in relation to the history of consumerism and the production of the modern subject. In relation to the first, we might reflect on a long history of denial of Africans as consumers—either through their portrayal as eternally rural or as being objects of charity—that is, as receiving commodities rather than by purchasing them as modern subjects. Green and Lascaris (1988) show that early advertising in

South Africa was aimed at the white settler. In the inter-war years, there was a growing American presence in the South African economy rather than growing black participation in the market. In the 1930s, ads were aimed not at the black consumer but at the "black specifier" (the person who decides what is to be bought [for his white employer]). Also in the 1930s, black job-seekers began to advertise themselves ("capable, clean houseboy, very quick and obliging, honest," read one ad in 1937). The latter implied an acceptance of race classification but also revealed new references to education. By 1957, a personal ad in *The Star* read, "Situation wanted: African undergraduate seeks position as clerk, general office work." By the late 1950s, the affordable transistor radio came to South Africa—and more and more black people made it a priority purchase. At this time, too, print media emerged aimed specifically at black readers (*Drum* magazine in 1951, *Bona* in 1956). Until the 1970s, Green and Lascaris observe, a schizophrenic marketing scene was in place in relation to black viewers, based on uncertainty as to whether (1) the black consumer would respond best to ads in black media, featuring black faces and black situations, with a message which had particular relevance for a black consumer (the assumption until then), or (2) an ad aimed at an ostensibly white audience would have such "aspirational pull" that black consumers would be irresistibly drawn into the target market (p. 41). It was only in the late 1970s/early 1980s that marketers started to look at similarities between race groups rather than concentrating on the characteristics which divided them—with Brazil rather than the United States and Europe as their case study and reference point. It was then that the crossover market emerged with a vengeance, and a system of marketing bands no longer based on race (though still revealing, in Green and Lascaris' terms, the realities of being black, white, and brown in South Africa today).

Consumerism is frequently equated with the production of the modern subject—an equal and modular citizen brought into being through the possession of mass-produced goods. What seems distinctive about postapartheid South African consumerism (though its current crossover appeal could be seen to have taken root by the late 1980s) is that it seeks to recoup the modernist moment described above but to do so through prevailing postmodern technologies—and within an active cultural project of desegregation. Advertising, such as examples I have looked at above, emerges, then, as an attempt to give content to modernist subjectivity and to engage with ideas about citizenship—and South Africa's future.[26]

Conclusion

In the first part of this chapter I showed that a study of Y Culture reveals the preoccupations of increasingly middle-class young black people in Johannesburg and the intricacy of their modes of self-making. The city itself becomes the engine for this self-stylizing. I have argued that the emergence of new stylizations of the self, embedded in cultures of the body, represents one of the most decisive shifts of the postapartheid era. Integral to this shift, I have sought to show as well, the use of a range of cultural texts, which, reframed within crossover media forms, become elements—accessories—in an aestheticization of the self.

I argued that a notion of the "gap" remains central in cultural theory, while also testing its limits and the notion of translatability on which it relies, and vice versa. Increasingly, I suggested, what is needed is a theory of the circulation of forms, one which necessarily draws on technological analogies. Despite this, I observed how consumer cultures (which draw on youth cultures such as Y/Loxion Kulcha) reopen the gap of desire. Thus, we need a cultural theory of contemporary forms which takes the surfaces of form more seriously as an analytic construct, registers the limits of the gap, and simultaneously is alert to its continual reopening as cultural forms and consumerism draw closer and closer together.

In the second half of the chapter, I considered ways in which a series of advertisements take up aspects of Y Culture's increasing remixing of race, and attempted more explicitly to reconfigure race along the lines of the market. The market, here, comes to the fore as a powerful vector for calming racial passions in a setting characterized by the emergence of a politically empowered black middle class and the presence of a substantial white minority that holds considerable economic power and cultural clout. The market becomes an important place for projecting racial conviviality and therefore a sphere in which the idea of living together is experimented with. As an earlier discourse of "nonracialism" has increasingly shown its limits, the market begins to project ideas of race which rework that earlier discourse.[27] Now, new work needs to be done on the intersection of cultures of consumption and poverty in South Africa. There, no doubt, the "gap" will prove more complex, more treacherous, and, potentially, more productive still.

Acknowledgments

Earlier versions of this chapter have appeared as follows:

Liberté de Style. Cultures de Consommation chez les Jeunes de Johannesburg in *Politique Africaine* 100, 248–272.

Stylizing the Self in Johannesburg: *The Elusive Metropolis*, edited by Achille Mbembe and Sarah Nuttall, Duke University Press, 2007.

Notes

1 In his book *The Black Atlantic: Modernity and Double Consciousness* (Harvard University Press, 1993), Gilroy introduces the idea of a transatlantic black culture—which he terms the "black Atlantic"—whose practices and ideas transcend both ethnicity and nationality. Black people, he argues, shaped a shared, transnational, diasporic culture, which in turn shaped the history of modernity. He explores this transatlanticism in black music and writing and reveals the shared contours of black and Jewish concepts of diaspora. Although he does not write about them in his book, both Brazil and South Africa partook of, and in turn helped to shape, this "black Atlantic culture."

2 George Makubalo emphasizes the productive force of language in constituting identity. He focuses on the embrace of the resources the urban/township environment affords through code switching between English and varieties that have sprung up in the polyglot townships of Gauteng. Crain Soudien writes about the difficulty of evading the racialized structures in which African students in a formerly Coloured school found themselves. He shows school student identity to be at once a fulfillment and a subversion of apartheid discourse. All of this constitutes the complexity that school students live with and negotiate.

3 Book prospectus for this volume, by Nadine Dolby and Fazal Rizvi.

4 I invoke notions of "citiness" and speak of Johannesburg as a metropolis, here, with a specific purpose in mind. The bulk of what has been written about Johannesburg focuses on issues of urbanization. Seldom is it spoken of as a city, in the sense that Paris, London, or Tokyo are commonly discussed. So, too, one rarely encounters treatments of it as a metropolis. Recent publications, in particular, tend to underplay its identity as a cosmopolitan center. Instead, its "pathologies" are highlighted in a willfully skewed reading that posits it as "the crime capital of the world." This, of course, is not a unique phenomenon: other cities (mostly outside Western Europe and North America) have been treated in this fashion. A case in point is Shanghai, a city long vilified, as Stella Dong (2001) has shown, as "the most pleasure-mad, rapacious, corrupt, strife ridden, licentious, squalid, and decadent city in the world" (p. 1). Still, the situation in Johannesburg's case is particularly striking and requires both attention and redress (see Mbembe and Nuttall, 2004.)

5 Loxion Kulcha began with a collection of hand-knitted beanies (hats) that then grew into urban street-wear, mainly denims, printed T-shirts, and sports shoes. Recent designs include branded overalls and men's suits.

6 The name "Stoned Cherrie" plays on a series of puns and local references. "Stoned" refers in part to the violence of the 1980s in the townships but also to being high on marijuana. "Cherrie" recalls the fruit of the same name but this particular spelling also refers to a slang term, originally from Afrikaans, meaning girl or woman or girlfriend. In 1965, for example, Casey Motsisi, writing in *Drum* magazine, wrote, "I had to invite that most fascinating cherie in this man's town, Sis Sharon with goo goo eyes" (see Motsisi, 1996). Thus, the term Stoned Cherrie contains numerous resonances, including the "retro" term for young township girls of the 1950s and 1960s. It places the girl/woman at the center of its frame of reference but also stands for a general sense of having a good time.

7 I am grateful to Lindsay Bremner for her discussions with me on these points.

8 Private security at the Zone is less apparent than in regular malls around the city. CCTV cameras can sometimes be seen but in general there are few security guards, and the outdoor precincts are not secured as such.

9 I am grateful to Isabel Hofmeyr for our discussions on this point.

10 For example, one set of T-shirts is emblazoned with the word "Sharpeville!" This is a reference to, but also plays on the colloquialism, "sharp!" which means "cool." It suggest that Jozi is a city with a past (a political struggle) but also a cool place to be.

11 Dolby (2000) argues that taste serves as "one of the anchors of race's re-articulation" but that it can also be "flimsy, changing, and unstable" (p. 13). She shows how commodities are plucked by school-going youth in Durban from global circulation and given a specific racial life. Taste, she argues, becomes part of a collective, structural way for students to imagine and produce race (p. 14).

12 A *pantsula* is a young urban person (usually a black man) whose attitudes and behavior, especially his speech and dress, are of the most popular current fashion. The term is sometimes applied retrospectively to *tsotsis* (gangsters) of the 1950s who dressed in expensive clothing, particularly trousers with turn-ups, fine shoes, and a felt hat. More recently, a diversity of urban slang and sartorial styles has emerged.

13 Steve Biko was born in 1946 in King Williamstown, went to medical school in Natal, and was cofounder and first president of the all-black South African Students Organisation (SASO). Until then, the struggle against apartheid had been "nonracial," but Biko asserted that black people had been psychologically affected by white racism, had internalized a sense of racial inferiority, and therefore that they needed to organize politically as a separate, black group. Biko's aim was to raise "black consciousness" in South Africa. He was banned in 1973 and assassinated in detention by apartheid police in 1977. His political and personal legacy lives on, despite South Africa's negotiated transition to democracy in 1994.

14 www.urbandictionry.com defines "miss-thang" as "a person who thinks they are, are, like so totally, like better than, like, you know everyone else, like." In other words, a woman who thinks she's way too cool. "Brother-man" would seem to speak for itself. "Jozi" is an increasingly popular term used by young residents of Johannesburg, referring not only to the city itself but to its surrounding townships, including Soweto and Alexandra.

15 "Translatability" emerges from the rise in the last decade or so of "translation studies." The latter focuses on such issues as how the translation is connected to the "foreign tex"; the relative autonomy of the translated text—and thus the impossibility of translation, as it is really a new text which is created; how the effects of translation are social and have been harnessed to cultural, economic, and political agendas, including colonial projects and the production of national literatures. Translation studies is beset by arguments between those who see language as hermeneutic and interpretative, opening up the gaps of meaning, and those who see it as communicative and instrumental, which seek equivalence with the original text. In sum, an analytics of the "gap" is at the heart of this work (see Venuti, 2000).

16 "Zol" refers to a hand-rolled marijuana cigarette.

17 Dorothy Masuka (1935–) is a famous singer in Southern Africa who sang with the African Ink Spots and later with Miriam Makeba. She sang songs of political resistance which were banned in apartheid South Africa. She still sometimes performs in different parts of the world.

18 The way postapartheid youth engage with the world has been shaped by often violent histories of international connection (through migration from elsewhere in Africa and the diffusion of British and American culture) and by the fact of apartheid South Africa's international isolation (as the figure of the grotesque in the colonial historical narrative and the international sanctions and boycotts that cut it off from the rest of the African continent).

19 In the April–May issue, the editors write: "Our relationship with black Americans is only by virtue of us all being African descendants. The reality is that their true ancestors, the slaves that crossed the ocean in the dungeons of those ships, were taken from the West Coast of the continent. We aren't preaching any anti-African-American theories. As much as we appreciate the music, there really is no need to patronize us" (p. 52). Other instances in the magazine reveal that black South Africans turn to the apartheid struggle, and explicitly not to slavery, in the making of black identity. For a longer discussion of this, see Nuttall (2004).

20 YMag was conceived by the YIRED publishers as a counterpart to SL magazine (SL stands for "student life"), which targets largely white but also crossover youth audiences. The intention was to overcome the dominant industry model, in which youth magazines targeted limited "readership ghettoes" in order to attract specialized advertising. The relationship between the two titles was initially conceived as a move toward establishing the first multiracial youth-oriented product to succeed in South Africa. Y and SL share irony and parody as dominant rhetorical modes as well as crossover reviewing styles and the accessorization of media forms within a broader process of self-stylization. For a discussion of this see Nuttall (2004).

21 Cultural texts—books, for example—become forms of quotation: book reviews attest to the constant dismembering of the book, harnessed to specific textual genres as readers, reviewers, and magazine publics exercise the capacity to choose and discard: The book loses its supposed autonomy, its power as a self-contained artifact; there is no book in and of itself but only a textual fragment in the technological constitution of the self. For a more detailed analysis see Nuttall (2004).

22 This is a term one has to use with caution. I do so here to signal that while South Africa in general is not a "post-racial" society, aspects of its culture are experimenting with spaces one could tentatively refer to in this way, in that the imperative, driven increasingly by what is patently a cross-racial market for goods, is that race no longer signifies as it did before, and that class, based on money, increasingly structures certain kinds of social relations. This is not to say that race doesn't—and won't in future—reassert itself in unexpected ways.

23 It is fascinating to compare these ads with those discussed by Bertelsen (1998) that appeared in the years of the mid-1990s, immediately after political transition, as a measure of how much has changed in the public discourse of nation-building and identity. An ad for shoes is accompanied by the text: "When a new nation stands on its feet… ," whereas an ad for milk contains the text, "Why cry over split milk, when we can build a healthy nation?" For a detailed analysis, see Bertelsen's full text.

24 Telephone interview with K-Swiss manager, April 2005.

25 I am grateful to Dilip Gaonkar and Ackbar Abbas for their comments along these lines at a Summer Institute on Media Cultures, Everyday Life, and Cultures of Consumption held at Hong Kong University (Hong Kong, June 2005).

26 I am very grateful to Isabel Hofmeyr for her discussion of these ideas with me.

27 Nonracialism, a term used widely during the antiapartheid struggle, and intended to signify the idea of a society freed from the credo of race, had faded from public political discourse in the 1990s, as the politics of black empowerment have moved center stage and have played an important role in shifting inherited institutional power structures. This has occurred at the same time as many more choices have become available to people in terms of racial identification, especially in metropolitan centers and especially in the sphere of culture.

References

Bertelsen, E. 1998. Ads and amnesia: Black advertising in the new South Africa. In *Negotiating the Past: The Making of Memory in South Africa*, ed. S. Nuttall and C. Coetzee. Cape Town: Oxford University Press.

Bogatsu, M. 2003. Loxion kulcha: Cultural hybridism and appropriation in contemporary black youth popular culture. Unpublished honours research paper. Johannesburg: University of the Witwatersrand.

Brown, B. 2003. *A Sense of Things: The Object Matter of American Literature*. Chicago: University of Chicago Press.

Burke, T. 1996. *Lifebuoy Men, Lux Women: Commodification, Consumption and Cleanliness in Modern Zimbabwe*. Durham: Duke University Press.

Butler, J. 1993. *Bodies That Matter: On the Discursive Limits of 'Sex'*. New York: Routledge.

Butler, J. 1999. *Gender Trouble: Feminism and the Subversion of Identity*. New York: Routledge.

Campbell, R. 1999. Review of *Thievery Corporation*. *SL*, February, 105.

Chakrabarty, D. n.d. *Historical Difference and the Logic of Capital: Towards a Different Marxism*. Unpublished manuscript (cited in Mazzerella, 2003).

Comaroff, J., and J. Comaroff. 2001. Millennial capitalism: First thoughts on a second coming. In *Millennial Capitalism and the Culture of Neo Liberalism*, ed. J. Comaroff and J. Comaroff, Durham: Duke University Press.

Davis, A. 2000. Review of *Magnum Chic* by Harper Engler. *Ymag* November, 130.

Dolby, N. 1999. Youth and the global popular: The politics and practices of race in South Africa. *European Journal of Cultural Studies* 2(3), 291–310.

Dolby, N. 2000. The shifting ground of race: The role of taste in youth's production of identities. *Race, Ethnicity and Education* 3(1), 7–23.

Dong, S. 2001. *Shanghai: The Rise and Fall of a Decadent City.* New York: Perennial.

Farber, T. 2002. Loaded with labels: The meanings of clothing amongst urban black youth in Rosebank, Johannesburg. MA thesis, Johannesburg: University of the Witwatersrand.

Frith, S. 1996. Music and identity. In *Questions of Cultural Identity*, ed. S. Hall and P. duGay, 108–127. London: Sage.

Foucault, M. 2001. *The Hermeneutics of the Subject.* Paris: Gallimard.

Gaonkar, D., and E. Povinelli. 2003. Technologies of public forms: Circulation, transfiguration, recognition. *Public Culture* 15, 385–397.

Gilroy, P. 1993. *The Black Atlantic: Modernity and Double Consciousness.* Cambridge, MA: Harvard University Press.

Gilroy, P. 2000. *Between Camps: Nations, Cultures and the Allure of Race.* London: Penguin.

Green, N., and R. Lascaris, 1988. *Third World Destiny: Recognizing and Seizing the Opportunities Offered by a Changing South Africa.* Tafelberg: Humand and Rousseau.

Gule, P. 2000. Review of *Yesterday I Cried* by Iyanla Vazant. *Ymag* October, 89.

Klandermans, B., M. Roefs, and J. Olivier. 2001. *The State of the People: Citizens, Civil Society and Governance in South Africa 1994–2000.* Pretoria: Human Sciences Research Council.

Makubalo, G. 2006. "I don't know…it contradicts": Identity formation and the use of English by high school learners in a desegregated school space. Presentation to SANPAD symposium, University of the Witwatersrand, January.

Masemola, T. 2000. Dlala Mapantsula. *Ymag* June–July, 47.

Mazarella, W. 2003. *Shovelling Smoke: Advertising and Globalization in Contemporary India.* Durham, and London: Duke University Press.

Mbembe, A. 2002. On the power of the false. *Public Culture* 14, 629–641.

Mbembe, A., N. Dlamini, and G. Khunou. 2004. Soweto now. *Public Culture* 16(3), 499–506.

Mbembe, A., and S. Nuttall. 2007. 'Afropolis.' Introduction to Johannesburg—The elusive metropolis. In *Johannesburg: The Elusive Metropolis*, ed. A. Mbembe and S. Nuttall. Durham, NC: Duke University Press.

McGregor, L. 2005. *Khabzela.* Johannesburg: Jacana Books.

McKinney, C. 2005. Language, identity and (subverting) assimilation in a South African desegregated suburban school. Unpublished paper.

McKinney, C. 2006. Talking "white," talking "black": "Race" and language practices of South African youth in desegregated schools. Paper presented at SANPAD symposium, University of the Witwatersrand, January.

Mhlongo, N. 2004. *Dog Eat Dog.* Cape Town: Kwela.

Morrow, W. 1998. Multicultural education in South Africa. In *Vision and Reality: Changing Education and Training in South Africa*, ed. W. Morrow and K. King. Cape Town: University of Cape Town Press.

Motsemme, N. 2002. YFreedom—Nthabiseng on blackness in post-apartheid South Africa. *WISER in Brief,* 11(2), 7.

Motsisi, C. 1996. *Dictionary of South African English on Historical Principles,* p. 37. Oxford, U.K.: Oxford University Press.

Mpe, P. 2000. *Welcome to Our Hillbrow.* Pietermaritzburg: University of Natal Press.

Mstali, B., T. Masemola, and T. Gule. 2000. Manga-Manga, *Ymag* June–July, 19.

Nappy Head. 1998. Into yam, bongo maffin. *Ymag* October–November, 9.

Nkosi, L. 1983. *Home and Exile and Other Selections.* London: Longman.

Nuttall, S. 2004. Stylizing the self: The Y generation in Rosebank, Johannesburg. *Public Culture,* 16(3), 431–452.

Povinelli, E. 2001. Consuming geist: Popontology and the spirit of capital in indigenoud Australia. In *Millennial Captialism and the Culture of Neo-Liberalism,* ed. J. Comaroff and J. Comaroff, Durham, NC: Duke University Press.

Soudien, C. 1998. "We know why we're here": The experience of African children in a 'coloured' school in Cape Town, South Africa. *Race, Ethnicity and Education* 1(1), 7–29.

Soudien, C. 2003. Routes to adulthood: Becoming a young adult in the new South Africa. *IDS Bulletin* 34(1), 63–71.

Soudien, C. 2004. "Constituting the class": An analysis of the process of "integration" in South African schools. In *Changing Class: Education and Social Change in Post-Apartheid South Africa,* ed. L. Chisholm, 89–114. London: Zed Books.

Soudien, C., and Y. Sayed. 2003. Integrating South African schools? Some preliminary findings. *IDS Bulletin* 34(1), 29–42.

Trend Youth. 2005. University of Cape Town Unilever Institute of Strategic Marketing, in partnership with the youth marketing consultancies Youth Dynamix and Instant Grass.

Venuti, L. 2000. *The Translation Studies Reader.* London: Routledge.

Watts, M. 2005. Baudelaire over Berea, Simmel over Sandton? *Public Culture* 17(1), 181–192.

10

Identities for Neoliberal Times
Constructing Enterprising Selves in an American Suburb

PETER DEMERATH AND JILL LYNCH

"The business of America is business."

—Calvin Coolidge, 1925

"It's all to do with self-control."

—Student poem, "Dilapidation," 2003 Wilton
High School literary magazine

Introduction

Neoliberalism has been defined as the dramatic expansion of the free market and according to Basil Bernstein, "market relevance" has become its key orienting criterion (1996, p. 86). Cindi Katz and her colleagues have described the formation of the "neoliberal subject" as characterized by "the devolution of more and more choice to a seemingly ever more autonomous individual who must rationally calculate the benefits and costs of all aspects of life" (Mitchell, Marston, and Katz, 2003, pp. 417–418).[1] More specifically, Michael Apple recently argued that neoliberalism demands, "the constant production of evidence that one is in fact making an enterprise of oneself" (2001, p. 416), and can demonstrate what the biological anthropologist Emily Martin refers to as "earnable competence" (2000, p. 140). Although social scientists achieve a deeper understanding of the drivers and effects of neoliberalism and its attendant "enterprise culture" (Olssen, 1996; Rose, 1992; Torres, 2002), the processes through which "neoliberal subjects" are formed, and the range of identity characteristics they take on, remain unclear. Accordingly, this project set out to understand how youth in a center of "fast capitalism" see the future, and how they are equipping themselves for it.

Drawing on data from a longitudinal ethnographic study, the chapter makes the argument that changes in family structure and parenting style, intensified engagements with electronic and commodity culture, and student-centered pedagogies have ceded young people in this U.S. suburban community significant power to direct their own socialization and education. These trends have fostered the production of an authoritative subjectivity in many of these youth that underlies a habitual disposition to seek to control social experience, including education, in part to allay their anxieties over uncertain futures. A subset of students had adopted a specific assemblage of identity characteristics and practices that were oriented toward self-advancement, and, indeed, enterprise. These students had extremely strong agentic beliefs, deeply held attachments to individual success, and highly specific aspirations. They made habitual judgments about what forms of knowledge and cultural capital were needed for them to successfully compete, and they struggled to habituate to stress and fatigue. In this sense, the chapter describes situated instances of what Sherry Ortner calls "psychological capital," which underlies "…the things that make for different social effectiveness" (2002, p. 13). As such, the chapter interprets these models of selfhood as emerging techniques of self-discipline that are adapted to the neoliberal order (Foucault, 1983, 1988).

Contemporary Contexts of Suburban Youth Socialization

Many writers have commented that the most important characteristic of U.S. suburban adolescents today is their "aloneness" (Csikszentmihalyi and Schneider, 2000; Hersch, 1998; Nichols and Good, 2004): Growing numbers of youth are seemingly being left to socialize themselves—and each other. In addition, Eckert has argued that U.S. middle-class family ideology stresses participation of the child in decision-making, as well as parent–child negotiation, which accords the child a certain level of adult status and gives them experience in dealing with adults on a more equal footing (1989, p. 116). The cultural psychologist William Damon has more forcefully asserted that a lopsidedly child-centered ethic has led parents to routinely defer to the views of their children, treat their sensibilities gingerly, and, in sum, parent them in an "overindulgent" manner (1995, p. 19). (See also Buckingham, 2000; Milner, 2004.)

Other researchers point out that young peoples' engagements with popular culture and markets have intensified across the globe, affording them greater access to areas of "adult" life from which they had traditionally been excluded, and more choices regarding how they spend their time, labor, and money (Canclini, 2001; Nespor, 1997; Schneider and Stevenson, 1999).

Many writers are observing that culture today is shaped more by the market than by the state and that identities themselves are powerfully shaped by consumption (Dolby, 2003; Milner, 2004).

Children are becoming one of the most prized targets of "niche marketing" (Buckingham, 2000, p. 147), and, indeed, Willis has asserted that it is the market that "supplies the most attractive and useable symbolic and expressive forms that are now consumed by teenagers and early adults" (2003, p. 403). Spring (2003) and Milner (2004) both point out that schools themselves are now consumer sites given over to the training of consumer-citizens, where the promise of increased levels of schooling is not happiness but greater consumption.

Self-Formation in Modern and Neoliberal Times

The chapter's conceptual framework derives largely from cultural historical activity theory, which regards young people as cultural innovators (McRobbie, 1994) whose identities emerge from their negotiation and "orchestration" of competing discourses and social structures (Holland, Lachicotte, Skinner, and Cain, 1998). Such an approach can show, as Paul Willis has recently written, how social agents "see," respond to, and embody the "structured world of power," and how, both resisting it and reproducing it, are "achieved in and through the radical unprefigurability of culture" (2004, p. 170).[2]

Scholarship on social change and identity suggests that under conditions of Western modernity, as affiliations beyond the family grow, individuality grows such that "opportunities for individualization proliferate into infinity" (Simmel, 1964, p. 151). Giddens has observed that under such conditions the self faces a "puzzling diversity of options and possibilities" and thus becomes a "reflexive project" characterized by incessant efforts to exert control (1991, p. 3). Moreover, given the unprecedented pace, scope, and profoundness of social change, Giddens holds that modernity is a risk culture: individuals must think in terms of risk and risk assessment more or less constantly, as, for example, they attempt to "colonise the future for themselves as an intrinsic part of their life-planning" (1991, p. 125). The making of the subject (Foucault, 1972, 1983, 1988) is central to Giddens' formulation, particularly how power, as expressed through the structures and discourses of modernity, subjects the body to the "internal discipline of self-control" and how "bodily discipline is intrinsic to the competent social agent" (1991, p. 57). We draw on two additional formulations of the relationship between identity and power: Bourdieu's work on the making of the contemporary habitus (1977) and what Foucault refers to as "techniques of the self," practices through which subjects constitute themselves "that are basically related to power and knowledge" (1988, p. 10).

These models of self are certainly linked to the Western notion of the "free-standing, self-contained individual" (Strathern, 1991), which contrasts greatly with the ways in which anthropologists have characterized the social bases of personhood in much of the developing world. The youth identities described in this chapter, of course, also reflect distinctly American cultural attachments to individual growth and development. Indeed, over 40 years ago, the American sociologist Jules Henry wrote, "ours is a driven culture," and furthermore, that the "ideal American is an inexhaustible reservoir of drive and personality resources; one who, while not using up what he has, yet exploits his personality to the best advantage" (1963, p. 16).

Setting and Methods

The research reported here is based on a study of student class culture conducted between 1999–2003 in Wilton, an affluent "historic" suburb of a large midwestern city that over the last decade has become significantly more diverse in terms of its socioeconomic makeup. There are pervasive and pronounced community expectations for success, which we have understood in the context of a local trope known as "The Wilton Way." These expectations, the local culture of competition, and instrumental strategies students and parents adopt to get ahead are detailed in another paper (Demerath, Davidson, Lynch, Milner, and Peters, 2006). We mention them here to be clear that the construction of these enterprising selves occurs in a middle/upper-middle class community with deep-seated norms concerning individual advancement and social mobility. At the time of the study, Wilton High School (WMS) itself was well-resourced and in 1998 was nationally recognized as a "Blue Ribbon High School." During the 2000–2001 school year, the school had 1649 students, of whom 86% were classified European American, 10% Asian American, and 4% African American; 88.2% of the graduates of the class of 1999 planned to attend a college, university, or technical school. The school offered a series of "enriched" and AP (advanced placement) classes, and an extracurriculum that included a wide variety of varsity athletic programs, clubs, and societies and award-winning programs in music, theater, and the arts. There was a cappuccino machine in the cafeteria by the check-out counter.

The project was designed as a four-year ethnographic study in order to describe the experiences and perceptions of a diverse group of students as they moved through high school (the school had two principals during this period, both of whom have been given pseudonyms for the purposes of this chapter: Principal Callahan, during the 1999–2000 school year, and Principal Trent, from 2000–2003). Data were collected by a diverse research team through participant observation and informal interviews in classrooms and other relevant in- and out-of-school settings; over 60 tape-recorded interviews with teachers, administrators, and students, including a diverse sample of eight high- and low-achieving male and female students from the class of 2003 and their parents; and consultation of school documents and popular culture discourses and social narratives on youth, parenting, and schooling.[3] In addition, a grounded survey consisting of 44 forced-choice and 16 open-ended items was administered to 327 female and 278 male students in March, 2002.

The Production of Authoritative Subjectivity: Individuated Adaptations in Isolated, Highly Mediated, and Competitive Contexts

Data from the study as a whole suggest that these enterprising identities found among the more high achieving students have their basis in an authoritative subjectivity that was more widely distributed among the entire student population. We describe the production of this authoritative subjectivity in detail elsewhere (Demerath and Lynch, 2006), and given space limitations, here provide a summary. Briefly, we have come to think of various salient points of the networks of youth socialization as a complex set of feedback loops, which constantly shape, and are shaped by, youth (see Nespor, 1997). This last point is important, as it reflects newer insights concerning the mutually constitutive nature of cultural complexity (Buckingham, 2000; Hannerz, 1997; Heath, 1999). Project data suggests that parents, electronic and commodity culture, and school policies and pedagogies in this context all share a tendency to attribute great authority to young people, and to defer to their views and sensibilities. It is in this sense that these socializing influences seemed to be producing and reifying an authoritative subjectivity in these youth oriented around the self as arbiter of experience and judgment. Importantly, in following Foucault's observation of how power works through, and not against, subjectivity (see Rose, 1992), we regard this authoritative subjectivity as seemingly a necessary precondition for the development of these identities for control and success, to which we turn next.

Techniques of Self-Advancement in Market-Driven Contexts: Identities for Control and Success

Translocal and Local Cultures of Competition

As Varenne and McDermott noted in their comparative study of suburban schools (1998), students and parents in Wilton generally evinced a keen awareness of being in competition with others. For example, when we asked students in an AP U.S. history class "What drives you to work so hard?" A sophomore Asian-American student responded, "It's harder for our generation to live the same lifestyle as our parents do." A mother of an enriched European-American student spoke of "wanting her to stay with the flow, caught up with the pack, even with all those other kids." Parental bragging about children's accomplishments was commonplace, as was posting AP test results on refrigerators and discussing the colleges to which children were applying and gaining admission. One of the African-American male focal students, intent on winning a college scholarship, was already calculating his odds of being able to do so with a 3.8 grade point average in his freshman year.

Discourses of Excellence and Success

Not surprisingly, discourses of "excellence" and "success" imbued the community and school. The district motto was "Where Excellence Is a Tradition," and a sign affixed to the high school itself noted that it was in one of the state's "Best Communities." The capacious commons area of the school had flags from nations around the world draped from the ceiling, with the school's blue ribbon banner featured prominently in the center of them. Also in the commons was an array of what we have come to call "technologies of recognition": The WHS Hall of Fame; framed photos of National Merit finalists; Students of the Month;

members of the Socratic Society; recipients of the Junior Book Awards, and farther on toward the athletic wing, teams and individual athletes with notable accomplishments. Throughout the school's hallways, framed artwork adorned the walls, and classical music emanated quietly from speakers. When Principal Callahan welcomed the class of 2003 to WHS, she concluded her remarks by saying, "Welcome to an outstanding national treasure." The important point here is that these discourses also functioned as feedback mechanisms in terms of contributing to the construction of these students as adult-successes-to-be.

The Press for Control and Underlying Assumptions about the Self: Causal Agency

One of the striking characteristics of the high-achieving students in the study was the extent to which they saw themselves as ongoing projects, and accordingly, attempted to exert great control over their socialization and education. These students held strong beliefs concerning the role of effort in determining life-chances and the role of the self in developing confidence. They were extremely effective self-advocates and had precociously circumscribed aspirations.

At the same opening assembly mentioned above, the class of 2003 was told by the current senior class president, "the staff works very hard to set you up for success .... Life is 10% what happens to you and 90% how you react to it." Three years later at a talk sponsored by Bears, Inc., the official parent booster organization, a former local college football star told the students, "It's nice to have others, but it depends on *you*, because everything in the world depends on *you*." One survey item asked students to rank the following influences in determining a person's future: individual effort, parents' background, social support, and quality of education; 71.5% of students ranked effort at the top. Indeed, in a lively discussion on the origins and perpetuation of social inequality in an enriched social studies class, two European-American female students made the following comments:

Tiffany: Our parents have worked very hard to send us to good schools, but some of them haven't tried as hard.
Susan : Some of them don't have the will[4] (field notes, 11/30/99).

Confidence and Self-Advocacy

When Principal Trent took over at WHS in the fall of 2000 she expressed surprise at "how empowered the students were." Indeed, 75.5% of surveyed pupils described themselves as a "confident student," and when asked, "Where does this confidence come from?" a number of students referenced themselves (several simply said, "Me," or "Myself"):

This confidence comes from me. I don't care what anybody else's opinion about me is, except for mine. (9th-grade European-American male)

My confidence comes from the satisfaction I get from getting good grades. (9th-grade European-American male)
It comes from my drive to be successful and get what I want. (11th-grade European-American female)

Importantly, of the minority of students who reported not being confident, many of them reported deleterious effects of the in-school culture of competition:

I feel that I have to be the perfect student, straight As, the perfect weight (110 pounds), the perfect size (6), and the perfect fashion googoo.[5] (9th-grade European-American female)

This confidence seemed to partly underlie students' habitual attempts to exert control over their educational experiences, including profligate schedule changes; routine questioning of their teachers' authority; critiquing how instruction was delivered; judging the utility of what they were learning; and attempting to personalize relationships with their teachers (see Demerath, 2006). A senior administrative assistant commented, "These kids today aren't afraid to advocate for themselves."

Colonizing the Future: Precocious Aspiration Circumscription

Aspirations was another area in which the compulsion to exert control was apparent. Beginning as freshmen, the high-achieving students in the study had strikingly precise ideas about what they wanted their future lives to be like—and work, jobs, and career achievement were certainly central. As a 9th-grader, one female student said:

Some of us, like, think really far ahead. You know, like, if I don't do this assignment, then my grades are going to go down and my GPA's going to fall, and then I can't get into the college I want, or whatever (student interview, December 14, 1999).

Throughout the study, college-bound students referred to their majors in the present, rather than the future tense—even as underclassmen. In the "Stellar Senior" segment on the WHS News student-run television program, a typical question was, "Where do you plan to go to college and what is your major?"

When asked on the survey what they wanted their "future life to be like," most students responded with great specificity, both in terms of their expectations, and their strategies for realizing them:

"I want to be an architect or fashion designer so I will do whatever is necessary." (10th-grade European-American female)
"Become a pilot, save up some money, open a microbrewery." (11th-grade European-American male)

It seems reasonable to conclude that these students' impulses to predict, foretell, and control derive in part from their anxieties about living in a future characterized by uncertainty, declining social support, and acute competition. Such total efforts could produce somewhat dizzying effects at times, such as the following statement from one of the high-achieving European-American focal students in an interview during her sophomore year: "I am a lot more focused on what I need to be focused on and I need to be focused on that."

Attachments to Success

Several students said openly in interviews that everyone's goal was to be "the best," and that they themselves wanted to be "the best" or "the top." What student voices from the study illuminated, though, was the depth of these attachments to personal success. In an English class one of us observed several student speeches that dealt with "success" in some way. Most notably, a wrestler brought in a framed Hallmark-type card with a printed message of support about success and learning from failure. He explained that his mother had given it to him in his freshman year when he had first started wrestling on the varsity level and was losing a lot of matches. He began his speech by holding up the framed card and saying, "I love my mom, and I love success, so I love this." Indeed, high-achieving students in Wilton seemed most animated when discussing evaluative criteria or their own accomplishments. These students often gave up their passing time to wait for teachers to grade their tests. When we asked a class of AP U.S. history students how being successful made them feel, an Asian-American junior female student immediately said, "Being successful makes me feel awesome!" (Another, whose older brother was one of the highest-achieving students to graduate from the school, said, "Relieved.")

Self-Conscious Cultivation of Work Ethic

Another central component of these identities for success was the self-conscious development of an extremely strong work ethic. The consensus was that most students worked very hard to get good grades. The motto on the back of the 2000 WHS men's volleyball team's T-shirts was epigrammatic of this belief: "Wilton Men's Volleyball: Learning Success Through Hard Work." Several of the high-achieving "enriched" focal students mentioned staying up until 1:00, 2:00 or even 3:00 in the morning in order to study for tests. David, a high-achieving European-American male focal student said in the spring of his senior year,

> I told myself long ago that you may not be the smartest guy, you may not be the fastest runner, but if you work hard, there's a lot of people who you'll go past [student interview, May 12, 2003].

Work ethics are nothing new, but the degree to which these young people rationalize them and self-consciously cultivate them may be. The deep-seated adoption of this work ethic married to the success orientation seemed to be behind the constant compulsion of the high-achieving students to be, or do, something, "productive." Indeed, when, as a junior, we asked David whether he was able to have time to have fun, he replied, "It depends what month it is.... That's what the summer's for." At one point during that interview with David, we asked him what he had done the night before:

David: I had no homework last night. And so, I mean I just—I don't even know what I did last night. I should have done something productive. I didn't [chuckles], but...

Peter : What do you mean, "something productive"?

David: I should have read a book. I should have worked on my vocabulary for the SATs. I should, you know, I should have done something that's going to help me in the long run. Now, I mean, granted, you know, my brother and I, we went out and played baseball in the back yard, and, you know, shot baskets, and... I guess that's productive, in the sense that I'm building a deep relationship with my brother, but... it's not... not academically or anything like that [student interview, May 24, 2002]

Envisioning the Self in Imagined Markets: Aspiring to Success and Acquiring New Forms of Cultural Capital

Many students articulated aspirations marked by success and affluence, and some expressed particular desires to not have to go through the same class struggles as their parents. A high-achieving African-American student said, "I just don't want to have to start on the bottom like they did and have to work up. I feel like ... they've worked up, so I have to ... start up, and continue from there." High-achieving students frequently used business, and to a less extent, military language to describe their academic challenges and triumphs. This seems to suggest the extent to which they saw education as a high stakes commodity-based venture. Students sometimes referred to their academic work as "product," had a keen eye for where "cheap As" could be had, and if not, "battled back," "reinforced," and closely monitored their course progress until they had an A in "lockdown."

The frequent student judgments of curriculum and instruction reported elsewhere (Demerath, 2006) could also be interpreted as the development of a valuable kind of cultural capital that Bourdieu referred to as *critical discourse.* Bourdieu argued that the process of "becoming critical" was one way in which middle-class children begin to distinguish themselves from others and socialize themselves into class membership (1984). Students also seemed self-consciously aware of developing the sorts of people skills desired as cultural capital in the corporate world. A notable feature of the student culture was the degree to which students from different social locations and groups got along, supported, and even socialized one another in school. Students seemed to value being able to move fluidly between groups, proclaiming with pride that they had different kinds of friends, especially as they moved through the grades. One female European-American student said as a senior, "I've got a lot of connections to a lot of people."

Perhaps more importantly, many of these high-achieving students became highly skilled negotiators, in part due to the leeway offered them in many of their student-centered classrooms. Referred to by Eckert as "adult handling skills" (1989, p. 112) these abilities enabled some students to develop potentially exploitable relationships with other people—including their teachers and counselors. When we asked one high-achieving student how she had managed to negotiate a senior-year schedule of two courses per semester—well below the district minimum of five—so she could work at her job 40 hours per week, she responded:

> You build rapport with people over time, and then you can work things out, you know? You scratch my back and I scratch yours, just like in the business world, you know? [field notes June 5, 2003.]

Indeed, an AP social studies teacher characterized the school culture as a "business culture."

Embodied Costs

Although these students had varying degrees of success in coping with such heavy schedules and expectations, fatigue, and particularly stress were mentioned throughout the study. Several high-achieving students said they were tired all the time, and in fact, in an AP U.S. history class, one student said, "We're tired every day. Ask it on your next survey." Data from the survey at hand indicated that 70.2% of students reported being stressed out "frequently" or "all the time," and that there were important gender differences in this area: Although female students had significantly higher cumulative grade point averages than male students, they were also much more likely to report being "stressed out," either "frequently" (64.9% of females; 45.5% of males) or "all the time" (17.9% of females; 12.3% of males), and to identify their schoolwork as the most important source of stress (48.3% of females; 31.6% of males; $x2 = 44.56$; $p = .0001$). Indeed, one focal student from the study experienced changes in her menstrual cycle that her gynecologist attributed to stress from school, the college application process, and her work schedule. She was prescribed birth control pills to remedy the problem.

Students who reported high levels of stress were more likely than those with low levels of stress to: (1) report that they were "very much" in competition with other students in and outside the school ($\chi^2 = 16.9407$; $p = .0497$); (2), describe themselves as a "confident student" ($\chi^2 = 32.7589$; $p = .0001$); and (3) eat dinner with their family infrequently ($\chi^2 = 82.8074$; $p = .027$). In addition, students who spent less time alone during school days were less likely to report high stress (OR = 0.2784; 95% C.I.: 0.1157, 0.6702; p = .004). Finally, there was some evidence to suggest that students who reported that they "often knew better than their teachers what or how they ought to learn" were more likely to report high levels of stress (OR = 1.991; 95% C.I.: 1.10, 3.61; p = .023). Considered together, then, these data suggest that students that were doing many of the things that were expected to bring them success were likely to experience high levels of stress.

When asked on the survey how they dealt with their stress, response categories that emerged from the data included failing to cope, taking medication (such as antidepressants), crying, and being physically aggressive (a striking number of students had punching bags). Most notable for the purposes of this paper were the responses that alluded to a conscious or unconscious ability to adjust to more or less ever-present levels of stress:

> Stop, breath, recover, continue. [11th-grade European-American male]
> I don't, I just keep going. [12th-grade European-American male]
> I deal with it by playing sports and filling my need for competition because it relaxes my mind. [9th-grade European-American male]

In this vein, as a junior, David expressed impatience with fellow students who complained about being stressed out: "You have to learn to deal with stress. Because stress is going to be a part of your life."

Conclusion

This chapter has described the reflexive identity projects of suburban American youth as they attempt to "colonize" their futures within the neoliberal order. The chapter identified elements of an accelerating competitive individualism in this context that may be understood as the kinds of "psychological capital" necessary for successful enterprise. The first part of the paper argued that the contexts of youth socialization in this community tended to share a tendency to attribute great authority to young people and defer to their views and sensibilities. It was in this sense that they seem to contribute to the production of an authoritative subjectivity in these youth oriented around the self as arbiter of experience and judgment. This subjective stance seemed to be a necessary precondition for the identities for control and advancement found in a subset of higher-achieving students that were described in the main portion of the chapter.

The British social scientist Nikolas Rose recently described the "enterprising self" as follows: "The enterprising self is thus a calculating self, a self that calculates about itself and that works upon itself in order to better itself" (1992, p. 146). The second part of the paper detailed identity constructs involved in the making of such "enterprising selves" in this setting, and underscored those aspects of self-development that occur on affective and subconscious planes.

As such, it related pronounced local expectations for advancement, and the ways in which school-based discourses of "excellence" and "success" seemed to contribute to a subset of self-formation patterns oriented around control and competition. We wish to emphasize that the authoritative dispositions seemed to underlie the unending quest for control that was a central component of these identities for success, and to mention that gender, ethnic, and class differences with regard to the development of these identities are discussed elsewhere (see Demerath, Davidson, Lynch, Milner, and Peters, 2006).

Primary dimensions of these enterprising identities included strong agentic beliefs in students' capacity to influence the kinds of people they are and will become, affective attachments and aspirations to success and affluence, habitual judgments about the instrumental value of various forms of knowledge and cultural capital, and a self-conscious development of a strong work ethic resulting in a habitual proclivity to be "productive." The final, and perhaps most important element of these identities was an ability to habituate to stress and fatigue. In sum, the constellation of identity characteristics described here seem to constitute new techniques of self-discipline that are adapted to the neoliberal order.

Notes

1 See also Katz, 2001.
2 The project has benefitted especially from the diverse optics of the rest of the team: Henry R. Milner, April Peters, and Mario Davidson.
3 Demerath's earlier research on youth identity and culture in Manus, Papua New Guinea (PNG) (1999, 2001, 2003) is used to generate a comparative perspective on the setting at hand that is consistent with the theme of the book. This lens is elaborated in related work on Wilton.
4 Here and elsewhere extensive quotations are identified as having been recorded in field notes or in formal interviews which were tape-recorded. Brackets ([]) mark text that has been inserted for clarification. Three ellipses (...) indicate a pause in the dialogue. Four ellipses indicate that a segment of protocol has been omitted. Italics indicate an emphasis of the speaker.
5 We interpret this student slang as referring to a person who exemplifies impeccable taste in clothing.

References

Apple, M.W. 2001. Comparing neo-liberal projects and inequality in education. *Comparative Education* 37(4), 409–423.

Bernstein, B. 1996. *Pedagogy, Symbolic Control and Identity: Theory, Research, Critique.* Lanham, U.K.: Rowman and Littlefield.

Bourdieu, P. 1977. *Outline of a Theory of Practice.* Cambridge, U.K.: Cambridge University Press.

Buckingham, D. 2000. *After the Death of Childhood: Growing up in the Age of Electronic Media.* Cambridge, U.K.: Polity.

Canclini, N. 2001. *Consumers and Citizens: Globalization and Multicultural Conflicts.* Minneapolis, MN: University of Minnesota Press.

Csikszentmihalyi, M., and B. Schneider. 2000. *Becoming Adult: How Teenagers Prepare for the World of Work.* New York: Basic Books.

Damon, W. 1995. *Greater Expectations: Overcoming the Culture of Indulgence in Our Homes and Schools.* New York: Free Press.

Demerath, P. 1999. The cultural production of educational utility in Pere village, Papua New Guinea. *Comparative Education Review* 43(2), 162–192.

Demerath, P. 2001. The social cost of acting "extra:" Students' moral judgements of self, social relations, and academic success in Papua New Guinea. *American Journal of Education* 108(3), 196–235.

Demerath, P. 2003. Negotiating individualist and collectivist futures: Emerging subjectivities and social forms in Papua New Guinean high schools. *Anthropology and Education Quarterly* 34(2), 136–157.

Demerath, P. 2006. Are student-determined goods good for students? Unseen effects of student identity, policy, and pedagogy in a U.S. suburban high school. Unpublished manuscript, Columbus, OH.

Demerath, P., M. Davidson, J. Lynch, H.R. Milner, and A. Peters. 2006. The "Wilton Way": A middle class logic of self-advancement in an American high school and community. Unpublished manuscript, Columbus, OH.

Demerath, P., and J. Lynch, 2006. The construction of enterprising selves in an American suburb: Identity and subjectivity for neoliberal times. Unpublished manuscript, Columbus, OH.

Dolby, N. 2003. Popular culture and democratic practice. *Harvard Educational Review* 73(3), 258–284.

Eckert, P. 1989. *Jocks and Burnouts: Social Categories and Identity in the High School.* New York: Teachers College Press.

Foucault, M. 1972. *The Archaeology of Knowledge and the Discourse on Language.* Trans. A.M.S. Smith. New York: Pantheon.

Foucault, M. 1983. The subject and power. In *Michel Foucault: Beyond Structuralism and Hermeneutics,* ed. H.L. Dreyfus and P. Rabinow, 2nd ed., 229–252. Chicago: University of Chicago Press.

Foucault, M. 1988. The ethic of care for the self as a practice of freedom. In *The Final Foucault,* ed. J. Bernauer and D. Rasmussen, 1–20. Cambridge, MA: MIT Press.

Giddens, A. 1991. *Modernity and Self-Identity: Self and Society in the Late Modern Age.* Stanford: Stanford University Press.

Hannerz, U. 1997. Borders. *International Social Science Journal* 49(154), 537–548.

Heath, S.B. 1999. Discipline and disciplines in education research. In *Issues in Educational Research: Problems and Possibilities,* ed. E. Condliffe Lagemann and L.S. Shulman, 203–223. San Francisco: Jossey–Bass.

Henry, J. 1963. *Culture against Man.* New York: Vintage.

Hersch, P. 1998. *A Tribe Apart.* New York: Ballantine.

Holland, D., W.J. Lachicotte, D. Skinner, and C. Cain. 1998. *Identity and Agency in Cultural Worlds.* Cambridge, MA: Harvard University Press.

Katz, C. 2001. Vagabond capitalism and the necessity of social reproduction. *Antipode* 33(4), 709–728.

Martin, E. 2000. Flexible bodies: Science and a new culture of health in the U.S. In *Health, Medicine, and Society,* ed. S. Williams, J. Gabe, and M. Calnan, 123–145. London: Routledge.

McRobbie, A. 1994. *Postmodernism and Popular Culture.* London: Routledge.

Milner, M. 2004. *Freaks, Geeks, and Cool Kids: American Teenagers, Schools, and the Culture of Consumption.* New York: Routledge.

Mitchell, K., S.A. Marston, and C. Katz. 2003. Introduction: Life's work: An introduction, review and critique. *Antipode* 35(3), 415–442.

Nespor, J. 1997. *Tangled Up in School: Politics, Space, Bodies, and Signs in the Educational Process.* Mahwah: Lawrence Erlbaum.

Nichols, S., and Good, T. 2004. *America's Teenagers—Myths and Realities: Media Images, Schooling, and the Social Costs of Careless Indifference.* Mahwah: Lawrence Erlbaum.

Olssen, M. 1996. In defence of the welfare state and publicly provided education. *Journal of Education Policy* 11, 337–362.

Ortner, S. 2002. Subjects and capital: A fragment of a documentary ethnography. *Ethnos* 67(1), 9–32.

Rose, N. 1992. Governing the enterprising self. In *The Values of the Enterprise Culture: The Moral Debate,* ed. P. Heelas and P. Morris, 141–164. New York: Routledge.

Sangari, K. 1987. *The Politics of the Possible.* Cultural Critique 7 (Fall), 157–186.

Schneider, B., and D. Stevenson. 1999. *The Ambitious Generation: America's Teenagers, Motivated but Directionless.* New Haven: Yale University Press.

Simmel, G. 1964. *Conflict and the Web of Group Affiliations.* New York: Free Press.

Spring, J. 2003. *Educating the Consumer-Citizen: A History of the Marriage of Schools, Advertising, and Media.* Mahwah, NJ: Lawrence Erlbaum.

Strathern, M. 1991. Partners and consumers: Making relations visible. *New Literary History* 22(3), 581–601.

Torres, C.A. 2002. Globalization, education, and citizenship: Solidarity versus markets? *American Educational Research Journal* 39(2), 363–378.

Varenne, H., and R. McDermott. 1998. *Successful Failure: The School America Builds.* Boulder, CO: Westview.

Willis, P. 2003. Footsoldiers of modernity. *Harvard Educational Review* 73(3), 390–415.

Willis, P. 2004. Twenty five years on: Old books, new times. In *Learning to Labor in New Times,* ed. N. Dolby and G. Dimitriadis, 167–196. New York: RoutledgeFalmer.

11

Disciplining Generation M

*The Paradox of Creating a Local National
Identity in an Era of Global Flows*

AARON KOH

Introduction: The Anxieties of Globalization for Singapore

Singapore takes globalization *seriously*. This is evident from the way in which the city-state continues to mobilize globalization as a "problem-space" (Collier and Ong, 2005) where globalization is heralded to pose more problems for Singapore vis-à-vis its economy and culture. These "problems" are, however, often engineered with "solutions" to augment a "legitimatory ideology" (Brown, 2000, p. 96). In other words, when "solutions" are offered to "problems" facing Singapore, it only reflects positively the managerial skills of the state and further enhances their legitimacy to intervene and rule.

Although the condition of Singapore's economy, whether it is performing or under-performing according to and in response to "global" conditions, is always the center of attention, increasingly cultural managers in Singapore are also watchful over the deleterious effects globalizing forces can have on its culture. By culture, in the context of this chapter, I am referring somewhat narrowly to issues relating to Singapore's national identity and the attendant concerns about Singaporean youths (between the age of 15 to 29) lacking a sense of (cultural) belonging and a national identity.

There is an anxiety that because Singapore has to remain "open" in order to embed in capitalism's presence, its openness will enable the flows of globalization (often castigated as the perilous influence of the "West") to destabilize its national identity, values, and ethos. In other words, globalization, it is surmised, will affect the fragility of its culture. Whether one regards this as a national paranoia or a disguise for the Singaporean government to perpetuate a culture of control, from an analytic point of view, globalization as a phenomenon is associated with a fear of uncertainty and capitalized as a resource (Thrift, 2005) for the government elites to "shape, normalize, and instrumentalize the conduct of institutions and persons in the name of making 'globalization' manageable" (du Gay, 2000, p. 116).

At the level of the economy, for instance, the anxieties of globalization for Singapore have recently led the government to form a high-powered research council to spearhead three niche research areas, namely, biomedical sciences, environmental and water technologies, and interactive and digital media with the overarching aim of using R&D as a driver for economic growth and to enhance Singapore's competitiveness in the long haul (Chang and Loo, 2006). In addition to this, other pro-globalization policies such as the Foreign Talent policy have been put in place to attract expatriates with highly specialized skills to work in Singapore, as it is often argued that there is a shortfall of talent in Singapore and that foreign talent will help "to enlarge (Singapore's) economic pie" (Peh, 2006; see also Koh, 2003). Such is the extent of what technocrats in Singapore would do—what Aihwa Ong (2005, p. 339) would call "neoliberal calculation"—to engineer an "ecology of expertise" where "the value of knowledgeable, risk-taking, and entrepreneurial subjects" will continue to fuel the economic engines of Singapore's economy.

Although the Singapore government appears to be able to "arrest" the anxieties of the vagaries of its economic performance, how then does Singapore manage the "problem-space" of identity politics where mobility in terms of flows of ideas, images, and people, etc. has the transformative effect of destabilizing its national identity? This chapter aims to present how Singapore utilizes its ideological state apparatus, namely, the media and school, to create a crisis construction (read: problem) of a lack of national identity among Singaporean youths and, through a national curriculum implementation called National Education (akin to citizenship education), aims to remediate this lack (read: the solution).

However, I argue in this chapter that in the context of globalization, this cultural experimentation of constructing a national identity and creating a sense of belonging is fraught with ruptures, as a new global youth culture and new communication technologies potentially offer liminal spaces where other sources and expressions of identities are up for grabs. These liminal spaces further allow youths to perform "elective belonging" rather than a sense of belonging bound by the "national" and "local" (Savage, Bagnall, and Longhurst, 2005, p. 29). This reality creates conflict with the official curriculum which it continues to engage in the politics of "fixing" a territorial-bound, local, national identity.

There are four parts to this chapter. I first begin by giving the chapter a contextual understanding of the socioeconomic and historical beginnings of Singapore's economic imperative to "go global." This is followed by a theoretical section mobilizing Stephen Collier and Aihwa Ong's (2005) conceptualization of Deleuze's terms *assemblage, reassemblage* to provide a nuanced understanding of the way in which technocrats in Singapore make globalization work (with the promises, and against the anxieties, of globalization). Next, the chapter presents a few media accounts of the representations of Singaporean youths who are in want of a national identity and sense of belonging. This is followed by a description of the context for implementing National Education (hereafter, NE) so as to understand the ideological project of NE, which aims to remediate the lack of a national identity, and to engage in a politics of fixing a preferred national identity over other identities.

"Go Global": Singapore's Socioeconomic and Historical Beginnings

To understand why globalization matters to Singapore, and why education is instrumental in its nation-building, it is necessary that the chapter begins with a cursory socioeconomic and historical account of Singapore. By any account, Singapore is an "improbable nation" (Lee, 2006); improbable because it is a small country of well over 4.3 million people with no natural resources of its own to draw on for local consumption or export. However, its geographical location as a site of an *entrepôt* port was to be Singapore's advantage and also the beginning of Singapore strategic take to "globalize," although *globalization* was then not a lexicon used in the heyday of the development of Singapore's colonial economy. As an entrepôt port, Singapore was a confluence of vibrant economic activity that drew together the East-West trade between China and India, which later extended into the industrializing countries of the West (Trocki, 2006; see also Ooi and Shaw, 2004). In a sense, "going global" was already a discursive operation in the colonial days of Singapore's economic foundation that later became even more pronounced in the many prescriptive measures of Singapore's economic policies.

Its history also records a failed merger with Malaysia in 1963, motivated by economic reasons as it was thought that Singapore would, in economic terms, benefit from a larger domestic market as a result of the merger. However, because of an unresolved clash of political ideologies Singapore separated from Malaysia to become an independent state in August of 1965 (Lau, 1998). This historical moment has been translated into a discourse of nation-building that celebrates Singapore's strong political will and its tenacity to succeed despite the odds. More importantly, it is also in response to this "crisis" of being jettisoned from a merger that the survival rhetoric has been repeatedly mobilized as the motif in the discourse of Singapore's nation-building (Chua, 1995). From merger to independence, it is evident that economic development is of top priority, and a national concern. And economic engineering in the long haul is the government's maxim, so much so that its government leaders have repeatedly made the clarion call for Singaporeans to "go global but stay local." Indeed, as one economist has observed,

> Engineering prosperity is at the heart of Singapore …. It does not ignore the aspirations of the Malay, Indian, and Chinese communities that make up Singapore or the fullness of their different cultures and heritage, … consistently creating prosperity is the public persona that Singapore, as a society, projects to the outside world (Ghesquiere, 2007, p. 6).

Ghesquiere is right when he says that despite Singapore's heterogeneous racial population comprising a disproportionate mix of Chinese (76.8%), Malay (13.9%), Indian (7.9%), and Others (1.4%), known also locally as Eurasians who are usually construed as people of European descent (Singapore Department of Statistics, 2006), making Singapore an economic powerhouse has become a collective will for Singaporeans, as its sheer size (and, in economic terms, this means a smaller market) continues to be mobilized as a *vulnerability* and a national constraint in the Singaporean national imaginary. "Going global" has therefore become "local-babble," a truth regime for the economic trajectory and survival of Singapore, which is why, given that its only resources are its people, the Singapore government heavily invests in education.

Singapore's population of approximately 4.3 million boosts a literacy rate of 95% with 61.6% attaining secondary and higher qualifications (Singapore Department of Statistics, 2006). Such is the extent and the importance of investment in education that as one commentator aptly puts it, education in Singapore is "schooling for economic growth" (Spring, 1998). Indeed, one needs no further proof but to notice the recent changes in Singapore's education landscape, which has been noticeably realigned to prepare its youth for a global economy (Koh, 2004). With a new Critical Thinking program infused into its curriculum, Project Work (which promotes a spirit of inquiry, creativity, and collaborative teamwork) and the use of IT, it is hoped that these new curriculum initiatives will engineer "thinking students" and "technopreneurs" who will invent new knowledge, niche areas, and new enterprises that will continue to steer the engine of growth for Singapore's economy. This is all part of the "Thinking Schools, Learning Nation" (TSLN) education policy that saw a major educational change in Singapore in 1997.

Yet, there is always a subliminal fear that with these requisite skills that prepare Singaporeans to "go global," many with the credentials or right capital to venture abroad may not return. Admittedly, Prime Minister Lee Hsien Loong raised the concern in his recent 2006 National Day speech (akin to the State of the Union address in the United States) that Singaporeans are increasingly talent scouted by overseas multinational companies (Lee, 2006). Although no actual statistics are given, what should not go unnoticed is that because of the anxiety of a "brain drain" and the backlash of Singaporeans not returning, the government has spearheaded the formation of an Overseas Singaporean Unit (OSU) with a purposeful mission of engaging Singaporean diasporas and maintaining strong links with them. This is a direct admission that the mobility of Singaporeans is creating a new level of anxiety which may destabilize the construction of national identity and their sense of rootedness and belonging to the nation. Cultural geographers have theorized this empirical truth that the mobility of people has potentially disruptive and transformative effects in the "spaces" and "places" where identities are forged and located (Morley and Robins, 1995), and even more so in the contradictory spaces of "place-bound" identity.

Not unexpectedly, immediately following the PM's National Day Rally speech, the Ministry of Education followed up with the formation of a steering committee on National Education (which is a form of a citizenship education program implemented in 1997 as part of the TSLN policy) to reassess how it might revamp its National Education program to further strengthen the heartware[1] and rootedness of Singapore youths while they stay globally oriented (Ministry of Education, 2006; Davie and Yen, 2006). It remains to be seen what the new revised National Education would be like; suffice it to say that engineering a local national identity will see a renewed focus through the technology of curriculum change in the years to come.

At this point, mention must be made that Singapore is not the only country that is trying to grapple with the complexity of crafting a national identity and a greater sense of belonging in an era of global flows. In Hong Kong and Taiwan, similar trends of implementing citizenship education are also evident in their national curricula, although its form and content are politically shaped to meet the sociopolitical makeup of each country (see for example Morris, Kan, and Morris, 2000; Law, 2004). Likewise, countries like Ireland embed the teaching of national identity in its primary history curriculum (Tormey, 2006); Australia, Canada, and England (see Davies and Issitt, 2005) also have a differentiated citizenship education curricula as a core component in their education systems. This goes to show that the technology of curriculum is by no means innocent but is used teleologically for an ideological end: to shape the conduct of schooling youths and demand their undivided allegiance to their state as globalization continues to be constructed as an overpowering source of destruction that will dismantle (national) identity-making. In the context of countering the forces of globalization, the next section aims to provide a meta-analytic perspective on how Singapore manages globalization by drawing on Collier and Ong's (2005) conceptualization of Deleuze's terms assemblage, reassemblage.

Assemblage, Reassemblage

Against the arguments that globalization contributes to the deterritorialization and fragmentation of *culture, place, homeland,* and *identity* (Appadurai, 1996; Tomlinson, 1999), *assemblage* and *reassemblage* are useful concepts that illuminate how while globalization suggests a seamless, mobile and all-encompassing phenomenon, assemblage and reassemblage call into question the totalizing effect of globalization. *Assemblage, reassemblage* suggests a more promising empirical reality that the effects of globalization are manageable if effectual polices are *ensembled* to circumvent the uncertainty and sometimes destructive elements of globalization.

Drawing on the work of Gilles Deleuze and Felix Guatarri, Ong (2005, p. 338) borrows the term *assemblage* to "denote a contingent ensemble of diverse practices and things that is divided along the axes of territoriality and deterritorialization." When this term is applied to globalization studies, "assemblage" suggests that while globalization is taken to be a universal phenomenon, the (re)appropriation of globalization at the "local" level is far from a uniform and uncontested process. Rather, Collier and Ong (2005, p. 12) explain that,

> In relationship to "the global," the assemblage is not a "locality" to which broader forces are counterposed. Nor is it the structural effect of such forces. An assemblage is the product of multiple determinations that are not reducible to a single logic" ... *assemblage* implies heterogeneous, contingent, unstable, partial and situated.

However, it must be noted that in the case of Singapore, assemblage is always engineered by government elites, and contrary to Collier and Ong's claim that an assemblage is not reducible to a single logic, the space for assemblage in Singapore is motivated by the enduring logic of an ideology of survival and pragmatism (Chua, 1995). This gives rise to a "siege mentality" (Brown, 2000, p. 94) in the Singaporean imaginary and body politic that Singapore must continue to reinvent itself if it is to survive in the quickened pace of globalization.

Collier and Ong (2005) further gesture to the enabling conditions for the operation of globalization regarding the rationality and agentive role of actors. In other words, the duality of *assemblage, reassemblage* calls into play a conjunction of diverse practices, government practice, and administrative calculations to counter the fluidity of global flows. And when new global conditions arise, new elements are reassembled to respond to the contingency of the "problem-space" of globalization. In essence, one could say that "assemblage, reassemblage" is a theoretical shorthand for foregrounding the agentive role of the state (at least in the Singapore case) to intervene and reinvent new moves to make globalization more amenable to local conditions.

Elsewhere, I have made explicit how the Singapore government assembles and reassembles new elements in the form of diverse policies to live with globalization tactically (Koh, 2007, forthcoming). So has Weiss's (2005) analysis of an unprecedented change in Singapore's social policy to include gays and lesbians in the civil service. She argues that,

> ... the Singapore state's stance on gays and lesbians provides a particularly clear example of the state's negotiation of cultural predilections and yen for control, counterpoised against international normative and economic pressure to calibrate local policies toward the next rung up on the global economic ladder (Weiss, 2005, p. 273).

Weiss's argument is illustrative of the kind of assemblage, reassemblage that operates within the "problem-space" that globalization engenders. In a similar vein, the next section will illuminate how Singaporean youths are in a sense "assembled" in the media to portray them as lacking in values desired by the Singapore nation-state.

Disciplining "Generation M": Troublesome Youth and Media Representation

A current observable trend in government rhetoric and in the media is the recurring ideological discourse and criticisms directed at "Generation M." This is a term used by former Prime Minister Goh Chok Tong to describe the younger generation of Singapore as the generation of the millennium (2001). As this generation of youth was born after post-Independence Singapore, and also at a time when Singapore was already experiencing economic wealth and political stability, many young people today bask in material comforts. They are perceived to be either oblivious to, or nonchalant about, the history of Singapore. Therefore, Generation M is in a sense disconnected from Singapore's history and nation-building ideology which is constructed around an ideology of survival, embodying the ethos of thrift, discipline, and diligence (Chua, 1995). Not only is this ideology too distant and unfamiliar to them, Generation M is ironically acculturated in a competitive culture and consumerism where the accumulation of material wealth and success is measured in terms of the 6 "Cs": cash, car, condominium, credit card, country club membership, and educational certificates. Yet they are often admonished for the excessive consumption of rapacious capitalism, indulging in materialism and also exhibiting a Westernized lifestyle, symbolically or otherwise (Chua and Tan, 1999).

The frivolous behavior of Generation M has also been periodically subjected to public criticisms in the media.[2] First, it is chided for displaying amnesia of Singapore's history ("Serious gap," 1996). In another media report, there are those who unabashedly profess that they prefer a Caucasian identity rather than their own ethnicity (Lau, 1999). Then, it is reported that young Singaporeans are uncertain about what constitutes a Singaporean national identity (Teo, 2001). More recently, *The Straits Times* published the findings of a survey which revealed that as many as 53% of Singaporean teens indicated that they would consider emigrating (Lim, 2006). What is one to make of such media constructions of Singaporean youths?

I argue that all these media representations work to associate Singaporean youth with liminality and position them as "deviants" with a moral/cultural dilemma: a generation devoid of national roots and patriotism for Singapore, and therefore in need of "parental" discipline. In a time of globalization, what is also feared is that Generation M is enticed by a sense of individualism, especially that which is associated with the liberal West. Whether or not the frivolous behavior of young Singaporeans is as prevalent as is reported in the media, the Singaporean government clearly does not condone these values, which it perceives as antithetical to the Asian values and ethics that it zealously guards and promotes. A case in point is the response to the high percentage of Singaporean youths seeking to uproot to other countries, as reported in the press. A minister, for example, is quick to raise the alarm that there is an urgent need for "dialogue with the sons and daughters of our country, to understand and work with them to build a home they would call their own" (Lim, 2006, p. H4).

Singapore's eminent sociologist Beng Huat Chua (2000) contests the politicized representation of Generation M. He argues that the construction of Singaporean youth as manifesting an identity crisis is based on "a background assumption that identity formation and stability is entirely dependent on a notion of unchanging 'tradition'" (Chua, 2000, p. 16). The consumption of popular culture further provides youths with an image bank from which they can draw their identities. To them, observing the latest fad and fashion is not only "funky" and "cool"; it is also their expression of belonging and their construction of an image of a "new generation," which, as Chua (2000, p. 16) argues, is drawn from "a globalized image of youth." Ang (2004, p. 306) further qualifies that their identity bank may not be some generic "globalized image of youth," which is often mistakenly equated with American or Western youth culture, but significantly a more culturally specific one represented by the cultural image of regional Asia such as Tokyo, Hong Kong, South Korea, and Taiwan. Whatever their source of identity-making is, Chua's argument nevertheless suggests that the image of Generation M is perhaps a hype, which serves ideologically to pathologize the "disease" of globalization and legitimize a reinvention of the Singaporean identity. From a Foucauldian (1979) perspective, the discourse surrounding the wayward Generation M is a disciplinary tactic used to regulate and discipline Singaporean youth.

I concur with Chua's view by citing a recent study conducted by the Institute of Policy Studies to measure Singaporeans' attitude towards Singapore in terms of their national pride and psychological ties to the country (Lee, 2000). The finding reveals that Singaporeans are by and large proud of being Singaporean and feel a strong attachment to their country. This survey is also benchmarked against 23 other countries, and Singapore is ranked second against the others. If this survey is anything to go by, perhaps there is no cause for concern that young Singaporeans are unpatriotic. And if the survey is representative of Singaporeans, it can be concluded that the construction of Generation M as a generation with no cultural and national moorings is a form of ideological management used to work against the backlash of globalization. Ideologically, the construction of wayward youth also justifies the need to usher in a form of citizenship education to inculcate and revive Singaporean identity and patriotism.

It is no coincidence that National Education has been implemented as a core curriculum in Singapore schools since the launch of the "Thinking Schools, Learning Nation" education policy in 1997 (see Koh, 2005). As a national curriculum that received statewide attention, it is interesting to note that the state-led implementation of the National Education program did not emerge out of a void. As Taylor et al. (1997) have pointed out, education policy or any form of educational change is invariably informed by a significant history of prior events that justify and legitimize a policy or curriculum change. Read in another way, National Education is a form of reassemblage used to engage in citizenship reproduction. The next section will detail when and why NE began so as to understand the ideological management of "fixing" a national identity over other identities and citizenship reproduction.

Contextualizing National Education and its Challenges

In September 1996, the idea of National Education was first announced at the Teachers' Day Rally by then-Prime Minister Goh.[3] He alerted the nation to the fact that there was a "serious gap in knowledge" among the younger generation of Singaporeans, who knew little about the country's history. His claim was based on a survey conducted by a local newspaper and the Ministry of Education that quizzed students on Singapore's postwar history. The survey revealed that students had little knowledge of significant postwar historical moments such as the Hock Lee bus riots, the state of emergency from 1948 to 1960, and important historical figures such as Plen and Dr. Albert Winsemius.

Prime Minister Goh translated this "serious gap in knowledge" as a "problem" that needed to be addressed. This was because a significant 47% of the population was born post-Independence. The fear is that the post-Independence generation may not appreciate and understand Singapore's vulnerabilities and constraints, as these are the important messages that may be gleaned from the episodes of Singapore's postwar history. Importantly, Goh argued that a shared past would serve to provide a common bond for nation-building. It was in this context of a knowledge deficit about Singapore's history that National Education was conceived.

The implementation of NE was officially launched in May 1997 as part of the Thinking Schools, Learning Nation education policy where the teaching of critical thinking and IT skills were concurrently implemented. At the launch, then-Deputy Prime Minister Lee Hsien Loong continued the rhetoric of "a serious gap in knowledge" mentioned by Prime Minister Goh in the previous year. Lee (1997) reiterated that:

This ignorance will hinder our effort to develop a shared sense of nationhood. We will not acquire the right instincts to bond together as one nation, or maintain the will to survive and prosper in an uncertain world. For Singapore to thrive beyond the founder generation, we must systematically transmit these instincts and attitudes to succeeding cohorts. Through National Education, we must make these instincts and attitudes part of the cultural DNA which makes us Singaporeans.

Thus, he further urged teachers to "equip ... (the young) with the basic attitudes, values, and instincts which make them Singaporeans." This "common culture," he continued, is "the DNA to be passed from one generation to the next." Lee's assertion of creating a common, unified culture through NE should be understood as a direct admission of the cultural anxiety and moral panic of the state—a subliminal fear that globalization, although necessary for Singapore's economic survival and much desired by the government (evidenced by the recent Free Trade agreements being signed with the United States) may, at the same time, open the floodgates and subterranean influence of the liberal West and its attendant corrupting values, often associated with tropes of "excess" (Chua, 2000), as was pointed out earlier. This is why NE has been introduced to work against the backlash of globalization.

However, by opening itself to globalization, competing identities and "belongings" are also made available in "youthscapes," where youth practices and their consumption of transnational and "global" popular culture give them alternative avenues to formulate and participate in other modes of citizenship (Maira and Soep, 2005). Similarly, Chua (2004) has observed and argued that a significant increase in the intra-Asian cultural traffic consumption and production of East Asia popular culture (other than what is often mistakenly perceived as essentially American popular culture) is developing and contributing to the formation of a transnational East Asian identity. Herein lies another contending source of identity-making.

Lee's DNA theory of cultural transmission is therefore problematic, as it presupposes that "culture" can be transmitted in its purity without being shaped and reshaped intergenerationally and in the liminal spaces of "youthscapes." I am, however, not suggesting that cultivating a national identity is not important. Rather, my criticism is that as a curriculum package, NE has not responded to what globalization means for the construction of youthful identities. There is a complete disregard for "who the young are and what they might become" (Kenway and Bullen, 2005, p. 32) and their agentive role of constructing their preferred identities, whether this is inspired by their consumption of global/regional popular cultural forms and practices or transient youth subculture practices. Rossi and Ryan (2006) also allude to the challenge of inculcating a national identity through National Education as the landscape of Singapore is inundated with a mediafest of contending sources of identities that are within easy reach for the media savvy and well-connected Singaporean youths.

I also oppose the absolute sense that identity-making can be fashioned without taking into consideration the influence and intermingling (read: hybridization) of other contested sources of identities and other possible sources of "elective belongings" (Savage, Bagnall, and Longhurst, 2005) such as those that permit them to make global as well as virtual connections. In other words, I am alluding to what Robertson (1992), Featherstone (1995), Albrow (1996) and others have collectively argued for: the destabilization and *relativization* of identities in the global–local nexus. Stuart Hall's (1996, p. 4), argument on identity best sums up the flux and fluidity of identity formation:

> Identities are never unified and, in late modern times, [are] increasingly fragmented and fractured: never singular but multiply constructed across different, often intersecting and antagonistic, discourse, practices and positions. They are subject to a radical historicization, and are constantly in the process of change and transformation.

My critique of the NE curriculum aside, in my view, the pedagogy of NE has a managerial function of "narrating the nation" (Bhabha, 1990). It tells the story of how Singapore overcomes its odds, and like all other stories, the Singapore story also has a moral, didactic intent to interpolate subject-citizens whose loyalty to the nation remains unfettered in the tides of globalization. Not unrelated to the crisis construction of Generation M in the media as deficit in cultural mooring and a desired national identity, the implementation of a state-led curriculum intervention in the disciplinary site of schooling is revealing in the way in which technocrats in Singapore "reassembled" a curriculum to craft a more robust national identity.

Conclusion

As much as theoretical debates on identity tell us that identity is a construct, the Singapore case, oddly, reveals the operation of fixing a preferred national identity through the technology of the media and curriculum. The ideological thrust of NE, as I have showed, is to cultivate a sense of cultural mooring, belonging, and a place-bound identity.

However, at another level, the case of Singapore's implementation of NE is symptomatic of the kind of calculations that occur at the level of governance. Ong (2005, p. 338) uses the term "reassemblage" to refer to the way in which technocrats and political elites seek to reassemble new elements to reproduce subject-citizens for the global economy. But in the case of Singapore, "reassemblage" is to ensure that while Singaporeans go global, they remain rooted in Singapore. And what better site to begin the inculcation of national values and ethos than in the disciplinary site of schooling.

Yet as I have argued, while the NE curriculum aims to create and foster a greater sense of belonging and (national) identity, there is an omission of the understanding of "what contemporary globalizing means for the construction of youth identities" (Kenway and Bullen, 2005, p. 32). In other words, the NE curriculum has disregarded how contemporary "youthscapes" (Maira and Soep, 2005) are the alternative loci where youths can participate in alternative forms of citizenship and belonging, and of identity-making. The process of the suturing of the state and school in working against globalization is thus faced with an irreconcilable tension. This is because globalization and (re)territorialization (in the form of National Education) are in fact mutually complementary processes that dismantle any holistic conceptualization of a fixed, territorial bound identity (Bauman, 1998). Competing sources of identities and interests are located in the "in-between" spaces of the global and local.

Notwithstanding that the voices of Singaporean youths—the way they make sense of their own identities as opposed to the preferred "national" identity that the state demands of its citizens—are noticeably absent in this chapter, mention must nevertheless be made that the *represented* voices in media construction of Singaporean youths and the state-led National Education curriculum are illustrative of the kind of calculation and assemblage, reassemblage that take place in the "problem-space" of globalization for Singapore. Although it remains uncertain how successful the National Education program is, what remains certain is that Singapore will continue to work with the promises and against the anxieties of globalization.

Notes

1 The term "heartware" is a homophone for "hardware." It is often used by political leaders in Singapore to refer to the cultivation of a sense of emotional bonding and the affect for the country.

2 The news headlines referred to in this section are taken from *The Straits Times*, which is state-owned. Politically, the media in Singapore—in particular, the press—is the government's mouthpiece used to disseminate government policy and rhetoric (see Birch, 1993).

3 For details of the street poll conducted by *The New Paper*, and the survey administered by the Ministry of Education, see Goh (1996).

References

Albrow, M. 1996. *The Global Age: State and Society beyond Modernity.* Cambridge, U.K.: Polity Press.

Ang, I. 2004. The cultural intimacy of TV drama. In *Feeling Asian Modernities: Transnational Consumption of Japanese TV Dramas,* ed. K. Iwabuchi, 303–309. Hong Kong: Hong Kong University Press.

Appadurai, A. 1996. *Modernity at Large: Cultural Dimensions of Globalization.* Minneapolis, MN: University of Minnesota Press.

Bauman, Z. 1998. *Globalization: The Human Consequence.* Cambridge, U.K.: Polity.

Bhabha, H.K. 1990. Introduction: narrating the nation. In *Nation and Narration,* ed. H.K. Bhabha, 1–7. London: Routledge.

Birch, D. 1993. *Singapore Media Communication Strategies and Practices.* Melbourne: Longman.

Brown, D. 2000. *Contemporary Nationalism: Civic, Ethnocultural and Multicultural Politics.* London: Routledge.

Chang, A.-Li, and Loo, D. 2006. Research council approves 3 key areas to boost economy, *The Straits Times,* July 8, p.1.

Chua, B.H. 1995. *Communitarian, Ideology and Democracy in Singapore.* London: Routledge.

Chua, B.H. 2000. Consuming Asians: Ideas and issues. In *Consumption in Asia: Lifestyle and Identities,* ed. Chua, B.H., 1–34. London: Routledge.

Chua, B.H. 2004. Conceptualizing an East Asian popular culture. *Inter-Asia Cultural Studies* 5(2), 200–221.

Chua, B.H., and J.E. Tan. 1999. Singapore: Where the new middle class sets the standard. In *Cultural and Privilege in Capitalist Asia,* ed. M. Pinches, 137–158. London: Routledge.

Collier, S.J., and A. Ong, 2005. Global assemblages, anthropological problems. In *Global Assemblages: Technology, Politics, and Ethics as Anthropological Problems,* ed. S.J. Collier and A. Ong, 1–21. Malden, MA: Blackwell.

Davie, S., and Yen, F. 2006. Govt to review National Education. programme. *The Straits Times,* August 25, p.3.

Davies, I., and J. Issitt. 2005. Reflections on citizenship education in Australia, Canada and England. *Comparative Education* 41(4), 389–410.

Du Gay, P. 2000. Representing 'globalization': notes on the discursive orderings of economic life. In *Without Guarantees: In Honour of Stuart Hall,* ed. P. Gilroy, L. Grossberg, and A. McRobbie, 113–125. London: Verso.

Featherstone, M. 1995. *Undoing Culture: Globalization, Postmodernism and Identity.* London: Sage.

Foucault, M. 1979. Governmentality. *Ideology and Consciousness* 6, 5–21.

Ghesquiere, H. 2007. *Singapore's Success Engineering Economic Growth.* Singapore: Thomson Learning.

Goh, C.T. 1996. Prepare our children for the new century: Teach them well. Retrieved October 14, 2006, from http://www.moe.gov.sg/corporate/contactonline/ pre2005/rally/speech.html.

Goh, C.T. 2001. *Generation M*: Ministry of Information and the Arts.

Hall, S. 1996. The question of cultural identity. In *Modernity and its Futures,* ed. S. Hall, D. Held, and T. McGrew, 273–316. Cambridge, U.K.: Polity/Open University Press.

Kenway, J., and E. Bullen. 2005. Globalizing the young in the age of desire: Some educational policy issues. In *Globalizing Education: Policies, Pedagogies and Politics,* ed. M. Apple, J. Kenway, and M. Singh, 31–43. New York: Peter Lang.

Koh, A. 2003. Global flows of foreign talent: identity anxieties in Singapore's ethnoscape, *SOJOURN: Journal of Social Issues in Southeast Asia* 18(2), 230 256.

Koh, A. 2004. Singapore education in "New Times": Global/local imperatives. *Discourse: Studies in the Cultural Politics of Education* 25(3), 335–349.

Koh, A. 2005. Imagining the Singapore "nation" and "identity": The role of the media and National Education. *Asia Pacific Journal of Education* 25(1), 75–91.

Koh, A. 2007, forthcoming. Living with globalization tactically: The case of Singapore. In *Cultural Globalization in Southeast Asia,* ed. T. Chong, Singapore: Institute of Southeast Asian Studies.

Lau, A. 1998. *A Moment of Anguish: Singapore in Malaysia and the Politics of Disengagement.* Singapore: Times Academic Press.

Lau, E. 1999. Being Chinese is fine, 'but Caucasian is better. *The Straits Times,* December 18, p.5.

Law, W.-W. 2004. Globalization and citizenship education in Hong Kong and Taiwan. *Comparative Education Review* 48(3), 253–273.

Lee, G.B. 2000. Singaporeans—and proud of it. *Singapore,* May–June, 16–19.

Lee, H.L. 1997. Speech by BG Lee Hsien Loong, Deputy Prime Minister at the Launch of National Education on Saturday 17 May 1997 at TCS Theatre at 9.30 am. Retrieved October 14, 2006, from http://www.moe.gov.sg/speeches/1997/170597.htm.

Lee, H.L. 2006. Transcript of PM Lee Hsien Loong's National Day Rally English Speech on 20 August at NUS University Cultural Centre. Retrieved October 14, 2006, from http://www.gov.sg/NDR06Engspeechtranscript.pdf.

Lim, J. 2006. Youth seeking to uproot an 'urgent' concern. *The Straits Times*, July 27, p. H4.

Maira, S., and E. Soep, eds. 2005. *Youthscapes: The Popular, the National, and the Global*. Philadelphia, PA: University of Pennsylvania Press.

Ministry of Education. 2006. *Committee on National Education*. Retrieved October 14, 2006, from http://www.moe.gov.sg/press/2006/pr20060824.htm.

Morris, P., F. Kan, and E. Morris. 2000. Education, civic participation and identity: Continuity and change in Hong Kong. *Cambridge Journal of Education* 30(2), 243–262.

Morley, D., and K. Robins. 1995. *Spaces of Identity: Global Media, Electronic Landscapes and Cultural Boundaries*. London: Routledge.

Ooi, G.L., and B.J. Shaw. 2004. *Beyond the Port City: Development and Identity in 21st Century Singapore*. Singapore: Prentice Hall.

Ong, A. 2005. Ecologies of expertise: Assembling flows, managing citizenship. In *Global Assemblages: Technology, Politics, and Ethics as Anthropological Problems*, ed. A. Ong and S.J. Collier, 337–353. Carlton, Australia: Blackwell.

Peh, S.H. 2006. Foreign talent critical to S'pore: DPM. *The Sunday Times*, August 6, p.10.

Robertson, R. 1992. *Globalization: Social Theory and Global Culture*. London: Sage.

Rossi, T., and M. Ryan. 2006. National Education as a civics literacy in a globalized world: The challenges facing education in Singapore. *Discourse: Studies in the Cultural Politics of Education* 27(2), 161–174.

Savage, M., G. Bagnall, and B. Longhurst. 2005. *Globalization and Belonging*. London: Sage.

Serious gap in the education of Singaporeans. We are ignorant of our own history. *The Straits Times*, July 18, 1996, p. 41.

Singapore Department of Statistics. 2006. Retrieved October 14, 2006, from http://www.singstat.gov.sg.

Spring, J. 1998. *Education and the Rise of the Global Economy*. USA: Lawrence Erlbaum.

Taylor, S., F. Rizvi, B. Lingard, and M. Henry. 1997. *Education Policy and the Politics of Change*. London: Routledge.

Teo, L. 2001. I want to be proud of Singapore...but what about? *The Straits Times*, February 20, p. 1.

Thrift, N. 2005. *Knowing Capitalism*. London: Sage.

Tomlinson, J. 1999. *Globalization and Culture*. London: Blackwell.

Tormey, R. 2006. The construction of national identity through primary school history: The Irish case. *British Journal of Sociology of Education* 27(3), 311–324.

Trocki, C.A. 2006. *Singapore: Wealth, Power and the Culture of Control*. London: Routledge.

Weiss, M. 2005. Who sets social policy in Metropolis? Economic positioning and social reform in Singapore. *New Political Science* 27(3), 267–289.

12

Marginalization, Identity Formation, and Empowerment

Youth's Struggles for Self and Social Justice

DAVID ALBERTO QUIJADA

If U.S. society continues to treat youth—particularly, young people of color—as potential criminals and undermines their contributions to social justice, then democracy, freedom, and fairness will only be wishful ideals in times of increasing disparity and despair (Ginwright, Cammarota, and Noguera, 2005, p. 25).

Today's youth have been constructed as society's "last and lost hope," generating moral panics that seek to protect the "innocence of childhood" by demonizing and blaming youth, especially urban, poor youth of color, for societal problems (Giroux, 2004; Grossberg, 2005; Males, 2006; Sibley, 1995). Despite statistical reports that document a steady decrease in youth violence, crime, and delinquency, policy and legislation continue to target and punish youth, stripping away any civil liberties, rights, and protections they may have (Males, 1999). Fueled by public perceptions of youth as apathetic, violent, drug-addicted, and sexually promiscuous, the category of youth makes young people accountable for societal debates without talking with them. Such categorization continues to position youth developmentally, as a state of transition toward future realities and adulthood, thus overlooking their present conditions and contributions to social justice (Wyn and White, 1997).

In this chapter, I challenge adults' construction of youth and seek to examine how an ethnically diverse group of youth reflect on their experiences of a Summer Diversity Institute (SDI). Specifically, I discuss how youth use what I term *talking relationships* to understand both their marginalization and their privilege, and how talking relationships become a form of social justice in and of themselves. In the balance of the chapter, I first review the relevant literature on youth studies and youth culture. I then draw on specific ethnographic examples from my research at an SDI in Northern California that illuminate youth's agency and their formation of talking relationships as a form of social justice.

Youth Cultures, Agency, and Voice: The Category of Youth and the Lives of Youth

Youth studies cuts across disciplines but continues to confront a legacy of biological determinism rooted in psychological and physical stages of development that position youth and youth culture in opposition to adulthood (Johnson, 2001; Schwartzman, 2001). Framed as a liminal period of growth or transitional space between childhood and adulthood, the presumption is that youth do not engage in the social and political debates that inform their own and others' lives (James, 1986; Sibley, 1995). Discontent with arbitrary markers of time that implicitly and legally position youth in opposition to adulthood, many scholars argue that a distinction between the category of "youth" and the lives of youth must be made to understand the cultural and political complexity of youth participation in society (Austin and Willard, 1998; Stephens, 1995; Vadeboncoeur and Stevens, 2005). Youth studies, beginning with the Birmingham School, understood youth as a social construct embedded in relationships of class, community and social status (Hall and Jefferson, 1976). Bound in multiple contradictory cultural practices, policies and values, "youth" generates a power to control and define who youth are. For example, "deviance" and "adolescent" have been discussed as organizing tools which generate "moral panics" over youth (Cohen, 1972; McRobbie, 1994). By unpacking contradictory ideologies and practices that frame "youth," youth studies has been able to broaden individual and psychological interpretations of youth.

In this way, youth are no longer solely discussed as segregated from society or as passive consumers of culture who need protection and guidance. Rather than struggling to achieve autonomy, individuality, and interdependence, youth can be understood as active social agents in their own right and at the forefront of change and cultural innovation (James and Prout, 1990; Lipsitz, 1994; Valentine et al., 1998). From this perspective, youth can be understood through the subcultural affiliations they create, coupled with the marginalization they endure (Amit-Talai and Wulff, 1995; McRobbie, 2000). Such analysis has opened up possibilities to discuss youth in relationship to the global context by locating youth resistance and/or agency to dominant cultural and political maps of meaning (Maira and Soep, 2005; Tienda and Wilson, 2002).

Not without its limitations, agency and resistance theories have investigated youth cultural production through subcultural affiliations that disrupt consumption and mass culture (Gelder and Thornton, 1997). For example, street gang affiliation, style, leisure, and music represent spaces within which youth subjectivities "talk back" to social inequalities underlying youth's subordinated status and class position (Austin and Willard, 1998). In this capacity, the concept of youth agency not only affords opportunities to rethink the politics of representation but also generates new knowledge bases from which to invert domination (Lipsitz, 1994).

Most recently, youth activism has gained much attention in youth studies because it represents a way of rethinking youth within youth's own paradigms. It is also at the forefront of policy debates that are tied to globalization as witnessed in the 1999 Seattle World Trade Organization demonstrations (Shepard and Hayduk, 2002) or the more recent 2006 youth-led unity marches and school walkouts, which opposed immigration reform bill HR 4437: Border Protection, Antiterrorism, and Illegal Immigration Control Act of 2005 (Quijada, forthcoming). Youth activism's response to social and political issues reminds us that "youth culture is non-political only because it has been defined that way" (Corrigan and Frith, 1975, p. 231). In this way, youth contribute to wider definitions of culture that move away from traditional oppositional "us vs. them" youth–adult relationships that constrain youth's roles in society.

More then simply raising youth voices, recent scholarship has moved to investigate youth activism tied to social justice and today's democratic process, transforming how we understand youth and youth development (Ginwright and Cammarota, 2002; Ginwright and James 2002). No longer constrained by biological stages of development, youth and development are immersed in civic participation and cammunity involvement with implications for understanding policy and the role of the citizen (Ginwright, Noguera, and Cammarota, 2006; Ginwright, Cammarota and Noguera 2005; Lesko, 2001). This shift in youth culture research opens up spaces to identify youth cultural practices that rethink everyday democratic participation in the global context (Dolby, 2003; Weis and Fine, 2000; Maira and Soep, 2005).

Thus, this chapter underscores the importance of hybrid dialogical spaces in which youth—no different than other marginalized populations—listen, relate, (in)form, conflict, and learn with others to transform their own and others' social conditions. As Virginia Caputa (1995) argues, these social spaces are constituted by individuals who are continually silenced yet demand representation because they afford new possibilities towards social transformation. Although we know quite a lot about youth styles, leisure activities, dress, and subcultural affiliations, we know very little about how youth individually lead their lives, cocreate intersubjective meanings across groups, discuss their marginalization, and work in coalition as active social agents who contribute to the world. Rather then presume youth to operate in distinct worlds that do not afford possibilities to bond and struggle in alliance, here I discuss youth as contributing members of society who seek to better understand their own and others' social positions by advocating talking relationships.

Recognizing the present need for research that prioritizes the everyday experiences of youth who cross group boundaries to form new relationships across differences, I move to discuss participants' collective articulation of talking relationships as a form of social justice. In this capacity, youth's active participation in an SDI is less about "the activity" and more about participants' informed opinions and collective formation of talking relationships to confront diversity. Rather then highlight or celebrate what Angela McRobbie (1994) refers to as a "spectacular youth culture," I discuss everyday naturally occurring responses which allow us to rethink an overlooked and underanalyzed form of social justice that youth collectively create and advocate in community.

Methods, Participants, and Setting

Using data drawn from participant observation and ethnographic interviews, in this chapter I reflect on forms of youth engagement with talking relation- 'ships. I base my reflections on my experiences with a youth empowerment project I call "Diversity Now." Diversity Now (DN) is a nonprofit youth-led organization located in an urban Northern California city in the United States. Its mission is to promote social change by affirming diversity and challenging attitudes about oppressions underlying race, class, gender, and sexuality. DN deals directly with diversity issues by hiring and training youth interns to facilitate and create workshops that use hands-on activities and interactive theater (or guerrilla theater), to generate discussion about race, class, gender, and sexuality and to promote community service during the school year. DN also conducts an intensive 6-week SDI that meets 5 days a week for 8 hours with 1 day dedicated to community action, working directly with a social service agency of the participants' choice.

DN is a pan-ethnic youth empowerment project that attracts youth ages 12 to 19 from poor and working-class urban communities in the surrounding neighborhood. The study draws upon 28 participants (19 female and 9 male) who either participated in the project's 6-week SDI or were paid diversity trainers during the school year. The majority of participants (22) self-identified as black, African American, or of mixed race, with the remaining participants self-identifying as white, Latina/o, or Filipina.

Talking Relationships and Engaging Social Justice

SDI begins with a three-day wilderness camping trip with no electricity or flushable toilets. The majority of participants have never left their urban communities, much less been on a hike, or hiked a mile and a half carrying gear to camp. These participants, like other urban youth are categorized by constructions of youth that position them as apathetic, deviant, resistant, and self-centered. However, participants' active participation in workshops coupled with their reflections on their participation suggest otherwise. Even before participating in workshops, participants reveal a commitment to each other and to talking that facilitates learning and social justice. Hence, a distinction must be made between what participants bring to the project and what the project does for participants.

Participants bring to the project informed opinions about diversity that generate a context for learning that contradicts public perceptions of youth.

Participants' initial responses, when asked, "Why did you apply to the Summer Institute Program?" reveal youth as more than empty receptacles or blank slates of learning who passively receive and/or actively resist teaching. These responses are more than behavioral traits that fuel moral panics and blame youth for societal concerns. Instead, responses can be understood as collective efforts that youth mobilize to address societal concerns.

During the three-day wilderness trip, I asked participants why they applied to SDI. Although the majority of participants were enticed by the $600 cash stipend, overnight field trips, and meeting new people they also conclude as Adam does, "It's not the money! Being here I lose my whole summer break! I could be hanging out with friends." It was clear that participants seek to develop more awareness about their lives and those of others. Their responses reveal a concern for community and others beyond their individual needs. Rather then search for self or independence from others and disconnect from the world, they verbalize an interconnected world that they seek to share and comprehend with others. Participants seek to broaden their world views and learn from each other by building relationships that transcend apathetic slacker mentalities. Each seeks to become, as Andy states, "a more complete person," which includes meeting new people and understanding human interaction. For example, Tara seeks to develop critical interactions that challenge preconceived ideas about the world:

> I mean it's important to meet new people, but I just would like to be surrounded by people who think about things. A lot of people are not aware because I don't think we really think. I just want to be in an environment where we can talk and discuss social issues and get connected to each other.

Participants share Tara's concerns as they gravitate towards conversations that push them to discuss their biases. More than learning about homophobia or sexism, participants seek to discuss how they contribute, to and understand oppression. For example, Lester reveals the struggles he has when discussing homophobia:

> Sometimes, I get into fights with people. I don't know why, I want to get rid of those thoughts. I don't know how. A lot of my friends have them, too. But we don't talk about them, but I know we need to—so that we could just have a better way to live.

Another participant, Kyle, wants skills to learn how best to interact with others, especially people he disagrees with. As he explains:

> There's just some things about me that I can't show other people, but I want to change. I want to know that if I have a problem with somebody,

> I can still talk to them or at least try to solve it out, not make it one huge
> conflict because I recognize I have that tendency.

While SDI generates activities to discuss social positions (i.e., gender and
sexuality), central to the project is the unified commitment to talking about
social issues that participants themselves bring to workshops. Participants
seek to learn from their biases—not just for themselves but for others as
well. They understand that their direct experiences with racism, sexism, and
homophobia are individual experiences that must be discussed in relationship
to other positions. For the most part, participants gravitate towards talking
relationships in which they engage other participants—in other words, they
actively seek relationships and criticism. As Natalie describes, "I haven't really
gotten constructive criticism … you know somebody to tell me, 'Ok, I heard
you say that but this is what I think.' I want to learn about other people's opinions and beliefs." Similarly, Laura explains, "I don't want to just say my opinion and have people say, OK, that's your opinion. No, I want to know, what do
you think about my opinion?"

Misha was the participant with the most experience in diversity workshops,
and she was also the most critical of the talking relationships that took place in
workshops. For example, Misha observed and experienced a disconnect between
"talking diversity" and "relating diversity to people." She was turned off by
workshops that distanced people's experiences with oppression by theorizing
structures of power in institutional settings. Misha related her experience in a
recent diversity workshop where participants unconsciously used stereotypes
that were hurtful. Despite participant's awareness of power operating across
race, class, and gender to perpetuate social inequalities, they still wielded
words like "illegal alien" and "retarded" because they were not called out on
their assumptions. Misha describes how participants were quick to refer to
each other as, "pimps, ho's, and bitches," and uncritically joked, referencing
negative experiences as "gay." More specifically, Misha describes it this way:

> People knew about diversity, but they really couldn't relate it to people.
> There were a lot of stereotypes, and some were just off the wall. Some
> people said things that were uncalled for. They had no idea what they
> were saying, but it was out of line and it hurt. I guess that's what spurs me
> to learn. I just need to learn something besides, "OK, here's how power
> and inequality is structured in the United States, and here's an example
> of racism, oh, and here's another phobia." Yeah, I'm pretty aware of the
> problems and the injustices. But I want to know how to relate to it … you
> know, skills to understand people by talking.

Participants' active involvement in workshops should come as no surprise;
it emerges from a cultural process that advocates the critical engagement

of difference. Rather then situate their needs as separate and distinct, and maintain a youth culture in opposition to adulthood, participants seek to link their concerns to relational qualities such as talking, which is not age based or reliant upon subcultural affiliation. In this way, participants disentangle categories of youth by rethinking how groups come together and discuss diversity and social justice in their everyday lives.

Gender and Talking Relationships

Participants sit in a circle around a pile of miscellaneous items: hats, wigs, face makeup, scarves, and sweaters. There's an old mirror, a baby doll, action figures, crayons, a journal, board games, and all kinds of books including romance novels and classics like *Catcher in the Rye*. Each is waiting their turn to select an item and join one of two groups, "male" or "female." Participants have already volunteered myself and Kimberly, the program director, to perform each group's construction of gender, "broadly defined." Participants are minimally directed by a youth intern who says, "Choose a male or female identity with this stuff and have someone perform it."

Participants in my group actively contribute. They mold my body and direct my performance of female identity. Jason takes the lead by exaggeratedly applying blush and lipstick to my face. Pricilla reminds me, "David don't be so stiff, point your toes inward and sway your left arm away from your hip when you walk." Carlos puts a journal in my left hand and a pen in my right. Maribel says, "No, I think he should be on the phone," as she hands me her cell phone which I awkwardly balance. In five minutes they have put me together, and constructed a "traditional" gender role I am to perform in opposition to the other group's very gendered construction of male identity. Participants name me "Davida" and instruct me to sit and pretend to be writing in my journal as I wait for my cell phone to ring. I am to act upset because my date stood me up and my group emphasizes, "Try to cry if you can, or sigh a lot like you're sad and it hurts."

It is the second day of the SDI, and I already feel a connection to participants due to the intensity of our interactions in workshops that require both language and body to communicate. Embarrassed, I perform my role for the other group, who cannot stop laughing. Both Kimberly and I are shocked by the severity of our newly ascribed traditional roles. However, we are also encouraged by the "conversational context" that emerges as participants enthusiastically shout out questions while watching what they have scripted us to perform.[1] Participants' questions and comments merge with laughter: "David looks like a drag queen! I don't wear makeup, why does he? Why is Kimberly acting so tough with her chest out when she walks?"

Jessica hesitates as she moves to discuss rather then question, "Well, maybe if Kimberly don't do all that then she would be a dyke," which sparks others to respond back in unison, "Why she have to be gay?" Some participants look confused. Conversation shifts from the performance to the general concept of gender when one participant states, "I thought gender was talking about men and women." Tiffany pushes others to respond by asking, "What is a boy, anyway?" Cristina emphasizes, "We created her this way, and people do it all the time!" Now participants take sides: "It's not people, it's families!" "No, you learn that in school—how to act like a boy. 'Be a man don't cry!'" "It's the media, that's all we see." Some participants move to broaden the analysis by questioning, "Yeah, but who owns the media?" "What sells and who buys the image?" Others return to the "individual" stating, "Some people really act like that because it's who they are." The debate continues as Jamal questions, "Is it who they are or what they are told to be?" Brenda sitting in the back wearing sunglasses shouts, "But people get blamed if they act differently and don't conform." What emerges is a conversation that jumps from self-identification to social construction to group positioning with gender and sexual orientation overlapping and informing identity construction.

For participants, this activity is new, and so is the discussion that unfolds. The majority of participants comment that they have had few opportunities to discuss social issues in formal settings, arguing as Jen does, "This is the first opportunity I have ever had to talk about these things—to actually talk about real things (i.e., oppression)." Yet, despite this lack of experience, participants are prepared to ask questions, contribute, and take risks. Although participants are quick to discuss and engage each other's opinions, forming talking relationships across "diversity issues," I argue that such participation speaks more to a unified emerging *process* than to the content discussed or learned. Hence, rather than privilege the pedagogical moves of a youth empowerment project, I emphasize participants' collective understanding and concern with social issues as operationalized through the talking relationships they promote. In this capacity, participants seek out opportunities to talk and discuss social issues due to a unified, however decentered, concern they have for the world they live in and the relationships they form. Equipped and willing to talk across differences, participants seize the opportunity to engage in talking relationships towards social justice.

Talking Relationships: Beyond the Summer Diversity Institute

Although participants advocate talking relationships and understand their contribution to social justice, they struggled to locate relationships in their lives that equally valued such discussions. In general, participants were disillusioned by their interactions with diversity, regardless of the setting or people they encountered. They desired more from the minimal conversations they had with family members and friends.

For example, Tanya felt on the defensive when discussing social issues. Unable to delve deeply into conversations, she experienced "criticism" more than "engagement" in discussions with her parents, "My parents take my words apart and make me prove myself, yet they don't even contribute." Similarly, Daniel described most of his conversations as one-sided and detached. He admitted his frustration by stating, "I'm just talking to myself, anyways."

Despite the struggles participants experienced, they still felt compelled to challenge others' opinions because it's what dominated the few "real" discussions they could have. For example, Tara asked, "Why is it that the only meaningful conversations I can have with people is when I challenge their conservative beliefs?" She described her father as a right-wing conservative Republican who contradicts his Christian beliefs and does little to critically interrogate his position. Discontent with her father's process, Tara described how she is more troubled by his lack of engagement with her opinions than with his conservative beliefs,

> My dad is a total hypocrite because he's broken all ten commandments. He thinks gays are evil and against the Bible yet he doesn't go to church. And then he calls me lazy for not going to church. But it's like, no, I choose not to go to church because I think it's wrong and I disagree with it. I share my opinions, and all he can do is disagree.

Here, Tara recognized how institutions, whether familial or educational, organize ways of communicating that silence "talking" as a form of everyday activism. Not only did participants have to defend their positions but they also had to push parents and sometimes peers to talk and reveal a position. For example, Stephanie became frustrated by her continual attempts to initiate conversations that did not fall back upon consumption and leisure activities. Disillusioned by her mother's and older sister's depoliticized conversations, Stephanie emphasized,

> I mean they (mother and sister) don't even really look at the world. They can't even look at themselves. When we start to talk about a political issue that I care about they just stare at me and go, "So did I show you what I bought at Wal-Mart?" And then they just kind of ignore me.

Although participants tried to talk across differences, they also shared how tired they were of having to be the only person to "give evidence and prove myself to make a point." Such interactions played on participants emotionally, at times leaving them with little desire to talk. Rather than defend their opinions, bring up issues and challenge positions, participants often preferred to censor their responses and avoid conversations altogether. For example, Kyle, who self–identifies as black and has dated a mixed-race woman, avoids conversations with his parents about interethnic marriages. He could no longer listen to his mother's generalizations about white people,

> Like, if my family see a black person on the TV, they might be, like, "Oh he's cute, he's a good guy" or whatever. But then if they find out that he is going with a white person or married to a white person then they be like, "Ooh, he's a sell-out." Most of the times I just try to get out of the room because I don't be feeling like dealing with people like that. It kind of makes me sick for them to put that into people's minds. I don't feel that's right, so most of the time I just walk out.

Discontent with their "talking relationships," participants recognized that they needed new opportunities to discuss diversity, especially when it dealt directly with their own racial formation. For example, Misha acknowledged that she felt "stuck" in how to discuss her mixed-race identity with a mother who is white,

> You know, I've heard my mom refer to me as Black, and she's Caucasian, which is weird because we're talking to each other from different racial backgrounds. She's pretty understanding, but then there are things which I just feel like I can't relate to her about—that she doesn't get.

While Misha listened and took note of how her mother discussed race, she also found herself choosing what to listen to and engage with. Unlike Kyle, she couldn't walk away, stop listening, and avoid conversations, so she found herself censoring conversations because as she explains, "I feel like I don't want to insult her by telling her that she doesn't understand. So sometimes I'll choose who to talk to. I mean I'll just give you the basics instead of, like, getting personal with it." Misha's response speaks to participants' underlying concern with how to engage talking relationships as a form of social justice, and their desire to seek out and explore new talking relationships to promote thinking.

Talking Relationships and Social Justice: Jamal's Story

It's an exceptionally warm evening in June. Jamal and I arrive early to the film festival sponsored by DN. I've known Jamal—a youth DN intern—for several months now. We sit on a park bench eating take-out fried chicken box dinners. As we eat, I struggle to reflect on my nine months of participation in the DN project, the upcoming SDI, and my continued reluctance to ask participants directly about oppression and social justice. Jamal responds with some frustration, "Just ask them!" I realize Jamal can see what I cannot—that youth are not apathetic and disengaged, but ready to talk.

In part, Jamal's stance emerges from his own engagement with talking relationships as a facilitator and as a participant of diversity workshops. For example, when I ask Jamal to answer his own question, "What do you think about certain issues, like racism, sexism, and where do you stand on these?" Jamal initially hesitated, responding with a long, "Hmmmmm," but similar to other participants he delved deeply into homophobia by stating,

> Gay people are bad. Everybody was, like, "If you gay, you a fag and soft and you sugary sweet." That's all it was, that's what it was like growing up in my community and school, you better not be gay.

Jamal is willing to admit his homophobia, but is open to engagement and discussion. Yet, Jamal is aware that he has had few opportunities to openly discuss issues of oppression and social justice in his daily life, despite the fact that he lives in an economically depressed and violent community. He reflected,

> It's like, you know what is going on but you blindfold yourself … like even me growing up the last couple of years, I notice there was a lot of killings, but I really didn't notice it as much until like lately when it became, like, really close to home and friends and stuff, and I was like, "Well, a lot of people been dying." Well, it's like at first I've been blindfolded and I didn't want to see it. I'm, like, my neighborhood is not that bad [laugh]. Yeah, right. But there are some things, you know, that I blindfolded myself from seeing that I really didn't think was bad. Like, just because they selling drugs don't mean it's that bad or just because someone got shot at last night or just because the police raid your block every other month [laughing]. These are things we used to take pride in. Even now I still take pride in it. Like my block is so hard, police raid our block, shit, we get shot at, we have shoot-outs on my block, you know.

Although Jamal lives in a city with a homicide rate that is the fourth highest in the United States, he did not see his community as violent until he lost six friends in two weeks to gang violence. Challenged by the loss of his friends, Jamal generated new opportunities to engage in conversations about what is violence. Although Jamal acknowledges DN as a context contributing to his new awareness, he is quick to remind me that it is not the sole source, "It [(change)] was already in me but Diversity Now helps you see some things, if you're ready to see it."

Thus, rather than regard DN as the catalyst of learning and presume himself to be a passive student of diversity, he focused on his contributions to gain awareness through "talking relationships" that he and other youth share. Similar to other participants, Jamal seeks critical interactions to discuss his shared marginalization and think about his relationship to the world. Jamal is ready to ask questions and rethink the blindfold he referred to. In this capacity, he seeks to engage talking relationships that confront differing opinions and challenge his position on the same issue. On the other hand, he reminds me that, "Nobody, nothing can help you, no program can help you if you're not really ready." Drawing upon his own experience in DN, he emphasizes what was important to his process,

> I think it was everything, I can't just say one thing. It's just how you take it, how you see it, and how you talk about it. I mean, just because someone else comes from my same background, he is not going to take Diversity Now as I've seen it because I'm a different person. I interpret everything different than another, the next man, so it's just the way that I took it in. It's how we mix in all that we think is valuable and expose it, because I don't know everything and neither do you.

However, Jamal struggled with the process of developing new awareness and new relationships with people who were different from himself. He described how

> At first, I remember it felt kind of soft because, man, you kicking it with white people, you kicking it with hell of Asians and Mexicans, dude, you tripping [laughing]—that's how I used to be, dang, you kicking it with bisexual and gay people and stuff …

Jamal is aware of his biases and reflects on the positions that underlie his developing social and political awareness as linked to the talking relationships that emerge in the critical interactions he has developed across difference. Thus, Jamal does not view his self-awareness as a linear progression from what he thought once to what he thinks now. Instead he describes it as a complex process that changes the more he engages in issues of diversity and connects his life to those of others. Even now, as he facilitates diversity workshops for other youth, he strives for more talking relationships:

> I can't believe I'm doing this, like … I couldn't believe I was around so many different people.… It took me awhile to get that out of my mind. … Sometimes I jump back in to those same thoughts—and I be, like, what are you doing?

Conclusion

As I have discussed throughout this chapter, youth who participated in diversity workshops seek to resurrect talking as a form of activism. In this capacity, participants reveal a commitment to improve their own and others' lives through forming talking relationships.

What emerges is an awareness that—in opposition to prevailing beliefs—youth care about the world and seek opportunities to discuss their participation in it. Herein lies the struggle to rethink not what is beneficial for youth but how youth as active participants promote and advocate movements that rethink how youth and other marginalized groups are positioned, while building a context to delve deeply into social justice.

Note

1 See David Quijada (2002) for a discussion of conversational contexts as social justice. Specifically, I discuss the example of youth diversity trainers debriefing their workshop facilitation.

References

Amit-Talai, V., and H. Wulff, eds. 1995. *Youth Cultures: A Cross-Cultural Perspective.* London: Routledge.

Austin, J., and M.N. Willard, eds. 1998. *Generations of Youth: Youth Cultures and History in Twentieth-Century America.* New York: New York University Press.

Caputa, V. 1995. Anthropology's silent 'others' A consideration of some conceptual and methodological issues for the study of youth and children's cultures. In *Youth Cultures: A Cross Cultural Perspective,* ed. V. Amit-Talai and H. Wulff, 19–42. New York: Routledge.

Cohen, S. 1972. *Folk Devils and Moral Panics: The Creation of the Mods and Rockers.* Oxford, U.K.: Basil Blackwell.

Corrigan, P., and S. Frith. 1975. The politics of youth culture. In *Resistance through Rituals: Youth Subcultures in Post-War Britain,* ed. S. Hall and T. Jefferson, 231–241. Great Britain: The Anchor Press Ltd.

Dolby, N. 2003. Popular culture and democratic practice. *Harvard Educational Review* 73(3), 258–284.

Gelder, K., and Thornton, S., eds. 1997. *The Subcultures Reader.* New York: Routledge.

Ginwright, S., and J. Cammarota. 2002. New terrain in youth development: The promise of a social justice approach. *Social Justice* 29(4), 82–96.

Ginwright, S., J. Cammarota, and P. Noguera 2005. Youth, social justice, and communities: Toward a theory of urban youth policy. *Social Justice* 32(3), 24–40.

Ginwright, S., P. Noguera, and J. Cammarota, eds. 2006. *Beyond Resistance: Youth Activism and Community Change: New Democratic Possibilities for Practice and Policy for America's Youth.* New York: Routledge.

Ginwright, S., and T. James, 2002. From assets to agents of change: Social justice, organizing, and youth development. *New Directions for Youth Development: Theory, Practice, Research* 96, 27–46.

Giroux, H. 2004. Disposable youth/disposable futures: The crisis of politics and public life. In *American Youth Cultures,* ed. N. Campbell, 71–87. New York: Routledge.

Grossberg, L. 2005. *Caught in the Crossfire: Kids, Politics, and America's Future.* Boulder, CO: Paradigm Publishers.

Hall, S., and T. Jefferson, eds. 1976. *Resistance through Rituals: Youth Subcultures in Post War Britain.* London: Hutchinson.

James, A. 1986. Learning to belong: The boundaries of adolescence. In *Symbolising Boundaries: Identity and Diversity in British Cultures,* ed. A.P. Cohen, 155–170. Manchester, U.K.: Manchester University Press.

James, A., and A. Prout. 1990. *Constructing and Reconstructing Childhood: Contemporary Issues in the Sociological Study of Childhood.* New York: Falmer Press.

Johnson, H.B. 2001. From the Chicago School to the new sociology of children: The sociology of children and childhood in the United States, 1900–1999. In *Children at the Millennium: Where Have We Come From, Where Are We Going,* ed. S.L. Hofferth and T.J. Owens, 53–93. New York: Elsevier Science Ltd.

Lesko, N. 2001. *Act Your Age! A Cultural Construction of Adolescence.* New York: Routledge Falmer.

Lipsitz, G. 1994. We know what time it is: Race, class and youth culture in the nineties. In *Microphone Fiends: Youth Music and Youth Culture,* ed. A. Ross and T. Rose, 17–28. New York: Routledge.

Maira, S., and E. Soep, eds. 2005. *Youthscapes: The Popular, the National, the Global.* Philadelphia, PA: University of Pennsylvania Press.

Males, M.A. 1999. *Framing Youth: Ten Myths about the Next Generation.* Monroe: Common Courage Press.

Males, M.A. 2006. Youth policy and institutional change. In *Beyond Resistance! Youth Activism and Community Change: New Democratic Possibilities for Practice and Policy for America's Youth,* ed. S. Ginwright, P. Noguera, and J. Cammarota, 301–318. New York: Routledge.

McRobbie, A. 1994. *Postmodernism and Popular Culture.* London: Routledge.

McRobbie, A. 2000. *Feminism and Youth Culture.* New York: Routledge.

Quijada, D.A. 2002. Youth coalition building: Crossing community boundaries, raising consciousness and dismantling oppression. Unpublished dissertation. Davis, CA: University of California, Davis.

Quijada, D.A. Forthcoming. Reconciling research, rallies and citizenship: Reflections on youth led diversity workshops and intercultural alliances. *Social Justice.*

Schwartzman, H.B. 2001. Introduction: Questions and challenges for a 21st-century anthropology of children. In *Children and Anthropology: Perspectives for the 21st Century,* ed. H.B. Schwartzman, 1–37. Westport: Bergin and Garvey.

Shepard, B., and R. Hayduk, eds. 2002. *From ACT UP to the WTO: Urban Protests and Community Building in the Era of Globalization.* New York: Verso.

Sibley, D. 1995. *Geographies of Exclusion: Society and Difference in the West.* New York: Routledge.

Stephens, S., ed. 1995. *Children and the Politics of Culture.* Princeton, NJ: Princeton University Press.

Tienda, M., and W.J. Wilson, eds. 2002. *Youth in Cities: A Cross-National Perspective.* Cambridge, U.K.: Cambridge University Press.

Vadeboncoeur, J.A., and Patel Stevens, L., eds. 2005. *Re/Constructing "the adolescent": Sign, Symbol, and Body.* New York: Peter Lang.

Valentine, G., T. Skelton, and D. Chambers, 1998. Cool places: an introduction to youth an youth cultures. In *Cool Places: Geographies of Youth Culture,* ed. T. Skelton and G. Valentine, 1–34. New York: Routledge.

Weis, L., and M. Fine, eds. 2000. *Construction Sites: Excavating Race, Class, and Gender among Urban Youth.* New York: Teachers College Press.

Wyn, J., and R. White. 1997. *Rethinking Youth.* Thousand Oaks: Sage Publications.

Notes on Contributors

Catherine Beavis is Associate Professor in the Faculty of Education at Deakin University. She has jointly edited four books: (with Louise Laskey) *Schooling and Sexualities* (1996, Deakin Centre for Education and Change); (with Bill Green) *Teaching the English Subjects: Essays on English Curriculum History and Australian Schooling* (Deakin University Press, 1996); (with Cal Durrant) *P(ICT)ures of English: Teachers, Learners and Technology* (AAATE, 2001 Wakefield Press); (with Ilana Snyder) *Doing Literacy Online: Teaching, learning and playing in an electronic world* (Hampton Press, 2004). She has published in numerous journals, including *English in Australia, Discourse, Interactive Educational Multimedia, Research in the Teaching of English* and *Education, Communication, Information*. She has jointly edited special issues of *Australian Educational Researcher* 25(3) 1998, with Bill Green; *Papers: Explorations into Children's Literature* 11(2) with Barbara Kamler, 2001; and *Literacy Learning in the Middle Years* 11(2) with Marion Meiers, 2003. Her research focuses on the area of young people and new media, with a particular interest in computer games, the changing nature of text, and the implications of young people's experience of digital culture for English and literacy education in schools.

Elizabeth Bullen is a lecturer at Deakin University. She has published in the *Journal of Education Policy, Policy Futures in Education*, and *Journal of Youth Studies*. She is a co-editor (with Jane Kenway and Simon Robb) of *Innovation and Tradition: The Arts, Humanities, and the Knowledge Economy* (2004, Peter Lang).

Peter Demerath is Associate Professor in the School of Educational Policy and Leadership at The Ohio State University. He has published in Anthropology and Education Quarterly, American Journal of Education, Education and Society, and Theory into Practice. His 1999 essay published in Comparative Education Review was selected for the George Z.F. Bereday Outstanding Scholarship Award.

Catherine Doherty is a lecturer in socio-cultural studies in the Faculty of Education at Queensland University of Technology, Brisbane, Australia. With a background in sociology and applied linguistics, her research interests lie in the sociology of education with particular reference to pedagogical responses to global flows of people, educational products, and technologies.

Nadine Dolby is Associate Professor of Curriculum Studies at Purdue University. She is the author of Constructing Race: Youth, Identity, and Popular Culture in

South Africa (2001, State University of New York Press), and first editor (with Greg Dimitriadis) of Learning to Labor in New Times (2004, Routledge). She has published in numerous journals, including Harvard Educational Review, Comparative Education Review, The Australian Educational Researcher, the British Journal of Sociology of Education, and Teachers College Record. She has conducted research in South Africa, Australia, and the United States.

Michael D. Giardina is Assistant Professor of Advertising and Cultural Studies at the University of Illinois, Urbana-Champaign. He is the author of *From Soccer Moms to NASCAR Dads: Sport, Culture, and Politics in a Nation Divided* (Paradigm, forthcoming), and *Sporting Pedagogies: Performing Culture and Identity in the Global Arena* (Peter Lang, 2005) and editor of *Contesting Empire/Globalizing Dissent: Cultural Studies after 9/11* (Paradigm, 2006, with Norman K. Denzin), *Qualitative Inquiry and the Conservative Challenge: Confronting Methodological Fundamentalism* (Left Coast Press, 2006, with Norman K. Denzin), *Ethical Futures in Qualitative Research: Decolonizing the Politics of Knowledge* (Left Coast Press, forthcoming, with Norman K. Denzin), and *Youth Culture and Sport: Identity, Power, and Politics* (Routledge, forthcoming, with Michele K. Donnelly). His work on globalization, cultural studies, qualitative inquiry, and the racial logics of late-capitalism has also appeared in numerous journals such as *Harvard Educational Review, Cultural Studies/Critical Methodologies, Journal of Sport and Social Issues*, and *Qualitative Inquiry*.

Jennifer Kelly is an associate professor in the Department of Educational Policy Studies, University of Alberta. Her areas of research are youth, culture, racialization, and media within an educational context. Jennifer is the author of *Under the Gaze: Learning to be Black in White Society* and *Borrowed Identities*.

Aaron Koh is Assistant Professor in the Department of English, The Hong Kong Institute of Education. His research interests are globalization and education, cultural politics of education, and cultural studies in education. He is working on his first book, *Tactical Globalization*, which is under contract with Peter Lang, New York. His work on globalization, education, and identity politics has appeared in journals such as *Globalizations, Globalisation, Education and Societies, Discourse, Asia Pacific Journal of Education* and *SOJOURN*.

Jennifer Logue is a doctoral student in Educational Policy Studies at the University of Illinois at Urbana-Champaign.

Allan Luke is Professor at the Centre for Research in Pedagogy and Practice at Queensland University of Technology. Previously, Professor Luke was Dean at the University of Queensland in Australia and Chief Advisor to the Queensland Minister of Education. As Deputy Director General of Education for Queensland Schools in 1999-2000, he was instrumental in major research and policy initiatives, including *The New Basics, Literate Futures, and Productive Pedagogies*. Professor Luke is author and editor of 15 books, including, most recently, *Struggles Over Difference: Texts, Curriculum and Pedagogy in the Asia Pacific* (State University of New York Press, 2005) and *Bourdieu and Literacy Education* (Lawrence Erlbaum, forthcoming). He is currently co-editor of *Teaching Education* (Routledge), the *Review of Research in Education* (AERA), the *Asia Pacific Journal of Education* (Routledge), and *Pedagogies: An International Journal* (Lawrence Erlbaum).

Ritty Lukose, Assistant Professor of Education, University of Pennsylvania, has published in *Cultural Anthropology* and the *Journal of Social History*. Her research interests include youth, globalization, consumer culture, and gender. She is completing a book manuscript, *Learning Modernity: Education and Youth Culture in Kerala, India. Professor Lukose is the 2003/2004 recipient of a Spencer/National Academy of Education Postdoctoral fellowship.*

Jill Lynch is an Assistant Professor in the Department of Educational Foundations at Ashland University. Her research interests include the nature of community in diverse contexts, youth culture and academic engagement, and school-university partnerships. She teaches qualitative methodology and inquiry seminars on popular culture.

Cameron McCarthy is Communication Scholar and University Scholar attached to the departments of Educational Policy Studies and the Institute of Communications at the University of Illinois. Among his most recent publications are *The Uses of Culture: Education and the Limits of Ethnic Affiliation* (Routledge, 1998); *Sound Identities: Youth Music and the Cultural Politics of Education* (Peter Lang, 1999); *Reading and Teaching the Postcolonial: From Baldwin to Basquiat and Beyond* (Teachers College Press, Columbia University, 2001); *Foucault, Cultural Studies and Governmentality* (SUNY Press, 2003), and *Race, Identity and Representation in Education*, Second Edition (Routledge, 2005).

Sarah Nuttall is Associate Professor of Literary and Cultural Studies at the Wits Institute for Social and Economic Research (WISER) at the University of the Witwatersrand. A South African Rhodes Scholar, Dr. Nuttall is co-editor of *Text, Theory, Space: Land, Literature and History in South Africa and Australia* (Routledge, 1996), *Negotiating the Past: The Making of Memory in South Africa* (Oxford, 1998), *Senses of Culture: South African Culture Studies* (Oxford, 2000), *Beautiful-Ugly: African and Diaspora Aesthetics* (Duke, 2006), and author of *Literary Cultures and Life Worlds: Essays 2001-2005* (Double Storey, 2006). She was a Visiting Professor in English and African American Studies at Yale University from September to December 2003. She has published in numerous journals, including *African Identities, Interventions: International Journal of Postcolonial Studies, Journal of South African Studies*, and *Public Culture*.

Parlo Singh is Professor of Education and Head of School—School of Education and Professional Studies, Griffith University Gold Coast Campus. Her research interests are in the areas of cultural identity, pedagogy and schooling, and she has published extensively in these areas. Parlo Singh has also received numerous awards for excellence in teaching in higher education. Her pedagogy is informed by her research work. She is the co-editor (with Erica McWilliams) of *Designing Educational Researchers* (Post Pressed, 2004), and has published in *Educational Theory*, *Asia Pacific Journal of Education*, *Journal of Educational Inquiry*, *Journal of Education Policy*, *TESOL Quarterly*, and *British Journal of Sociology of Education* (in press) among others.

David Quijada is an Assistant Professor in the Program in Education, Culture, and Society at the University of Utah. He is past recipient of a Chancellor's postdoctoral research fellowship at the University of California-Berkeley. His dissertation, *Youth coalition building: Crossing community boundaries, raising consciousness and dismantling oppression* received an honorable mention award from the Council on Anthropology and Education (American Anthropological Association).

Fazal Rizvi has been a Professor in the Department of Educational Policy Studies at the University of Illinois since 2001, having previously held academic and administrative appointment at a number of universities in Australia, including as Pro Vice Chancellor (International) at the Royal Melbourne Institute of Technology and as the founding Director of the Monash Center for Research in International Education. At Illinois, he directs an online program for teachers around the world in Global Studies in Education. See gse. ed.uiuc.edu. Attached to this website is an open access space consisting of resources useful to teachers in internationalizing their curriculum. His next book, *Globalizing Educational Policy* will be published in late 2007.

Angharad Valdivia is Research Professor of Communications at the Institute for Communications Research at the University of Illinois at Urbana-Champaign. Professor Valdivia is the author of *A Latina in the Land of Hollywood* (University of Arizona Press, 2000), editor of *The Media Studies Companion* (Blackwell, 2003) ; *Feminism, Multiculturalism, and the Media: Global Diversities* (Sage: 1995); the communication and culture section of the Routledge International Encyclopedia of Women (2000); and co-editor of *Geographies of Latinidad* (Duke, 2006). She has published essays in the *Communication Review*, *Global Media Journal*, *Journal of Communication*, the *Journal of International Communication*, the *Review of Education/Pedagogy/Cultural Studies*, the *International Journal of Inclusive Education*, *Women and Language*, *Chasqui*, and in many edited anthologies. She is working on a book length manuscript entitled "*The Gender of Latinidad*."

Index